R CREDIT CARDS ✳ ANTI-AMERICANISM
BOYS ✳ BELIEVE BARS
AMES BLUNT ✳ BOTC Z
D CAMERON ✳ CELEI E
LE'S DREAM DATES ✳ CHEFS' FAMILIES
RANDS ✳ CORRIE BABES ✳ TOM CRUISE
OCKS ✳ DIET APPLES ✳ DUBAI ✳ ENERGY
ES ✳ FAIRTRADE TOWNS ✳ FOOD HALLS
TER'S BUFFET BARS ✳ ZAC GOLDSMITH
ATCHER, PHILOSOPHER ✳ HELPDESKS
AKS HUNKS ✳ INCONVENIENT TRUTHS
RNET CAFES ✳ IPOD POPES ✳ ITV PLAYS
IS ✳ JK AND JOEL ✳ THE KAISER CHIEFS
YLE ✳ LEMSIP ✳ LOST ✳ BOB MARLEY TAT
IRS ✳ PIERS MORGAN ✳ NAZI HATE POP
RS ✳ OSCAR PARTIES ✳ OVER-SHARING
IANS CALLED DAVID ✳ PORSCHE SUVS
CE PROMISES ✳ QUEUES ON EVEREST
EADY MEALS ✳ RECRUITMENT VIDEOS
IES ✳ RALF SCHUMACHER ✳ SKY THREE
TEAK BAKES ✳ SUPERLOOS ON TRAINS
THAI-INFUSED CRISPS ✳ SANDI THOM
P ✳ UNNECESSARY GREETINGS CARDS
WORK EXPERIENCE ✳ XANAX ADDICTS
✳ XENU ✳ YOUTH ALPHA ✳ YOUTH NEWS
CELEBRITIES SAVING THE PLANET . . .

IS IT JUST ME OR IS EVERYTHING SHIT?

Also by these authors

IS IT JUST ME OR IS EVERYTHING SHIT?:
THE ENCYCLOPEDIA OF MODERN LIFE, VOLUME 1

IS IT JUST ME OR IS EVERYTHING SHIT?

VOLUME 2

THE ENCYCLOPEDIA OF MODERN LIFE

STEVE LOWE AND ALAN McARTHUR

sphere

SPHERE

First published in Great Britain in 2006 by Sphere

A CIP catalogue record for this book is available
from the British Library.

ISBN-13: 978-0-316-029964
ISBN-10: 0-316-02996-3

Typeset in Palatino by M Rules
Printed and bound in Great Britain by
Clays Ltd, St Ives plc

Sphere
An imprint of
Little, Brown Book Group
Brettenham House
Lancaster Place
London WC2E 7EN

A Member of the Hachette Livre Group of Companies

www.littlebrown.co.uk

IS IT JUST ME OR IS EVERYTHING SHIT?

VOLUME 2

THE ENCYCLOPEDIA OF MODERN LIFE

A

Abstinence programmes

Jesus. Did not approve of having all the sexy sex. Prophylactics may sound like the sort of word you'd find in the Bible ('And He did say unto the Prophylactics . . .'), but it isn't. Prophylactics are a modern scourge, a modern scourge that are sadly prone to bursting and making you die. Jesus, just to be absolutely clear about this, did not like them. He didn't put them on his head at parties. And he didn't put them on his willy.

This is, roughly speaking, the main lesson of abstinence programmes: Godly guidance in how not to do it. What makes this quite a difficult campaign is that it's aimed at teenagers, who, as we know, often get quite worked up about the sex, finding the whole thing something of a turn-on.

The non-doing-it movement has in recent years been backed by George Bush, Pope Benedict and, of course, Ann Widdecombe. It will solve so many problems: STDs and pregnancy in the West, AIDS in Africa, all sorts. Britain's own radical reverends are now stepping up their campaign with rows over 'purity rings' breaking out in British schools. Purity rings aren't some sort of exotic sex toy; they're rings you wear as a pledge not to boff before marriage. 'With this ring, I wed Jesus, who doesn't do it,' is what the wearers say.

The wearers are dedicatedly not into joining what Silver

Ring Thing movement founder Denny Pattyn called 'the cesspool generation'. Ooh, smelly. Again, a Silver Ring Thing is not a sex toy. Just so we're clear on that.

But how can anyone think that sex is not going to happen because of Jesus? How is the sex not going to happen? In fact, an eight-year study in the US showed that 88% of people taking pledges of abstinence fall off the non-shag wagon before marriage – at which point they have nothing for the weekend (some of them don't even know what a weekend is). One common result: joining the pudding club. You don't get a special ring in the pudding club. You don't even get a pudding.

In the spirit of even-handedness, we have thoughtfully created some advertising slogans for future campaigns against having it off, ever:

PHALLIC SNEEZES SPREAD DISEASES
DON'T GO ROUND DOING IT!
DO DO DON'T DONG DONG, DO DO DON'T DONG
ONLY LET GOD TOUCH YOU, NOT SOME
    HORMONE-CRAZED SEX NUTTER
GET OFF THAT PENIS!
JESUS!

Ads for Credit Cards

'Don't put it off, put it on'. Let's be clear about this: there is absolutely nothing wrong with putting things off.

'Things get more exciting when you say "YES"'. That's right: seize the day!

Your life is not exciting enough, quite simply, because you haven't borrowed enough money. That much should be self-evident. Borrowing money may make you taller. You will have a nicer smile, and have read more books – while still finding time for that all-important jet-skiing holiday. It's possible that, by borrowing money, you can end all wars. Certainly if you get one of Bono/American Express's Red Cards (where a tiny percentage of your capricious spending is forwarded on to the poor, starving African babies) and you spend, spend, spend enough with it – you know, really absolutely totally ruining yourself – you could end famine. All of this while living in a cool contemporary apartment drinking crisp white wine.

This is the abiding message of ads for credit cards. In 2005, posters for HSBC credit cards bore the slogan 'Magical Christmas Cards'. So that's 'magical' meaning 'running up large debts so that more of your money ends up with the bankers'. It's magic only in the sense that it involves a trick.

We should trust our banks: they look after our money and everything. Yes, they make more every month from skanking people with late payment fees than you are likely to earn in your entire life, but that's only fair. With the UK public clearly in the middle of a cash crisis, still the adverts offering more credit come thicker and faster. Anyone would think the only way our economy is remaining afloat is by getting everyone to embrace really quite terrifying levels of financial insecurity – borrowing squillions to buy tat, and driving up house prices and rents with mortgage-mad buy-to-let mania (Britons owe over a trillion in mortgage debt alone). Britain is booming! Don't let your fear of bailiffs spoil it. Do bailiffs give you a new Audi and a spangly top? They do not. Credit does. So I know which side I'm on.

It's amazing how early you can start getting the plastic habit. Mastercard's new Splash card even entices under-18s to get involved. This despite cases like the 19-year-old who sought help from the Consumer Credit Counselling Service because he had £48,000 of debt with 19 lenders. The debt of Panama before reaching your 20s? Now that's a reason for teen angst.

Mastercard have defended the Splash card by saying it's the parents who control the limit and spending. Sadly, though, that would be the same parents who are working 70 hours a week because they owe eight billion pounds to credit card companies because they kept saying YES to trinkets and baubles because 'they are shiny'. Kids would be better off saying NO and shipping their parents off to Dr Tanya's House of Big Spendaways. Or get that Supernanny woman to put the shits up them.

Airbrushing fags out of history

Sorry, but it did happen. I know, it's shocking. But some people smoked. I'm getting all upset just remembering it, to be honest. It was barbaric. Ronnie Kray apparently smoked 140 cigarettes a day – and that should tell you everything you need to know.

Not us twenty-first century-ites, though. Oh, no. We don't even know what cigarettes are. What are cigarettes?

Given the stresses inherent in our era, it seems like we might have picked the wrong century to quit smoking. But as other dangers pile up, it is kind of good to know that we have tidied away one of the dangers: passive smoking. And the related danger of passively looking at pictures of cigarettes.

France's National Library airbrushed a Gitane from a poster of the famously chain-smoking philosopher Jean-Paul Sartre (it might make people feel *nausée*). The US Post Office corrected a stamp of blues legend Robert Johnson to remove the cigarette dangling from his lips. You can go down to the crossroads to do a deal with the devil, just as long as you don't buy any fags while you're there. Why not also alter his mouth to make the miserable bugger look a bit smilier too? 'Cheer up, Rob.' 'Can't. Got hellhounds on my trail.'

The Beatles have become such a smoke-free zone that you almost suspect that the next time you hear 'A Day in the Life', new lyrics will find Macca going upstairs to have a vegetarian sandwich. In 2006, the *Capitol Albums Vol. 2* box-set removed cigarettes from three smoking Beatles. Before, a cigarette was airbrushed from Paul McCartney's hand on the *Abbey Road* cover – and the song-titles were altered to 'You Never Give Me Your Money (To Buy Fags)', 'Carry Those Fags' and 'Her Majesty (Doesn't Like Fags Much, But Her Sister Likes Them A Lot)'.

Amstrad health and beauty

You have to feel sorry for affable *Apprentice*-winner Tim Campbell (who once described himself, rather brilliantly, as 'a very small fish in a big world') when you consider the task awarded to him for scooping the Top Job on the runaway ratings-grabbing show: marketing an Amstrad-branded beauty device that pumps electricity into your face.

'So, you want me to enter the image-sensitive health and beauty market, a smoke and mirrors world where aspiration is all, with a brand name mostly associated with green-screen 1980s word processors and a very gruff man with a stubbly beard? Right. And it pumps electricity into your actual face? Okay. Yes, I understand it's safe, it's not that, it's . . . So that's the actual prize, is it?'

Amstrad cleverly overcame the possible image problems by giving their revolutionary health and beauty product the very Primrose Hill name of Integra Face Care System. And that's going straight into *Top Santé*, surely? Face Care System. Caring. Systematically. For your face.

The £129 Integra applies electricity to the face (mostly 'on a subsensory level' – that is, you can't feel it doing anything) to 'improve circulation and muscle relaxation by varying the shapes of the impulses or waveforms' ('waveforms': a word that does not exist, but presumably helps your face turn wavier), thus providing 'stimulation by micro-current for you to treat your own face in the comfort of your own home'. I'm feeling visibly more beautiful just thinking about it.

Series-two winner and 'former check-out girl' (© all the newspapers) Michelle Dewsbury* was installed as head of Xenon Green, which sounds like a docusoap on Mars, but is in fact a computer recycling company. Christ, what will the third winner get put in charge of: emptying the bins?

Sir Alan 'Sir Alan' Sugar, by the way, once sent his wife a birthday card signed 'From Alan Sugar'. Well, we've all done it: worked hard on a heart-rending, confessional message of love before bottling out at the last moment and putting down 'From Alan Sugar'.

He also sent a fax to a videorecorder manufacturer in China which read: 'DEAR MR CHING CHANG CHONG, WE HAVE RECEIVED YOUR VIDEO. IT IS SHIT.' Sugar PR man and *Apprentice* regular Nick Hewer told the *Sunday Times*: 'It was all spelt out in bold. In capital letters . . . His use of language is very explicit, but he has this real ability to communicate.'

There are people out there, right now, all over this land, treating their own faces in the comfort of their own homes.

Anti-Americanism

You cannot escape the point: America has produced a vibrant culture that is the pleasure and envy of millions. These people have given us not only *The Cannonball Run* but also *Love in An Elevator* by Aerosmith. That's right.

But despite all these achievements, a wave of anti-Americanism is sweeping the globe. In Indonesia in April 2006, people rioted against *Playboy* – not because it was porn per se, but because it was American porn. 'Down with Yankee bongo' – that might have been the slogan. Apparently, even Japanese porn was deemed comparatively harmless – which is weird, considering it basically consists of women dressed up as little girls.

In Britain, we have certainly traditionally ridiculed Americans for being clamorous, rotund morons who have to be forcibly stopped from eating the furniture (the latest craze in US supermarkets is to buy paper plates in bulk: so no one has to wash up after dinner – how sick is *that*?). This is all good clean family fun. But now it's getting out of hand with supposedly rational souls seeing Islamists holding up posters proclaiming, 'God is great and America is Evil' and thinking: 'Hey, I'll have some of that. Surely I can harness that enthusiasm for the forces of good . . . Hey, you know what? America *is* a Great Satan. Eight quid – that's what going to see *Big Momma's House 2* cost me . . . the bastards!'

But the Americans need not fear, because leading the charge against the 'they had it coming' hordes, is . . . Tony Parsons. Writing a year after 9/11, he said the US should be hailed for its considered response to the atrocities: 'So a few al-Qaeda tourists got locked without a trial in Camp X-Ray? Pass the Kleenex. So some Afghan wedding receptions were shot up after they merrily fired their semi-automatics in a sky full of American planes? A shame, but maybe next time they should stick to confetti.' ('Pass the Kleenex', by the way, does seem rather an unfortunate choice of phrase.)

Perhaps there is another way. Perhaps people who just happen to have all been born in the same country, are not some strange homogeneous Other. Have they not flesh? (And plenty of it quite often.) Do they not bleed? In the same way that the people of Lower Dicker will tend to despise the people of Upper Dicker (something to do with a drill not being returned), not all Americans feel as One. It's a simple matter of divorcing the idea of the American state going round doing all the bad things from the people who live under it. They aren't the same thing. And they didn't even all vote for Idiot Boy. That map of the States after the last presidential election – the sea of blue down the coasts, the red down the middle – didn't tell the whole story. In most of the blue states, nearly 50% voted red; and vice versa. These are a diverse people.

So now, more than ever, we must demonstrate our solidarity with this fine (if often quite fat) people – perhaps by watching some Wesley Snipes films while eating floppy cheese. We must remain confident in the potential of the American people. We believe they are deserving and capable of human liberty. If they would just pull their fat fingers out of their fucking arses. I thank you.

Articles in newspapers reporting polls in magazines

For example, saying that Heston Blumenthal's restaurant The Fat Duck has been knocked off the number-one spot as the world's best restaurant as voted by some people for *Restaurant* magazine. Or that the Keith Chegwin-fronted nudeathon *Naked Jungle* was the worst programme ever made, according to some bloke in a magazine.

Reading a magazine does not constitute gathering the news. It constitutes reading a magazine.

What next? Mark Lawson's new column reveals 'Woman Finds Happiness With Sister's Widower . . . riveting True Story in *Take a Break* . . . Of course they still miss her . . . And the next thing they knew, they were having sex.'

B

'Baby Asbos'

In October 2005, the news was 'leaked' that the government was considering introducing 'Baby Asbos' to help further the 'respect agenda'. These measures, actively considered by Tony Blair and his anti-social behaviour tsar Louise Casey, would help tackle the problem of criminal behaviour within a section of society previously beyond the arm of the law: the under-ones. Including, of course, foetuses.

Such young people, although currently not considered capable of committing a crime in the eyes of the law, can seriously disrupt communities, harassing neighbours, defacing walls and engaging in abusive acts. Groups gathering together on street corners were often found to be 'very threatening and scary'.

As the law stood, full-scale Asbos could be given only to people over the age of one. But the 'baby Baby Asbo' – or 'Basbo' – may, for example, see a troublesome nine-month-old being barred from verbally abusing neighbours or from entering parts of an estate. It would be a lighter sanction than a full-blown Asbo. Anyone served with one would be 'highly unlikely' to be 'named and shamed' (although, clearly, such powers would have to be held in reserve).

Senior police officers claimed measures for dealing with under-ones might be necessary as a 'last resort'. Surrey Chief

Constable Bob Quick said that some one-year-olds were 'streetwise enough to know the consequences of their actions'.

More recently, the Prime Minister went further in identifying future criminality, claiming, 'we can identify such families virtually as their children are born.'

He went on to explain that you can tell just by looking at the eyes, claiming they were: 'Coming to get me. You can see it in their eyes. It's all in the eyes! THE FREAKY LITTLE EYES!'

'Bad boys'

'We know it's wrong, but they're just so . . . so . . . likely to commit random acts of violence! Yeah?'

Aisleyne from *Big Brother 6* revealed she was 'addicted to bad boys'. On meeting Mark Croft, Kerry Katona told *Closer*: 'My new man is a bad boy'. Inside, she revealed he's a 'naughty man'. So what are we talking? Stealing hubcaps? Or just all the Hobnobs? It's not clear.

For today's thrill-seeking chick, a right bad 'un is the ultimate accessory. Essentially, if your man has never been had up for GBH while dealing out crackpipe from his Harley Davidson motorbike, is he even a man at all? BOOOORING!

In *Observer Woman* magazine, Meg Mathews (yes, she's still here) revealed: 'Bad boys are always the most attractive . . . When I look back at all my exes, they've all of them either been in borstal or prison or rough-and-ready or rock-and-roll. The last one was in prison for 10 months. I thought it was great. I thought I was in *Married To The Mob*. I used to go on the visits all dressed up.' Dressed up as what, though? On past form, it could be anything from a Phoenician slave-trader to Little Bo-Peep.

Next week: 'My new man is Radovan Karadzic. He's been on the run from the UN War Crimes Tribunal for murder, plunder and genocide since 1996! Genocidal Bosnian Serbs? Saucy!'

Believe bars

The popular chocolate-and-caramel confection rebranding itself as a New Age exhortation for England to 'come on' was, even in a crowded field, easily the weirdest bit of 'Come On England' marketing attempting to ride the perceived national obsession with England's World Cup performance. Maybe they were inspired by Shakespeare's classic evocation of all things England: 'This sceptr'd isle, This earth of majesty, This seat of Mars . . .'

You have to wonder who the US confectionery giant supported in other territories. And also about the long-term brand-association effects on people who took it seriously – those who genuinely bought into the idea that, by eating a lot of Mars bars, maybe even enough to reach the bulb at the top of the Believe-ometer in the adverts, they would somehow propel England to a frankly unfeasible World Cup victory.

'I just got fat. I was on about nine or ten of the sweet bastards a day. King-size, some of them. And England were still shit. *Really* shit. I can't believe it. Maybe I just didn't eat *enough* Mars bars . . .'

Belief was a good theme for the English team, though. Belief – that is, irrational conviction – was very much what this show was all about. If there were a World Cup in bullshit and hubris, England would have romped home in spectacular fashion. The grandiose, deluded mission statements ('It is our time'/'We will win it'); the entourage of merciless consumers ('Shopping's coming home . . .'); the overpaid executive who was ultimately fairly clueless – they represented 'the nation' all right. For a spectacular society that values going down the shops, talking a good self-obsessed New Agey fight and never delivering anything much in the way of 'goods', these were very much our boys.

'Against the envy of less happier lands,/This blessed plot, this earth, this realm, this . . . De! De! De-De-De! De-De-De-De! ENGLAND!'

Big Brother firsts

There's a first time for everything – even having a wank with a champagne bottle on live telly. Each year, *Big Brother* contestants are encouraged to score more *Big Brother* firsts. Otherwise, viewers might decide that it's just the same as last year and stop watching, and then where would we all be?

Big Brother 5, for example, saw the first *Big Brother* fight. Emma and Victor were eventually pulled apart by security guards. It was most exciting. Recalling the scrap on a Channel 5 talking-heads-celeb-clip programme, the editor of *More* magazine declared: 'It was brilliant. I was shaking watching it – anything could happen.'

During *Big Brother 6*, remaining whities Maxwell and Saskia started acting as though they were under siege. Viewers were enthralled by what appeared to be the first *Big Brother* to divide along racial lines. Mmmm, racy! That same year, Kinga famously broke another taboo by seeming to masturbate with that champagne bottle. Viewers were shocked. Susan of Torquay complained: 'It gives young people a bad name.' Mostly, of course, *Big Brother* gives young people a really good name.

Australian *Big Brother* saw the first two people – Michael Cric and Michael Cox – evicted for sexually assaulting a woman. On hearing of their eviction, she wept: 'I'm really sorry, guys. I feel so bad.'

Big Brother 7 saw the show become a twisted sister. *Now* magazine called it 'pure gratuitous evil'. The *Sun* accused producers of casting too many 'sex-obsessed crazies, weirdos and unstable attention-seekers' (which, for the *Sun*, is a bit rich). We had Pete, the first Tourette's sufferer. And Shahbaz, the first potential suicide. After he walked, executive producer Phil Edgar-Jones explained: '[Shahbaz] found it a very positive experience. He's got himself an agent.'

Yet still they come. Before the 2006 show began, *Big Brother* founder Jon De Mol told the *Daily Mirror* that he was '100% sure that if we announce a show where we say we'll take 10 people and put them in an airplane and there are nine parachutes and one person is probably going to die and the nine who live will all get $1 million, we will get enough contestants for a daily show'. Of course, the same would also be true for no parachutes.

But, despite all these television breakthroughs, a nagging doubt remains. No matter how many firsts *Big Brother* pulls out of the bag, after a while it's still hard to escape the fact that it's mainly just another load of numpties hugging and crying and giving each other massages and that.

To be honest, I don't really trust my jaded palate to be sufficiently shocked or thrilled by anything *Big Brother* might offer:

- First bumcam? Well, it's certainly an eye-opener, of sorts.
- First face transplant? Surprising what they can do these days, I suppose.
- First Black Mass? Interesting-ish. But where's bloody Satan?
- First use of napalm on nearby villages? That's just being deliberately provocative.
- First uncovering of the Holy Grail? Seen it in films already.
- First putting evicted contestants back in the house, thus causing people who have never voted/been on a demonstration/written to their MP taking to the streets with revolution in their eyes, outraged by having their 'rights' taken away, shouting 'That's our money! That is our fucking money, that is what that is!'. Oh no, hang on . . .

Binge-drinkers assuming kung fu poses in pitched fights with bouncers and/or police

If the hard-hitting documentaries are to be believed, this is very common. It is also *highly* futile.

Honestly, are you even fooling yourselves?

Blackberries

What exactly the fuck do you think you're doing to yourselves?

Cherie Blair

Now, you'd struggle to make the case that Cherie Blair has remained immune to criticism throughout her husband's premiership. But in amongst all the lambastings for New Age freeloading and buckshee election coiffures, she has resolutely hung on to the image, in the popular and media consciousnesses, that she is cleverer and 'more political' than her husband. Eminent left-wing journalists have urged her to stay on in public life. Under that steely, flat- and friend-buying exterior, we are led to believe, beats a softer – or should that be harder? – political heart.

But it's difficult to work out where this reputation for political sharpness and principle comes from. You never hear Cherie Blair saying things like: 'In years to come, may we not hold as an image of these times, Little Ian McCartney, stricken on a hospital bed recovering from two emergency heart operations, quite possibly about to die, being duped into signing documents approving peerages for backdoor big-money loans from billionaire donors. Multicultural billionaires, of course . . . which makes it better.'

Or she might say: 'What a legacy! An Airforce One-style presidential plane for the PM; political language gutted of all meaning; a PM hocking himself up with £4m of mortgages on the strength of his forthcoming memoirs deal, while also trying to suppress civil servants' perfectly legitimate memoir criticisms of his lying and obfuscation in the run-up to the disastrous Iraq War; the disastrous Iraq War. I could go on.'

Then she might go on: 'Packing government committees with unelected business people and policy wonks; creating a situation whereby the richest 1% of the population now receive more of the nation's income than at any time since the 1930s; Byers and Milburn consulting for Iraq and NHS profiteers; a groundswell of support for the far right; a government lushing itself up with cushy pension deals while exhorting everyone else to work until they drop. I could go on.'

Then she might go on: 'David Cameron; the lowest mandate for a government ever; so toadying to the US that we would fly in the face of every single other country on the entire face of the whole planet in refusing to call for an immediate ceasefire in the Lebanon; Labour Party membership decimated, and Labour members' influence ever diminished, even to the point of setting up a shadowy Supporters' Network of people who can only reply to absurdly phrased multiple-choice questions via e-mail making Labour less a political party and more like a fairtrade banana republic.'

But I've never heard her say anything like that. I've only ever heard her say:

'Hello, is that a woman Labour MP? Cherie here – you know, the one with the reputation for shrewd politics. Vote for Tony's war, there's a good girl. Human rights? Yeah, loads of them. I love him, you know.'

'Hey, Tony – sign these Downing Street postcards for me and I'll pop them on e-Bay.'

'I know the Queen, you know.'

'That'll be $100,000, please' (– to the organisers of a charity book tour of Australia).

'What's that Silvio, another biscotti? Don't mind if I do. What's the point of holidaying at the expense of a grotesque plutocrat if you can't have a biscuit? Garibaldi? No, he was a bastard.'

'All I did – boo hoo – was get a crook – boo hoo – to buy me a couple of flats. I didn't – boo hoo – know – boo hoo – that there was anything – boo hoo – wrong with being so – boo hoo – grasping. I only – boo hoo – wanted to make – boo hoo, sniffle – loads – whimper – of cash.'

'Gordon Brown is a fat, miserable freak who should have made his move years ago. The twat.'

Except we should make it crystal clear that she didn't say the last one. What with her being a lawyer and all.

James Blunt

James Blunt is the perfect singer-songwriter for the busybusy-busy generation who don't have time to consider what a song might actually mean. Literary conceits swallow up valuable minutes which might be spent . . . oh, I don't know, cracking up or having a really massive latte.

Given these constraints, the smartest, sharpest title for a song about a woman being beautiful is surely 'You're Beautiful'. And why call any song that concerns the pain of saying goodbye to a lover anything other than 'Goodbye My Lover'? From this perspective, it's hard to see why anyone gets stewed up about this songwriting game. It's quite straightforward. A fucking monkey could do it.

'Goodbye My Lover' was the emotional core of Blunt's huge-selling debut album *Back To Bedlam*.* As the title implies, the song in no way involves saying 'hello' to a lover. The situation departs from the pleasures that come with welcoming a lover almost completely. It could equally have been called 'Farewell My Lover'. Or: 'See Ya! My Lover'.

Blunt – the 'epitome of 21st-century chic', according to the *Mail* – has probably said goodbye to quite a lot of lovers. If the tabloids are to be believed, he can't keep it in his trousers: sort of like a posh-rock Darren Day. But those were merely casual lovers. The lyric of 'Goodbye My Lover' explores the crucifying angst of losing a woman who Blunt apparently 'pretty much considered the one'. Interviewed on *James Blunt At The BBC*, the Queen-guarding balladeer called the story 'very tragic'. And, in many ways, he is right.

The song begins by questioning whether he failed his departed lover, before his thoughts turn back to the early flowering of romance, depicting himself as some sort of victor (that would be the army background, presumably). His powerful presence caused his new lover temporarily to lose her sight. So he decided to take, not forcibly but with a certain righteous zeal, what he considered his property by an everlasting, possibly even divine, covenant. Continuing this reverie, Blunt imaginatively plants his mouth over various parts of his ex-lover's body before recalling how they would both sleep under the same sheets. This is the reason he can then claim intimate knowledge of her physical odour.

In the chorus, he repeatedly bids his lover farewell before revealing she was probably the only woman for him in the world. The implication is that he can never love again. That's it. He is spent. Goodbye to love, perhaps.

The second verse finds the war-hero-turned-singer still urgently envisioning his former girlfriend and imploring her to remember him, too. He has watched her at various times, he reveals, while she was crying, while she was smiling and also while she was sleeping (but not for that long, he also assures her – not so long that it would become fucked-up). You see, he would happily have sired offspring with this woman and spent all his born days with her. Actually, you know what? If she isn't there, if she has definitely disappeared for good, then he is genuinely unsure about whether he can carry on living. It's not quite, 'Don't leave me or I'll kill myself!' But it's not quite not that, either. Self-harm, possibly?

The chorus then repeats the claim that she was his only hope. Everything is ruined. And so on.

We're nearing the end now, but he must still detail the haunted nights; the nights when, lying in bed, he actually feels her hands. Honestly, it's like she's really there. She's not, though, as I hope we've established. At the song's climax, he brings out what we have already surmised: that this heart-rending experience has left him an empty husk. To emphasise this point, he repeats it six times.

Don't make the mistake of thinking his life has any meaning. Because it hasn't. Okay? Selling lots of records in America? He's not bothered.

'People have said it sounds like she died or something like that,' he admitted.

He's very hunky with his top off and all that. But wouldn't you chuck him too? The moaning twat.

* Bedlam here refers to the famous London mental hospital. However, in 1930 the Bethlehem (of which the common name is a corruption) moved from St George's Field, Southwark, to the outer London suburb of Beckenham. The long tree-lined streets of semi-detached ennui do not in any way conjure up the spirit of 19th-century chaos; they do, however, perfectly evoke the spirit of James Blunt. I expect that's why he called his album that.

Boobs specials

How was the March 2006 *Nuts Boobs Special* special? *Nuts* is full of boobs week in, week out, so what's 'special' about an issue of *Nuts* with boobs in it? Boobs it has. Special it is not.

The men's weeklies contain roughly 70 pictures of women

per issue, around a third of whom are topless. That's twenty-three and a third pairs of boobs. Or 46.66 (recurring) individual boobs. That's a lot of boobs. With such a high boob count, a few extra will make little impact. To stand out as 'special' you'd need to, say, put that many boobs on each and every page. But then the pictures would be quite small. And where would they put all the stuff about John Terry?

Or maybe the *Boobs Special* was a fact-packed public-service extravaganza about breastfeeding, and infant nutrition generally: 'Women – don't feed your baby foods high in salt, sugar and preservatives on a Tuesday'.

It wasn't.

Or maybe it was a fascinating and insightful discussion of boob-politics through the ages, considering how primitive sculptures from ancient civilisations tended to depict full, ripe breasts as symbols of life-giving force, health and wealth. The Egyptian goddess Isis was often portrayed with milk flowing from her breast; the Greek goddess Artemis had a dozen breasts – and you could definitely see how *Nuts* might be interested in *that*.

They might then go into in some detail about how it was Christianity that wanted breasts repressed and covered up, comparing it with the polar opposite attitude in periods of freedom like the French Revolution – where Liberty, as per the Delacroix painting, is bare-breasted.

They could conclude by wondering whether they are reversing the gains made by the boob in the 1960s sexual revolution with their mania for very skinny women with unfeasibly big tits ('breasts on sticks', as Sally Feldman put it in the *New Humanist*), created by a combination of plastic surgery and desktop airbrushing: the beauty myth indeed, they might have concluded.

They didn't.

Men's mag editors do like to deconstruct their activities, though, and place them in a wider social context. On the need for soap stars and tabloid babes to bare all, *FHM* editor Ross Brown said: 'When you become a celebrity, you automatically tick the box saying, "Are you prepared to be photographed in your knickers and pants?"' Which could be interesting news to, say, Walter Wolfgang.

Further explaining the high concept behind all the norks-aloud covers, Paul Merrill, launch editor of *Zoo*, said of the trademark shot of the model's breast partially concealed by her hand (devised to keep WH Smith's and the supermarkets happy): 'We call that shot "hand-bra". We use that a lot.' Considering a cover showing a model whose hair extensions cover her nipples, he added: 'This is hair-bra.

'Then we have knee-bra, where she's sitting down hugging her knees.

'And boob-bra, also known as girl-on-girl-bra, where you have two girls' breasts touching.

'Oh, and this is clever . . . [Points to a cover showing two images of Abi Titmuss facing each other] Look, she's being her own bra [!].

'When we get really bored, we even use a bra-bra.'

Most insightful. But boobs specials? You want to take your hands off your tacker for five minutes and give Trading Standards a call.

Boozy adverts

That is, adverts trying to get you to booze. By which I don't mean adverts for booze. It's fairly obvious that adverts for booze will involve booze. I'm not a mental. I mean adverts that involve booze but are not for booze. Like adverts for banks.

A recent ad campaign for Smile, the online bank, tried to lure punters with an offer of '12 bottles of wine when you open a Smile current account'. It's no doubt a highly reputable company, but I'm sure someone once advised me not to do financial deals with people who offer me alcoholic drinks. My gran maybe.

Supermarkets are always encouraging you to booze, too. They do this in many ways, principally by stocking lots of booze. Shelves of the bloody stuff, sirenically inviting you to share in its delicious, boozy goodness.

But sneaking it into adverts for cheese?

A February 2006 national press campaign by Sainsbury's most definitely purported to be about cheese: 'Save 25% off selected cheeses,' it said. Okay.

There was Red Leicester (a cheese), Cheddar (cheese, obviously), Gorgonzola (the cheese) and Brie (admittedly, not a cheese – ha! just checking you were paying attention; of course, it is in fact a cheese).

But printed on the Brie section of the ad were two badly drawn cartoon characters, one saying to the other, 'Why not try a glass of Shiraz with the Brie'.

Not even a question mark. A statement. You – that is, I – will get shitfaced on the popular red wine variety Shiraz, much beloved of Australian viticulturists and enjoyed by fans of fruity robust *vin* the world over. And all you were doing was idly considering some photographs of cheese. Now here you are, pissed up, with a load of warm Brie you didn't even want. I don't even like Brie.

Yeah, well, chew on this bit of cheese, J. Sainsbury.

According to impeccable academic sources, wine and cheese don't even go together. I know! The '70s lied to us.

The University of California's Department of Enology and Viticulture (wine and vine studies – or Faculty of Booze) says that mostly they don't complement each other, and that the wine suffers most. So there.

Quite a job for an academic, mind, sat round in sunny California, munching cheese and sousing yourself with fine wines before deciding: 'Hey, you know what? These things don't really go. Or maybe they do – I'll just check again . . . Bob, more Stilton.'

As a bonus for Americans, this is exactly the sort of research that will really, *really* piss off the French.

Botox bollox

The biannual *New Beauty* (according to the *Sunday Times*, 'The new magazine for the Botox generation') has helpfully collected '40 Uses for Injectables'. It's 'highly experimental', but Botox can potentially 'inhibit the nerve impulses that make you feel hungry'. Furthermore, sticking it into the armpit can 'completely shut off the production of perspiration'. So Botox can save you from sweating or getting the munchies. That's right: just like Barbie.

It's not all post-sweat, post-comestible fun, though. High-powered London bankers are injecting Botox to stop looking all frowny and stressed after regularly working eighteen-hour days. One told *Time* magazine: 'It's important to look your best . . . like you can take it in your stride.'

Of course, injecting yourself with bacteria to look like you're not tired when you really are *very* tired would make you a living metaphor for the age. Which is sort of cool. Hopefully, we're on our way to a big-bosomed, non-frowning utopia. Hey, maybe we should all dye our hair blond and put in blue contact lenses, too? Wouldn't that be perfection?

When the 'Botox generation' dies, what will its ashes look like?

Bratz

Look, here's saucy leatherclad Roxxi, one of the Bratz Rock Angelz, playing a flying-V rock guitar and showing off her midriff and high-heels. Kind of like when Britney dressed up as a Nazi dominatrix. 'Hi! My name is Roxxi,' says Roxxi. 'My twin calls me "Spice" because I like to spice things up!' Twins, eh? Eh? Wicked!

Bratz are taking over. You might have thought they were just a range of dolls, purple-spangly teenage dolls in 'funky' outfits slathered in make-up. But you would be wrong. The Bratz doll is not a doll. Well, it is a doll, anyone can see that. But it's also, according to Paula Treantafelles, who initially created the range, a 'self-expression piece'.

How this 'self-expression' piece expresses itself is mainly through the prism of having the right trinkets, phones, accessories and shoes. (Without shoes, the Bratz dolls have no feet. It's kind of a metaphor.) They are 'the only girls with a passion 4 fashion!'. It's a sort of WAG training course for six-year-olds.

Doll designer Lui Domingo insists: 'We are not making a deliberate effort to sexualise these dolls. We are making them fashionable, and coincidentally the fashions these days are rather sexy.'

Not trying to sexualise them? They look like a series of Hollywood central casting whores made out of plastic!

Then there's the passion 4 dating guyz: the 'Secret Date' range of Bratz included a dolled-up doll, plus a mystery date (one of the Bratz Boyz) and – oh yes – champagne glasses! Why not go the whole way and chuck them naked into a jacuzzi? Bubblicious!

Then there are The Bratz Babyz – sort of what babies would like if they decided to become strippers. And there's a 'Babyz Night Out' fashion pack and 'Brattoo Parlor' playset. Because if there's one thing babies need it's more nightz out and tat-toos. They could go out and compare their new markings: 'Look, I've got a spider, what about you?' 'Mine says "Mum".'

Bratz Big Babys (yet another range) have 'Designer Diapers' – lovely frilly knickers, which they set off with these highly peculiar coquettish poses. Oh yes, and earrings. And a bikini bearing the slogan 'I Blow Bubbles'! This is also a coin-cidence. The fashion among babies is definitely for looking like little sexpots. Oh no, hang on . . .

Even the Bratz Babyz Ponyz have coloured highlights and makeup. So they're sexualising ponies now? Come on – if you're sexualising ponies, you're definitely taking the sexual-ising way too far. Or is this a coincidence too? Are there slave-to-fashion ponies out there now, right this minute, having their tits done?

Hey, I know! How about a Babyz Self-Harm Kit? Or at least just supply the Secret Dates with Rohypnol. Or is that going too far? How does one judge? Anyway, let us be thankful that children are not generally impressionable or easily led – or we may end with a generation of stifled, consumer-crazed fuck-ups. Another one.

Britain, Britishness, the British Empire, British Citizenship Tests, Britishness lessons in schools, the proposed Britishness Day, New Britain, *Little Britain*, Fern Britton, etc.

Britishness is everywhere. Well, in British political discourse it's everywhere – no one else really gives a monkey's. There are new British citizenship tests for people who want to become British, a proposed Britishness Day (a day on which British people shalt be Exceedingly British), the BBC has been told 'promoting Britishness' might be added to its charter (BBC3 already complies with all those *Little Britain* repeats), and Gordon Brown has nailed the flag to his mast with his adherence to a new, strong, vibrant, albeit hazily defined, British identity. A hazily defined identity he proposes to be hazily taught in schools.

It's devilishly difficult to work out what would be taught, though, because a key feature of the Britishness debate is a refusal to give any specifics and say what 'Britishness' may actually mean. It's as if they have taken French philosopher Ernest Renan's adage that a nation is 'A group of people united by a mistaken view about the past and hatred of their neighbours' and focused entirely on the mistaken-view-of-the-past aspect. (They explicitly play down the whole 'hating the neighbours' side of things. Well, unless they've got oil, or vote the wrong way in the EU.)

In a speech to the Fabian Society in January 2006, Brown made Britishness the launchpoint of his proposed premiership, thereby cleverly reversing another famous maxim, Dr Johnson's one about patriotism being the *last* refuge of scoundrels. 'What is our Fourth of July?' he implored. 'What is our Independence Day? Where is our Declaration of Rights? What is our equivalent of a flag in every garden?'

That summer, of course, much of Britain would indeed boast a flag in very nearly every garden. Just not the British flag. Another flag. Which complicates things.

The job of defining Britishness can, it seems, lead only to a hasty retreat in bloody disgrace – like invading Russia. In his book *The Abolition of Britain*, the somewhat barking (actually positively medieval) right-wing commentator Peter Hitchens defines core British values as 'patriotism, morality, tradition and beauty'. And he comes out strongly against . . . central heating. (When it's cold, families congregate in one room; when it's warm, they go off and do their own thing and the edifice of the family fractures. Maybe that's why he's always arguing with his brother?)

So it's tricky. Nevertheless, you would think that someone trying to get us to fall in behind a common notion of Britishness would have the good manners to say what it is. They don't even define Britishness in the citizenship tests: based on the book *Life in the United Kingdom*, the new exam for all immigrants seeking a UK passport ignores history and culture entirely, focusing instead on how we say 'please' and 'thank you' a lot, and what to do if you spill someone's pint in a pub (I'm not making this up).

Some say British values are the best defence against terrorism. When the public voted for their chosen Britishness Day, the winner was 15 June, to celebrate the 1215 signing of the Magna Carta, which brought the tyrannical King John to heel and enshrined such key concepts as habeas corpus (the right to have the legality of your detention put before a court).

Certainly, nothing will ever come between us and these core values. Except Guantanamo Bay. And Belmarsh. But then, those places aren't even in Britain. Except for Belmarsh. Or are we so committed to 'British' values that we must demolish 'British' values in order to protect them? To paraphrase the US commander in Vietnam, maybe we need to destroy the village green to preserve it.

The closest we get to a proper science bit – as opposed to just feeling slightly teary while watching *Blackadder Goes Forth* – is a 2005 Commission for Racial Equality report called 'What is Britishness?'. By focus-grouping almost a hundred people of various ethnicities, they found Britishness included things like:

- Geography – that is, it's something to do with the British Isles. Nowhere outside of this area can truly be considered British. Not really.
- Values and Attitudes – including wholesome virtues like 'a strong work ethic, community spirit, and compassion', which are, of course, completely unknown in other nations (particularly the Germans), as well as 'drunkenness, hooliganism and yobbishness', which are bad virtues also unknown to other nations (except the Irish . . . obviously).
- Cultural Habits and Behaviour – for example, queuing, watching football, listening to the Beatles and Charlotte Church, and consuming 'fish and chips', 'English breakfast', 'curries' and 'beer'.

Britishness, then: it's Charlotte Church playing keepy-uppy in the rain while eating a fried-egg sandwich and listening to 'Tomorrow Never Knows'. Or, to put it another way: it's what the people who live in Britain just sort of bod about doing anyway. Not much of a unifying political vision, is it?

Given these findings, and in keeping with the need to display patriotism in our gardens, we present our own British citizenship test – which is, if anything, even more British than the real one:

1. By 1921, the British Empire held sway over:

   a) A population of between 470 and 570 million people, approximately a quarter of the world's population, and about 14.3 million square miles, about a quarter of the world's total land area.

   b) I am Scottish/Welsh and we never done it. We didn't fight for the Empire, our bosses didn't profit from it, we didn't own our own mines and industries and thus exploit our own, that was the English, blame them, the English did it, it was the English. Not us.

   c) I don't know, we only did Hitler at our school.

2. Name three Loyalist paramilitary groups.

3. How many pints can you get down your neck in an hour?

4. In 250 words or less, tell us what you love most about Britain. (Clue: don't mention benefits.)

5. What is the title of Charlotte Church's debut pop single?
   a) Crazy Chick
   b) Crazy Chicken
   c) Funky Chicken
   d) Kentucky Fried Chicken
   e) Dixie Fried Chicken
   f) Chickago Fried Chicken
   g) Chickin' Lickin' Fried Chicken
   h) Ain't Nobody Here But Us Chickens

i) I don't know, I'm more of a Cheryl Tweedy person myself. Chicken.

British American Tobacco

In what can be described only as bit of a 'satire: dead' moment, we can reveal that UK-listed cigarette giant BAT – recently outed as having paid only £13 million in corporation tax over the five years up to 2006, out of pre-tax profits of £9 billion – was the founding benefactor of the Centre for Corporate Social Responsibility (based at Nottingham University).

BAT – whose deputy chairman is Ken 'the beer-drinking face of capitalism' Clarke – relies for growth on poorer nations: Turkey, Iraq, Pakistan, India, Bangladesh, Vietnam and Nigeria. In 2004/5, its profits rose by 20%. Feeling poor? Have a fag. It's calming.

BAT has also been accused of smuggling its own cigarettes, and marketing them to kids.

And, really, nothing screams social responsibility like marketing cigarettes to kids.

Broadband service providers

While broadband service providers maintain the illusion of competition by vying to have the stupidest name, they actually collude in keeping us in a state of roiling panic.

One day, according to their fiendish plan, you might be up and me down. The next day, the situation might be reversed with me on top, cackling with a glass of something nice, while you're down in the pit feeling abandoned like an abandoned dog feels abandoned when it's been abandoned. Fucked, essentially.

It's the broadband whirligig of life that makes weak, impotent pawns of us all. In fact, when Polish sociology guru Zygmunt Bauman formulated his new theory of the 'liquid life', a scary new precariousness that sees the 21st century individual walking on quicksand, under perpetual siege, while seeking shelter from the storm in Pandora's Box (which is on fire), he had just lost his broadband connection and was being seriously dicked around by the helpline staff.

Or is it even more cosmic than this? Is it part of the divine plan, of which broadband companies are mere fucknutted minions? Is there some kind of karmic payback going on? Do we get the broadband service we deserve? Or are we randomly picked out for this torture because we're completely controlled, both physically and metaphysically, by complete bastards? They send our instructions down the broadband cable. It's possible. Well, probably it is – I don't actually understand how it works.

I think it's all of the above. And more.

C

Cabvision

'As an advertiser, have you wondered how to efficiently target an ABC1, under-35, affluent audience in London?'

I don't think you would need Peter Ackroyd levels of capital-obsession to claim that London is an interesting enough city to look at, and that one of the best ways of viewing it is from the back seat of one of those famous black London taxis. But this is to ignore the marketing opportunities opened by attaching a mini-TV screen to the dividing wall and pumping out adverts, news and film footage of people getting in and out of London taxis. It's a 'Total Taxi marketing solution'!

Presumably chastened by their above-ground competitors, some London Underground stations have now replaced the old-skool paper posters on escalators showing Claire Sweeney in *Chicago* with series of moving screens advertising spectacles.

Such innovations no doubt lead weary commuters to think: 'Tottenham Court Road? Why no, I appear to have been transported to the Tokyo of the mid-22nd century – as imagined by Philip K. Dick.'

Of course, if renowned sci-fi speedfreak Philip K. Dick, famous for predicting that technologised marketing would take over everything, were still alive to witness the modern age, he might have to reassess the extent to which technologised marketing has taken over everything.

Maybe change the title of 'Do Androids Dream of Electric Sheep'? to 'Do Electric Sheep Dream of Watching Telly in the Back of a Cab'? And, of course: 'Flow My Tears, the Hapless Taxi Passenger Said'. And: 'The Man in the High Dudgeon (Due to Adverts)'.

In an amazing metaphor for the modern condition, the traveller can't turn Cabvision off – only down.

Cafes that serve pre-cooked bacon
Out of a packet!

Cafes whose idea of a sausage sandwich is to cut a cooked sausage into very thin slices lengthways, then deep fry that cooked sausage for a considerable period of time, then put what are effectively sausage crisps – that is, crisps made out of sausage – between two dry slices of Value bread

There's a reason why sausage crisps remain excluded from the exhilarating new wave of crisp-style snacks, root-vegetable crisps, bagel chips, all of that. This is because sausage crisps – that is, crisps made out of sausage – are a very stupid idea. A very stupid idea that will attack your heart with a heart attack.

Cafes without toilets

Basically, what they're saying is: 'We've had your money, but we've not got a pot for *you* to piss in – now buzz off. And once you have buzzed off, go and fuck yourself.'

Calamity porn

The coffee-table tome of the Apocalypse will look amazing. Certainly, the dry-run – *New York September 11*, containing photos of that terrible day taken by the photographers from the illustrious Magnum photo agency – is an eye-catching, one might even say jaw-dropping, document. A vivid memento of one special day to remember.

The 2006 documentary on The Falling Man was built upon the premise that we cannot bear to look upon the image of the mid-air mystery man jumping to his doom and so end up censoring the image. This was good because it enabled everyone to print the image again, really big, just to prove that we are now brave enough to face the image. Look, here we are: facing it.

Photoshopped images of a future London after some future flood? Horrendous, yes. But also quite cool. After all, didn't New Orleans look dramatic? The picturesque hobos, the battered streets, the martial law surrounding the chain stores . . . and what a soundtrack: between all the blues and all the jazz, nature could not have wreaked havoc in a more culturally enriching setting.

For years, torture was a very worthy, late-Pinter sort of subject, but now it's family entertainment with pliers-on-body action adding real piquancy to the plots of hip television series like *Lost* and 24. The whole taboo has really lifted of late: after

9/11, the *New York Times* said that conversations 'in bars, on commuter trains, and at dinner tables' were now turning on the relative ethics of torture. It's almost worth a supplement spread: Torture Chic.

'Disaster movies will never be the same again' was one verdict, in the *Guardian*, on *United 93*. Oh, good. So they didn't die in vain. If nothing else, at least we can point to 9/11 as having revived a moribund movie genre.

At the time of writing, anyone hoping for a revival in fortunes for the cop buddy movie would be slavering in anticipation of Nicolas Cage and Michael Peña in Oliver Stone's *World Trade Center* – two men bravely fighting an evil even worse than Joss Ackland in *Lethal Weapon 2* (and he killed Patsy Kensit!). Hopefully, other moribund movie genres will also get a twenty-first-century calamity boost: personally, I can't wait for the first weird weather sex comedy. Or the first post-Guantanamo caper flick.

The acclaim for *United 93* was deafening. Apparently, it was 'unifying, and uplifting, at a time when the wars in Iraq and Afghanistan are going badly'. Which is, surely, kind of weird. Everything's fucking up! With our governments' efforts to rectify matters only seeming to derectify matters further! But look, here's some proper brave stuff. It's uplifting. More than the nightly news, certainly. I'm sick of that stuff.

Of course, artists are beholden to reflect the world around them, and if that involves getting off – in a simplistic way – on the drama of it all, then at least it's not standard-issue Hollywood escapism of rappers in fast cars. Or maybe, in fact, this is the new escapism: seeking respite from the fruitless drear by getting kicks from bloody, handheld, vérité docudramas on the more horrific flashpoints of the age. 'There's such a lot on at the moment. What do you fancy? There's the

Twin Towers film or the New Orleans film. Then there's *Fast and Furious: Nightmare in Najaf*. Oh, and *The Taleban Terminator*, about the British sniper in Helmand Province. It's apparently a bit like *Phone Booth* – only they haven't got a functioning telecommunications network.'

David Cameron

Here is the first draft of an appeal from Conservative leader David Cameron to 'The Kids' . . .

Dear The Kids

Hi! It's David Cameron here. Dontcha just love the environment? Big up to the biosphere. That's what I say. Like, totally.

OK, here's the deal. The under-thirty-fives don't vote Tory. Professionals in their thirties or forties have been turned off by our closet racist, dog-whistle anti-immigrant stance. The average age of our voters is fifty; the average age of our members is ninety-two. It is time for newness.

Up the gays! I mean it!

So here are my new priorities as the new leader of the new Modern Compassionate Conservative Party:

1. Kiss Muslim babies.

2. Bring hope to the poor. I love the poor. I mean, the less financially engorged. In particular, I like sullen young men in hoodies. I like to touch them. Jesus – not in that way! I mean reach out to them, give them belief. With the substitution of one little letter I will bring understanding to these poor,

deluded, feral children. Not hoodies – but goodies! Less knifing each other; more making tea for oldies. Goodies!

3. Institute the use of Smythson's stationery. My wife's a director, you know. Smythson's of Bond Street – for all your posh paper needs!

4. Go blue. No, green. Vote blue, but go green. Don't go blue, that would be awful. You'd be like that Blue Man Group with its stupid mime drum act bollocks. And nobody wants that. In fact . . .

5. Deport the Blue Man Group. I'm going to send those bald drumming bastards straight back to Vegas. No messing.

But don't let that give you the idea I'm prejudiced. Another aim of mine is to get ethnic and lady. Nine out of 10 Tory MPs is, like me, a white man. I consider myself ideally placed to sort this out, having been intimately involved with Black Wednesday.

Free Nelson Mandela!

The all-new New Tories are so new it's like we never even existed before. Maybe we didn't? I myself am so shiny and new that I had nothing whatsoever to do with the last Conservative manifesto – the one with all the NHS privatisation and sending the buggers back home. Nothing at all. Except I wrote it. I was Michael Howard's right-hand man – his writing hand, the one writing all the stuff about sending the buggers back home. Aside from writing the 2005 manifesto, though, I couldn't have had less to do with it. Apart from, as I say, writing it. That was me.

New! I'm new! Can't you read?! New!!!

With me, what you see is what you get. And what you see is a man riding a bicycle being followed by a chauffeur-driven limo that you pay for.

Look, we can all joke about my toff background, but just remember this means I was actually born to lead you. My lineage includes both the Royal Family and the Medicis. Although, where the Medicis were courted by Leonardo and Machiavelli, I've got Michael Gove and Adam Rickitt.

But just compare my smile, my eye contact, my cheery repartee with gruff old Gordon Brown. My hair is nicer.

Should you ever have any doubts about me or my policies, simply imagine me firmly shaking you by the hand, looking you square in the eye and saying: 'Have faith. Leave everything to me. It's perfectly safe.' Reassuring, isn't it?

Coal not dole!

And I care. I really do. I often weep openly for Gaia. I'll do anything for the environment, and have written a special New 'Compassionate Conservative' (yes, just like George Bush) New Programme to Renew the Old Environment. Here are my pledges for you to cut out and keep.

1. I will recycle plastic bottles.

2. I will take short-haul flights to glaciers to talk to journalists who have also taken short-haul flights to hear me talk about how important the Earth is. And it is.

3. I will use both sides of the excellent paper marketed by my wife – Smythson's of Bond Street, available to buy in the shop or via the website (Smythson's – for all your posh paper needs).

4. I will go 'aaaah' if I see any pictures of seals, and will become quite stern if I think for any significant period about carbon dioxide.

5. I will regulate and tax the rapacious big business interests who are raping the Earth for their filthy private gain. What? Shit. No. Not the last bit. Sorry, I was copying some points out of a Friends of the Earth pamphlet and did the wrong bit. I mean it about the seals, though. Just look at them! Aaaah.

It's all about balance. About balancing your concerns about the environment with not actually doing anything. Regulations, man, who wants to be tied down with that shit? Hang loose – that's what I say.

It's about seeming to echo your concerns about the NHS, cool trainers, Third World debt, while not actually doing anything. It's about shedding our old-fashioned, right-wing image and trying to look like a vigorous, young voice of Britain as it is, not as it was, while still being really quite right-wing. (Honestly – check out my voting record; you'll shit.)

As my good friend and 'intellectual godfather' Olly Letwin said, when explaining our radical new approach: 'It's quite a liberating idea to create an area between ignoring things completely and having to legislate or regulate them.'

Basically, I would say this to you: if the traditional ideological barriers between left and right have broken down, why not just vote for the right? Or, as you Kids would say: whatever.

He was the future once. But tomorrow belongs to me.

Peace, y'all.

Dave Cameron

Carbon offsets

Planting trees: what can possibly be wrong with that? Well, nothing usually. Except if those trees become figleaves. Figleaves to help cover up an enviro-hellstorm. Which they won't be able to do. Because figleaves are small, and enviro-hellstorms are big.

The wonder of carbon offsets shows that there really is no problem you can't solve by throwing more money at it, even if that problem is born from having money. Honestly, it's like a little miracle.

So Coldplay can feel OK about the CO_2 emissions of their super-success enormo-gigs by funding the planting of 10,000 mango trees in India. In this way, a recent broadsheet interview can proudly report the band flying 'by private jet to Palm Springs . . . The band can now afford to fly wherever possible'. (Of course, pretty soon there might not be any palms or any springs when they fly to Palm Springs – but that won't be their fault!)

In such ways, even an utterly atomised populace can change the world. Any problems? Well, only that it's largely bollocks. The science is disputed, but what is clear is that you cannot even accurately account for the amount of carbon that will be 'offset' by planting trees. Trees do temporarily 'trap' some carbon but, unfortunately, they also breathe some of it out again – it's just kind of what they do (I know this is disturbing, but trees are alive – not like in *Lord of the Rings*, but still . . .). And when the trees are felled, at least some of the carbon will be released back into the atmosphere. So landscape historian Oliver Rackham has compared the practical effect of carbon offset tree-planting to drinking more water to keep down rising sea levels. Even Friends of the Earth, who fucking love trees, say it's 'not a solution'.

In culinary terms, it's like living on a diet of doner kebabs and thinking that's all right because you've also got the slice of lemon, lettuce and pickled chilli in there.

The message is simple: the planet cannot survive on a diet of kebabs.

Celebrities taking celebrity reality TV shows far too seriously

During the filming of *Celebrity Masterchef*, the singer Paul Young was 'close to tears' as he revealed that getting into the second round would 'just mean so much to me'.

Don't get so bound up in it, mate. Put it into context.

'I'm Gonna Tear Your Playhouse Down'? 'Toast'. That was YOU.

Celebrity fragrances

Have rubbish names. There's Lovely by Sarah Jessica Parker; David Beckham's Instinct; True Star Gold by Beyoncé; Britney Spears' Fantasy and Britney Spears' Curious.

Britney Spears 'personifies daring . . . Curious by Britney Spears represents the young woman that pushes boundaries and revels in adventure.'

Yes, Britney Spears is indeed fairly curious, although not in the sense that she might suddenly, say, get really into botany. She's curious in a different way. And she's getting curiouser and curiouser.

True Star Gold sounds like one of those obscure petrol stations you only ever see in the countryside – like the ones in

Sussex with a logo that is almost exactly, although not quite, the same as the European Union's, if the European Union had produced its logo on a Commodore 64 and superimposed the British isles over the top.

Sean John's scent is Unforgivable. By which I don't mean it's unforgivable, although it probably is. It's actually called Unforgivable. Apparently, he personally chose the 'combination of breathtaking, addictive and slightly dangerous essences'. What are 'slightly dangerous essences'? Arsenic that's been very heavily diluted? Is Sean John slowly trying to poison the world literally as well as metaphorically now?

Also, why does he always look so miserable? Is he actually miserable? Or has he now taken the whole old-school-aristo thing so far that he's started modelling himself on the Queen?

Celebrity Hair Now

As in the magazine. Called *Celebrity Hair Now*. A special edition of *Now* magazine that focuses entirely on celebrity hair, now.

You shouldn't look here for stories about celebrity noses or teeth. Those would be the concerns of other magazines. Go find them. This one is about hair.

Of course, the title of this magazine is *Celebrity Hair Now*. From that alone, everything should be clear.

First, there is the Celebrity aspect: *Celebrity Hair Now* is a very celebrity-centric publication. Then there is the Now side of things: very little of worth is included in *Celebrity Hair Now* about celebrity hair *then*. It gets the odd mention. Mere context-setting.

But the dominant aspect of *Celebrity Hair Now*, the very

heart of the beast and not just the dressing on top, is the Hair. Of this, the preponderance at times verges on the overwhelming. There is rarely any let-up in this regard. You feel like you are drowning in Hair. I might have to cancel my subscription. It's *too much* hair.

'Change Yourself Today!' culture

Understand this: there is something deeply adrift within your personality. Be prepared to chuck it away and start again.

The urge to start afresh seems particularly strong in the New Year. A few hours after the bells have chimed, anyone remaining unaware that they are polluted rotters will soon be disabused of this by shelves crammed with books by Paul McKenna offering to Change Your Life in Seven Days. Or possibly Make You Thinner. Or Turn You Inside Out if You Fancy.

Newspaper headlines urge you to 'Change Your Life for 2006: Be happier, be healthier, be richer. The experts tell you how in our special guide' (*Independent on Sunday*). Why are these writers so obsessed with cleansing their souls and starting afresh? What did they do over Christmas to mire themselves so thoroughly? Did they find themselves shouting racial epithets in the middle of an orgy?

In March 2006, the self-helpish magazine *Psychologies* included a special dossier called 'Get Ready to Change'. It had the headline 'Are you ready to CHANGE?' Plus bullet points: 'Your life map: what needs to change?', '"How I got a new life"' and 'Test: how will you handle change?' A subliminal message arguably emerges here. And it's not: stay exactly the same as you already are.

A change, it's often said, is as good as a rest. I prefer a rest, myself, but there you go. The self is a tricky concept that has been the subject of anguished debate since time immemorial. Maybe the autonomous individual has a burning core of consciousness from which all else exudes. Maybe this is a myth to enforce positive feelings about ourselves and engender the illusion that we can determine our own way in the world. Perhaps we are merely the sum of our socio-economic relations with other human beings. Or simply the totality of all the words we ever speak and think. Alternatively, we could just be a set of genetically pre-programmed desires designed to propagate the species, a trillion mindless robots dancing . . .

Whatever, it's clearly a tangled affair. So thank the Lord we have Paul McKenna to sort it out.

Chantelle's Dream Dates

The E4 programme in which the *Celebrity Big Brother* winner Chantelle turns fairy godmother, whisking away a dateless girl in her pink stretch limo and offering them a chance to 'live the dream' – by going on a date with some bloke.

After meeting her lonely bachelorette, Chantelle heads down to Covent Garden to find her a likely lad. Then she goes out and apparently looks for someone with a face only his spots could love. His bum-fluff moustache indicates he's too young for this kind of challenge, so Chantelle explains: 'I was sort of thinking . . . toyboy?'

Then this young lad is shown a video of his perfectly attractive potential date and delivers his verdict: 'I think she's a bit rough looking and needs to glamour herself up.'

Then Chantelle shows her the film of him pointing out her alleged shortcomings and asks: 'So how does that make you feel about yourself?'

And she says: 'It does make me feel worse about myself, but it's nice to hear . . .'

'Nice to hear'? Really? Because having my physical appearance grimly picked apart by rude tossers would not be music to my ears.

Chefs' families

Start off by frying the garlic and the red onion in a touch of extra-virgin olive oil. When that's sizzling, drop in the chillis and the ground spices. After a couple of minutes –

Look at my kids! Look at them! My kids!

Now this is the crucial bit. Get the pancetta and wrap it round the chicken breasts. Make sure you have a little bit left over – we'll be needing that later for the dessert. Stick it in the oven at about –

Mum! Here's my mum. Taught me everything she knew – shit at cooking, mind. Only joking, Mum. I love you really. You old tart! Only joking. Freak.

Now mix the chocolate with the whipped cream until you form a marble effect. Make sure not to overmix. Before adding the Radox, just –

Uh-oh, Dad's here. 'The Colonel', I call him. Put *me* through my paces, I can tell you. But now I'm Mr Moneybags and he comes on *my* show. So there you go . . . all right, Dad? I'm fucking minted.

At this point, you'll need to coat the strawberries in liver. Add them to the pan and let them gently frown –

Look! At! My! Kids!

Now, aren't we a family? One big happy family? Except when we're all shouting at each other, but we even do that in quite an animated kind of way. Think of this as not just a cookery programme, but also a lesson in how to be more Italian. We're so Continental, it's mental!

At this point, I like to stuff my face with grated Parmigiano, feast on the family pet (look at it!), pour a southern Burgundy that tastes of appley snails over my head, and then cackle in the summer rain as I luxuriate on top of a roasting hot barbecue. Yeah!

Look! It's my kids! Look again! Kids! My!

LOOK AT MY KIDS!

Dick Cheney

Sometimes, one may have doubts about whether it's right to demonise one man as the figurehead for all gas-guzzling, planet-raping, profiteering bastardry. We might momentarily wonder whether such a complex individual can really be so baldly drawn as the pure, living embodiment of bug-eyed Republican evil. Then, for a relaxing day off, he gets pissed up and shoots another man in the face.

Dick Cheney hunts pensioners – releasing them into the Texas scrubland, then letting off 260 pellets of leaden injury right in their faces. Still, at least it gets him into the outdoors – his previous exercise having been confined to climbing greasy poles and counting his money.

Cheney has often been called the architect of the Iraq War (however, an architect would have made a plan – so let's just say it was 'his fault'). Even people supposedly on his side

(Lawrence Wilkerson, a former aide to Colin Powell) have openly wondered whether his propensity to ignore UN conventions makes him a war criminal. His enemies, however, *really* don't like him.

After the shooting, Cheney took a while to take responsibility for pumping buckshot into hapless Harry Whittington. It was a full 14 hours before the cops were called. Earlier, the local sheriff – alerted to the incident by the call made to the ambulance service – had been turned away from the estate by security guards who 'knew of no incident'.

According to our sources, the full 14 hours were taken up with an in-depth debate on how to play the issue. Cheney argued that if he could get Whittington classified as an 'unlawful enemy combatant' then he could not only shoot him in the face but also torture him. 'Let's waterboard the fucker,' Mr Cheney is reported as saying. He then suggested the excuse 'An Arab did it'. Ultimately, his final gambit that he should 'privatise responsibility' having fallen on deaf ears, he was persuaded to go on the telly and claim to be 'a bit sorry'.

Even then, he managed to turn his admission that he shot an old man in the face – 'I'm the guy who pulled the trigger that fired the round that hit Harry' – into a piece of sing-song circumlocution in the style of 'There Was an Old Lady Who Swallowed a Fly'.

I don't know why she swallowed a fly. But I strongly suspect part of the reason why Dick Cheney didn't alert the police until 14 hours after he had pulled the trigger that fired the round was because he was an old man who had swallowed a beer. Followed by another beer. Possibly to catch the first beer. Who knows?

Chinese Communist Party, the

Plimsolled peasants, the blind tide who have floated down re-routed rivers: hanging off girders a hundred thousand stories high. Everything everywhere expanding like a great big expanding thing that moves very quickly. In 1998, 16 of the world's 20 most polluted cities. We must build more. Build more and capture the last few places until the buildings eat the sky. Wonders accomplished far surpassing Roman aqueducts, Gothic cathedrals, the Burj al-arab. No one can breathe. It doesn't matter.

Everyone must live in a pod hotel and eat out. All the restaurants in China full – all the Chinese restaurants full of Chinese people, which, as we know from our dads, is 'always a good sign'. Now, 24 million chickens eaten a day. It's not enough. Soon they won't be able to wait, and will just eat the eggs. Everything laced with agricultural chemicals and animal hormones: women buying tits; men growing them. 'Western' technology bought or taken. A resplendent Olympics showcasing the all-new Re-education Through Labour event. Beijing sites of English public schools churning out Chinese public schoolboys. Polo. Party princelings and the rich renew their organs from slaughtered-to-order cultists and Christians. Power-brokers chasing 'wild flavours' gorge on SARS-carrying civet cats from the wild animal markets of southern China. Businessmen's prandial panda penises wreak disease and pestilence in foreign financial centres that are no longer houses of finance but merely houses of whores. Kids sent away to see how estate agents live. Kids who now can read but cannot read their history. *Teen Vogue* swearing allegiance to the Party. No longer an iron smelter in every garden – steel plants for all that want them, dismantled and labelled piece by piece and shipped in from Germany. Motorways upon motorways –

leading inevitably to motorway service stations; corrupt officials skimming off the top to leave potholes and cave-ins for unwary capitalist roaders. Families hitherto forced to work at opposite ends of the country now can work at opposite sides of the globe. A mature society, with proper vast inequality between the supra-rich and the super-poor.

They will solve the problems of the countryside by abolishing the countryside. All will be a constantly renewing urban sprawl, an end of days of peasants starving while they feed the cities; now they can starve in the cities – cities leaping through stages of development and redevelopment. And again. A billion five-car families buying widescreen refrigerators. A billion coal-fired arms dealers propping up revolving African despots. Socialism which you cannot eat becoming state capitalism which you cannot stop eating. Obesity: growth measured with a tape measure around the waist.

Production producing product-producers nestle everywhere, settle everywhere, establish connexions everywhere. The cheap prices of Chinese commodities are the heavy artillery with which the new system batters down all Chinese walls, bringing home brands as souvenirs. Baby milk. Toys and tractors. Soft war by penicillin production. If only we could make the West wear its shirt-tails a half-inch longer; the mills of China would be working round the clock. The world gorged on cheapness. Tesco and Wal Mart merrily marking up marks-ups that merely mark the end. The West desiccated and ruined – everyone reduced to surviving by selling one another their knick-knacks on eBay and servicing each other. The rest of the time is spent falling down manholes, the iron caps melted as scrap by kids to send East. Kids once more display posters of Mao. Snakeheads smuggling people in. The only good goods the Chinese goods.

Fish, wood, logs legal and illegal. Oil. Wood for wood; wood to make way for soy beans. 20% of the population; 7% of the arable land. Raw materials sucked in from the globe like a giant fishing factory-ship draining all the oceans at once, commodity prices trebling even in the instant that they are sold. Norwegian men fight in the street like dogs, over tree saplings. The West morally outraged by the combination of low wages and environmental degradation. The very idea! Taiwan purchased. A yo-yo of African despots, misery revolving; cash loans and ivory palaces bestowed upon the new dictators. China Radio International broadcasting as Radio Not Free Nairobi. But starvation-waged copper miners listen instead for accidents. More Chinese in Nigeria than the Brits ever had. Hard power. Oil wars. Chinese fiefdoms in the Middle East – Mad Max beyond the Terrordome. Mel Gibson strung up on an oil derrick like Christ.

Jailed journalists fail to report the unveiling of the statue of the Google founders – 1,989 feet high at the gates of the Forbidden City, next to the mural of Mao. Under it, the Google motto – now the organising principle of the Communist Party of China – 'Do No Evil'. Kids jailed for internet searching 'Tiananmen'. Twenty years for throwing an egg. Shi Tao – jailed for 10 years for emailing abroad how the paper he worked for covered the 15th anniversary of the slaughter in the Square. Yahoo helped identify him. Yahoo/Google/ Microsoft: will you let me search 'police informants' or 'accomplices to repression'? Murdoch: he knows a ruthless money-hungry elite when he sees one. Seek truth from facts – even if you have to make them up. Party and nation fused; run by arse-lickers, nepotistic yes-men and old-fashioned bastards. Lawless local government mafias getting fat on the wages of migrants; siphoning enviro-cash to build coal-fired coal burners, just for kicks, state loans disappearing in a puff of sulphurous smoke. 170,000 party members found guilty of corruption in 2004 – just the careless ones. Grasping at the organs of the living – imprisoned for the fear of funny-exercising Falun Gong. Churches putting party before god in their screeds. The organs of Christians (body organs, not big music ones with pipes – that would be stupid). The organs of the trade unionists. The organs of those jailed for having a picture of the Dalai Lama: look, he's 'Tibetan'. Tiananmen? An 'incident'. The Cultural Revolution? A couple of mistakes may have been made. 30 million dead of famine? I couldn't possibly comment. We prefer to be called the ruling party, as if someone else might get a go.

Acid rain already falling in Canada reaches all the way around the world and comes back. But it cannot be enough. Overproduced stock piles of baby clothes tower. Pauperised paupers pauper their pauper. Workers handed the shitty stick – and are then struck with it if they strike. The iron rice bowls are empty. A communist state which is not as 'socialist' as Germany – spending less than half the share of GDP on its people. 120 million migrant workers with no welfare. Housing sold off. Mass state redundancies. Releasing private firms from the commitment to fund healthcare and workers' kids' education. But it cannot be enough. Private and public blurred, with CP fingers over every sticky pie. Nobody knows where the join is. The CP keeps the water and energy costs low; they'll turn a blind eye to piracy and environmental destruction and twat anyone who gives you jip. Beating back social movements like bashing moles with a mallet. No one can stop this? There are 1.3 billion Chinese who need to consume like Americans. There is no alternative? The Three Gorges Dam – the world's most costly construction project, its opponents disappeared? 'It is not enough! I want a bigger dam! Get me more gorges!'

Onwards. Driving up commodity prices until you have to pay to stand in the breeze. Driving down prices to the point that they actually pay you to take pirate copies of VW Golfs off their hands. Everyone is eating everything, and everyone is being eaten. Everyone waiting for the Chinese Elvis. But she is in the army. The galleries have been closed. They are coming for the backward elements who do not shop at Accessorise. A billion boys and girls, no longer aborted, playing video games continuously for days on end. Once, kids denounced their parents. Now, parents bottle pressure up in kids. The kids lose themselves in online games; generations jump from buildings, believing they can live and die and live again, as in a game. But you cannot repair nature. The air is like sewage. But what do you want? Scenery or production? All relationships are burst asunder except relations to money and relationships to the party. Ancient traditions prove futile to resist, and are swept away. New traditions are ratified unanimously by the National People's Congress. All that is holey is propaned. A man stands stripped bare in a dry riverbed, clutching a pirate Harry Potter with an alternative ending. Everyone is melting.

Well, that's one school of thought, anyway. Who knows? Maybe sense will prevail. Or they might just run out of oil or get a bit tired out or something.

City status

Whenever I hear about another town being granted city status, I always imagine a hall full of councillors going: 'Yeah, yeah, yeah! We're a city now! We're a city now! Whereas

Skelmthwaite is still a town! Ha ha ha! Who's the city? We're the city! Yeah! Let's get the guys together and drive over there – show them some-bitches a bit of what we got.'

But I'm sure that's wrong. I'm sure that in fact they're much more mature about the whole matter.

'Contemporary', the word

These days, you can pass a building-site sign advertising new 'modern contemporary apartments' before turning the corner to see a new art gallery calling itself Contemporary and then sitting at a café beside someone reading an interiors magazine offering 'the latest in contemporary chic'. This isn't just rhetorical overstatement. This actually happens. I was there. I *was* that building site.

We live in 'contemporary' times. Arguably, all times are 'contemporary', in that when they are happening, that's when they are happening. But that is to overlook precisely how 'contemporary' these particular times are.

The message is plain: Leave the past behind. It was probably horrible anyway. And if it wasn't horrible, well, it's gone – which is slightly sad, so what's the point in dwelling? Britain is booming. Why would we want to recall times when Britain wasn't booming? We are young, wild and free. The cranes on the skylines are testament to this revival: how towns throughout Britain are developing 'contemporary new quarters' full of 'contemporary flats' or 'contemporary refurbs'. Just feel the nowiness of now. Get it while you can. It won't last forever.

What 'contemporary' means here is a slightly chilling continual present with places to eat called 'eat' and lots of white paint and glass.

Of course, being 'contemporary' is actually rather temporary. 'Now' always has this awful habit of becoming 'then'. And what happens then? Once you are no longer hip, hot and happening and start entering old age – 24, say – you have essentially reached the end of your usefulness and you might well find your support systems closed down – yes, just like Microsoft have been threatening to do for the millions still using Windows 98.

1998? That's *so* last century!

Cool brands

'Perhaps you had dreams of becoming an adventurer like Indiana Jones [when you grew up],' reckons a huge pullout ad for Diesel's 55DSL brand in the pages of *Dazed & Confused*. 'Or a world-class ballet dancer, maybe even an ace fighter pilot. Perhaps you wanted to be all three at the same time! Either way, you probably wanted to do something a little more exciting that what you do right now . . . 55DSL is looking for two young and gifted individuals to join our new Kick Ass Department. This isn't a joke, we really do have a Kick Ass Department and we really are looking for someone to fill our Junior Lucky Bastard position.'

Not joking, but really having a Kick Ass Department: how cool is that? The winning (junior) lucky bastards get to see cool stuff, film cool stuff (films are cool), blog about cool stuff (blogs are cool), supplying the content for DSL's new 55 Seconds campaign . . . Making someone's ads for them? Now *that's* cool. Diesel is cool. Not the fuel – although some maintain it's more environmentally friendly than petrol, as it's more efficient. No, Diesel the clothes.

The best brands are always on the hunt for cool. Cool-hunting: it's like fox-hunting, but cooler. Cool brands are not afraid to let cool kids show them the way to cool. If you can get them to do your advertising for you for free, then you're on to a double-winner.

And if you can't get the kids, then best rely on style journalists who, as we know, can always be relied upon to dance for beans. Cool brands get these cool consultants to show them how to be cool. These people are the consultants of cool. In return, they write about your brand and place it in photoshoots. So it's sort of like a bribe . . . only cooler.

Cool Brandleaders, a Brand Council initiative, saw a judging panel of cool people deciding which brands were the coolest. Among the chosen brands were the London Eye (standing in queues for hours? Totally cool) and Coca-Cola (diverting water supplies from Indian villages? Way cool).

One of the prime factors the judges identified was that cool brands never actively try to be cool. They never ask, 'Are we cool?' And they definitely don't say, 'We are cool.' According to photographer (and *Dazed & Confused* publisher) Rankin: 'If you have to try then you've already failed; if you want it too bad you're just chasing your tail.' Tails are not cool.

But brands must also work hard to keep their cool. Not abandon their original purpose or personality for the sake of cheap profit. Rankin's advice here is to 'stay focused'.

So brands must stay focused on being effortless. Which might be the same as staying unfocused about making an effort. You mustn't make an effort at being focused, anyway. Are you following all this? Or are you just not cool enough?

'Cool has nothing to prove/Cool dares to be imperfect,' claims Isabella Von Bulow of the Institute of Practitioners in Advertising in a cool poem she contributed to a cool book called *CoolBrands: An insight into some of Britain's coolest brands*. After noting that cool is 'visionary' and 'selfish', von Bulow concludes that cool 'fills a need'.

Poems about cool? How cool is that?

Cornish nationalism

Palestine, Kurdistan, Cornwall – a roll-call of trapped nations and oppressed peoples. The latter, shamefully, a country so close to our own. Kicked to the floor by the jackboot of the Blairite junta; a fetid bog of poisoned nationalist aspirations and fudge, oppression crashing on to their cliffs like the sea, gradually rendering their spirit unto sand.

Such is the view of political and intellectual heavyweights like Lisa Simpson of *The Simpsons*. In a special edition of the show, Lisa ran round the family home waving a Cornish flag, shouting, 'Rydhsys rag Kernow lemmyn' ('Freedom for Cornwall now') and holding a placard saying, 'UK OUT OF CORNWALL'. Mebyon Kernow (the Party for Cornwall), meanwhile, refers to the proposal for the Plymouth unitary authority expanding ever so slightly into east Cornwall as 'an invasion of Cornwall, a violation of its territorial integrity which must be resisted at all costs'.

The UK has an incredibly cunning way of being 'in' Cornwall – by overtly occupying it for only three months of the year, lying prostrate, eating clotted-cream ices or bobbing about on novelty inflatables. This is not occupation as we understand it from, say, Iraq. Certainly, if the Coalition had 'done a Fallujah' on Polperro I think I'd have noticed. Maybe High Command decided they'd never get the tanks up that steep hill near Liskeard on the A38? (It is *very* steep.)

To find notions of Cornwall as anything other than just another English county – albeit quite a handsome one; I mean, don't get the idea we're just taking the piss here – you have to go back to medieval times.

One of the very last mentions is from Italian-born scholar Polydore Virgil. In the introduction to his *Anglica Historia*, first published in 1535, he wrote: 'The whole Countrie of Britain . . . is divided into iiii partes; whereof the one is inhabited of Englishmen, the other of Scottes, the third of Wallshemen, [and] the fowerthe of Cornishe people, which all differ emonge them selves, either in tongue . . . in manners, or ells in lawes and ordinaunces.'

'Thee Cornishe', he added, 'do devilish maketh fudge. But they can patenteth not pasties, which they didn't invent. Alleth of the isles eate stuffe in pastrie; not just them; just because they were popular with tinne miners, it doesn't mean they invented it or have exclusive rights. It's not like champagne, which is clear-cut. They can't even agree whether you put swede in or not. And most of them are knockede up by Ginster's in a huge factorie usinge ingredients bussed in from all over the country. So I'm not taking that claim at all seriously.'

And what's this Spirit of Cornwall obsession with being Celtic? Cornwall, they remind us, is one of the 'historic Celtic nations' – that's historic as in 'ages ago'. If the Cornish do want to be a bit Celtic, best of luck to them, but it does seem a tad random. The Celts only arrived in 500 BC, after the Bronze Age. Long before that, in the fourth millennium BC, Cornwall saw the arrival of Neolithic tribes from mainland Europe – as did the whole of Britain. Before the Neolithics, there were just wandering tribes, wandering about. So if getting tribal is the thing, let's go back to that.

Sadly, all of these options breach the useful rule of thumb

that, if your political views are fundamentally and inextricably based on something that happened before, say, 1700, you probably want to take a long, hard look at yourself. Perhaps we could draw a line a bit later – say when the Great Western Railways came with their amazing steam horses? This rule goes for the Balkans, the Middle East and Yorkshire, too; otherwise things just seem to get silly.

Incidentally, Rick Stein's not Cornish; he's from Oxford. He is Judge Jules's uncle, though. That's a fact.

Corrie babes

I don't wish to sound prudish, but there's definitely something odd about seeing someone you've watched on the telly since they were a small child now all grown up with their front all over the front of *Front*. One minute it's all sympathy for the gymslip mum struggling gamely with her GCSEs (Sarah) or loving very much a dog (Maria); next it's 'Have I ever considered lesbianism? You never know!' etc. I'm sure this must be how their parents feel. And, in a way, are we not all their parents?

The *Sun*'s Charles Rae is certainly looking out for Sarah Louise Platt. She's been a bit silly. She hasn't been claiming her due benefits. 'If [she] only took advantage', rued Rae, 'of the £400 million [Educational Maintenance Scheme], she could be earning *and* studying.' Sarah could be taking home anything up to 30 pounds a week – which would not be deducted were she to take other part-time work while studying.

Next up, here's Charles advising Pauline Fowler on drawing up a will in advance of her marriage to Joe Macer: 'Without the will, Joe would get everything – leaving Pauline's kids and grandkids with nothing.' As adjudicated where? *Crown Court* that was on the Telly in the 1970s, Judge Judy presiding? A wine bar?

The *Sun* is literally mad for this sort of thing. The day after the 2006 Budget, they examined its effect on the Battersbys, the Peacocks and Little Mo: 'Everyone will be affected by Chancellor Gordon Brown's budget – and that includes our most famous soap families living in Weatherfield, Albert Square and Emmerdale.' They were, though, forgetting the Chancellor's exemption for fictitious characters.

Going one step further than the *Sun* (in this, as in so many things), David Blunkett was featured on the same pages, in a rare moment of not talking about his dog, assessing the Budget's impact on everyone's favourite teenage sorcerer: 'Harry Potter will welcome the rebuilding of his classrooms and the increase in money invested in the baby bond. It'll provide a nest-egg to help him set up home when he is 18, or see him through uni.'

Except a) he goes to private school; b) he won't go to uni, he's a fucking wizard; and c) he's made up, you stupid, stupid, really quite shockingly right-wing man.

By the way, worst affected by the Budget, in case you were wondering, was that nefarious shit Tom King out of *Emmerdale*, due to his 4×4 and the tightening of rules on setting up trusts for his sons. 'But on the plus side, duty on spirits was frozen again.' Drink yourself stupid, old man.

Cotswolds columns

Pigs! But also sheep. My sheep are very much the best sheep.

Behold, the new Countryside Alliance – it's small-beer

entertainers telling you about our new lives among the smells and the airs of the countryside. Before now, the only foxes I'd ever hunted were of the two-legged variety around the media haunts of Olde Soho. Now I can't wait to get my jodhpurs on for some illegal galloping across the downs with the locals. Shhh, don't tell, but apparently, if I'm very good, I might get invited to a cockfight. I know it's wrong, but it's actually so wrong it's right. And they rip each other's faces off right in front of your very eyes!

And don't worry, it's not all maiming wild animals down here on the Côte D'Wolds. It's dinner parties, too. For me, the best invite is always the post-shoot supper at some enormous country house. The locals are extremely keen on their London visitors. They can't stop asking us what it's like being on television. If we've ever met Jilly Goolden. That kind of thing.

But, even if I say so myself, and I frequently do, me and the other half particularly pride ourselves on our select gatherings. At our last soirée, Rory Bremner dressed up as the Queen. Kate Winslet played a harp while Sam Mendes danced around in a tutu. Anne Robinson poured beer down the back of the television. Liz Hurley wrote a sonnet.

Rebekah Wade had a fistfight with William Morris. The fat bloke who did *Trigger Happy TV* was set upon by the chickens. Then I spotted Kate Moss standing in the rain looking lost. Or was it Joanna Trollope? Or was it the fat bloke who did *Trigger Happy TV*? It really was quite a do!

To be honest, I'm not really sure why I'm here. It's fucking miles from London . . . Twenty more words? Okay: Doctor Foster went to Gloucester in a shower of rain. He fell in a puddle right up to his middle and never went there again.

Which I'm not at all surprised about. I fucking hate Gloucester.

Couples' columns

Here's a chance to look back fondly at everyone's favourite must-read column, 'We Hate Each Other's Guts', soon to be published in book form . . .

Her story

To begin with, it was pure, full-on hysterical attraction. Our appetite for each other was prodigious, as it was for many things: going to the cinema, cakes . . . And we were always at the centre of everything. We loved getting a crowd of friends over for food, wine and gossip round the kitchen table. We were like the Liz Taylor and Richard Burton of our scene. People loved us. But, even more than that, we loved us.

Our philosophy, on life and home, was to reflect the individual in each of us. To be diverse. Plus we complemented each other work-wise: we both wrote about our latest relationships for the gratification of others.

It's hard to say why things started to go bad. In retrospect, the strain started to show when he wrote a column headed: 'She's smelly, and has many annoying habits'. From there on in, I started developing sudden feelings of rage. I thought I was a patient person, but I found myself increasingly wanting to snap his fingers off backwards and shove them up his arse. This made me sad.

I wondered where this anger came from. Was I a bad person? Was I a stupid person? I didn't know any more. I explained these feelings in a new weekly column called 'I'm Seriously Considering Getting Out'.

At that point, he became worryingly unhinged. One morning, I woke to find he had left me the message 'DON'T FUCKING LEAVE' by scorching the grass on the bit of Hampstead Heath behind our garden flat with the hot coals left over from the previous night's barbecue. This was a sweet, romantic gesture of the kind that reminded me of our early days together. But deep down I had already realised that by nature I am a nomad. I love change, just to keep up my spiritual energy. So I moved out to live with our daughter's trampolining instructor.

I still think we were soul-mates. We were just soul-mates who grew to hate each other deeply. In a way, we sort of turned our mateyness into hatiness. We became soul-hates. We had to have the good times to get to the bad times. That's what I think, anyway.

His story

Mutual friends always said we had to meet. They realised we were very alike, that deep down we were both people of substance. I often feel like that: that we were both completely full of the same substance.

When we moved in together, our house was an open house. Everyone was welcome day and night. People came and went. They stayed for a drink or supper or perhaps tea or a cold drink and, because they felt so at ease, they often stayed longer. Sometimes, they came and went, and then came back again – after leaving, they'd soon realise they couldn't stand to be apart from us much longer. Always the people and the coming and the going. Always.

But nothing lasts, does it? I started to have my doubts about our relationship when I read an interview with a Sunday magazine in which she said: 'I'm starting to realise that I'm married to a prick.'

Then, later that week, I was listening to my iPod in the bath when I opened my eyes and saw her trying to pull the lampstand through from the hall to throw into the water. Luckily, this ill-thought-out murder attempt failed – although, ironic-ally, I was the one always saying we should get a longer lead! But from then on, I knew we would never find that freshness or innocence of the early days.

Not long after, my book *I Feel so Much Hate towards My Wife and, Indeed, All Women* was published, which some took as a fictionalised account of our marriage. Thereafter, she seemed increasingly distant. When I burned the words 'DON'T FUCKING LEAVE' on to the Heath for her to see out of our window, I thought that would convince her to rethink, but it only seemed to heighten her feelings of insecurity.

Deep down, I think she was scared of how happy I could make her feel. In a funny way, I think I was *too* good as a lover and as a friend. There was so much goodness, she didn't know what to do with it. There was a surfeit. I fulfilled her too much. To the point of over-filling her. There was spillage.

I still think about her all the time. I would say that, yes, I'm obsessed, but not in a way that stops me getting on with my life. I don't just prowl around her neighbourhood in the early hours of the morning. There are many other neighbourhoods I prowl around in the early hours of the morning, too. But that's life, isn't it?

Tom Cruise

Writing a piece for *Time* magazine on 'The People Who Shape Our World', Tom Cruise waxed miracle about *Mission: Impossible 3* director J.J. Abrams: 'It's hard to convey with brevity the extraordinary experience of knowing and working with J.J. Abrams. First of all, is there anything in a name – J.J.? Look at the Jays we have now – Jay Leno, J. Lo, Jay-Z – but he's got two Js. He was born to impinge and invade pop culture.'

There are many reasons to find Tom Cruise a worry. There's his fully functioning WWII fighter plane. The way he thinks all psychological problems can be cured by 'vitamins and exercise' (he might himself consider a brisk walk down to Holland & Barrett). There's all that stuff about the silent birth thing. Those films. But, given that he believes we are descended from super-intelligent aliens, it is perhaps not wholly surprising that when he turns his hand to journalism, the results are so utterly off their head and, well, look like they have been written by an alien.

Maybe there is something in a name. 'TC' was, of course, the nickname for Top Cat, the cartoon alley cat who ruled his manor with cheek and charm; – and Tom was, of course, Top Gun. Then there's Terry Christian, who presented *The Word*; – and Tom Cruise uses words.

Anyway, Cruise finished his lavish eulogy by revealing that J.J. is a 'loving husband to his beautiful wife (can you believe this coincidence?) Katie and father of three glorious children. Gotta give it up for that J2.'

Can we believe that Abrams, like Cruise, also has a wife called Katie? Well, yes. Super-aliens: no. Two women being called Katie: I'm not feeling that to be too much of a stretch. It's quite a common name: Katie Melua; Katie Price. That's two more, right there.

Christ, don't tell him about Eamonn Holmes or he'll really freak.

Current affairs presenters brandishing pens

The new weapons in the war between journalists and politicians: ballpoint pens. Be careful: the tops are off.

For the fearless televisual interrogator, there is little mileage in thinking up tough questions with which mercilessly to skewer abject sophistic postures. You've got a pen, you'd better use it.

The phrase 'the pen is mightier than the sword' is meant to imply that the written word can be more damaging than, well, a sword. Emily Maitlis knows this is bollocks and jabs her pen like it is a sword. Not a metaphorical sword. She actually looks like she'd take your eye out with it. Don't, for God's sake, suggest she's creepily over-earnest: she'll slam that Bic right through your gizzard.

Paxman uses his completely differently: to twiddle round his fingers to express his unending boredom with the party political round. As he twiddles, he is perhaps conveying his belief that our mediatised politicians are purposely closing down all options on real change, fobbing us off with bogus notions of choice and a minuscule range of options that congregate around the mythical 'centre ground of British politics'. That's one interpretation, anyway.

The main question is: what do they have these pens for? Do they jot down thoughts as they go along? 'Blears: Arse!', maybe. 'Ask him re: boyz'. 'Piss bum poo willy pants'. Stuff like that.

I bet Maitlis does sudoku.

Actually, no, I don't. (I'm shit scared of her.)

Cut-glass milk bottles

The design of the humble milk bottle could reasonably claim to have married form and function. Even if it hasn't, milk bottles do the job of bottling milk very effectively. So while improving on the design of milk bottles may be possible, it's not particularly worthwhile. While there are still people hungry – or even just slightly peckish – in the world, there surely isn't much rational scope for going round R&Ding milk bottles.

So what are we to make of the cut-glass milk bottle – that is, a milk bottle with cut-glass, crystalware-style detailing on the side – made by hand and costing £103 each? Many items appear to have perfected a design for up-yourself living, but this surely takes the malted milk biscuit.

Designer Sam Sweet, says *Grand Designs* magazine, 'reinterprets familiar objects and gives them a contemporary twist – the cut-glass milk bottles are about the value of individuality. By remaking the common milk bottle by hand and decorating it, Sam thinks it's much more likely to be reused than a mass-produced one.'

As a model for reuse and recycling, the milk bottle would, as it stands, be a disaster. The humble, 'common' milk bottle, left on people's doorsteps to be collected and reused for many decades past – it's just wasteful.

Forgive me, *Grand Designs*, if I'm not pitching my contribution to the debate at what you might feel to be an appropriate level, but I do have to ask: *are you out of your fucking minds*?

Because if you are, check out the milk bottle design I've been working on for the past fortnight: take two ordinary milk bottles, smash one into tiny fragments and coat the other in glue. Now roll the gluey bottle in the broken shards and glass-dust. Let dry to produce a new milk bottle that not only looks utterly crap but is impossible to pick up without lacerating your fingers and palms. Then dip it in uranium. This will make any milk go off and sadly irradiate you, but it glows like a bastard.

Now *that's* a stupid, pointless design for a milk bottle. Can I have my award now, please?

D

Daily Express, the

The World's Greatest Newspaper. Particularly, or indeed only, if your main interest is in who killed Princess Di.

Design classics that by common consent don't work

The Alessi Juicy Salif lemon squeezer has, according to one retailer, 'earned its place in the Olympus of design. It now stands among the divine.' If you make even a cursory survey of modern design – inquisitive to decode everyday objects, or just wanting to translate some of the conceited consumerist jabber in the back of the colour supplements into English – you will almost immediately be confronted by this divine, Philippe Starck-designed juicer. It is indeed The Law with design books/exhibitions/critics that they must worship at Starck's lemon-squeezing altar, if not pop a picture of the citrus-related masterpiece on the cover.

It's a stone-cold design classic, retailing for around forty pounds. And it doesn't work.

The aluminium lemon juicer, which resembles a tall, skinny, angry spider, has been hailed by *Culture of Design* author and academic Guy Julier as 'beautifully dysfunctional' – that is to say, it doesn't work.

Two-for-one lunchy/design guru Sir Terence Conran said of the Juicy Salif: 'It's intriguing, tactile and desirable, and even though it squirts juice all over your shirt, it's fun to use.'

Fun? What if it goes in your eye? Is that fun too? Why don't all these crazy design gurus just spend all day squeezing lemons straight into their eyes? Or would that just be stupid? Stinging-eyed freaks.

Certainly, Starck doesn't seem to have been entirely on top of his brief. Apparently, company supremo Alberto Alessi was 'surprised and intrigued' when he received the lemon-juicer design from Starck: 'Not [just] because the design was exceptional, but because he had asked Starck to design him a tray.'

Starck said: 'My juicer is not meant to squeeze lemons, it is meant to start conversations.'

Conversations that presumably go: 'Why have you got such a shit lemon squeezer?' 'I don't know.'

Did I mention that it doesn't work?

Dyson vacuum-cleaners, meanwhile, have attained – certainly in the popular consciousness – the hallowed status of all-conquering saviours of British design, the object that proves We Can Still Do It. Workshop of the world? That's us, that is. (Via Malaysia.)

Dyson purchasers are three times more likely to be loyal to the company than those of any other vacuum-cleaner manufacturer. They're yellow and you can see some of the bits inside, so it deserves some loyalty.

It's novel, certainly; like a small Pompidou Centre that cleans your house. But on closer inspection the legend crumbles into dust. Dust you might have to clean up with a different brand of vacuum-cleaner, because *Which?* magazine has found Dysons 'unreliable'.

Anthea Turner, the housework freak, said of the Dyson 'The Ball' DC15: '[It] looks like the Early Learning Centre on wheels . . . Just because some bloke designed this, doesn't make it good.'

According to exhaustive consumer tests, the Germans make the best vacuum-cleaners. Damn them to hell!

Detox socks

Detox rocks. And no form of detox rocks more than detox socks.

These socks hold on detox patches through the night so all the toxic nasties can pour out of your feet. You then wake up with socks full of tox.

Maybe these can then be sold on as tox socks. Because all the detoxing that modern life offers must also require you to do an awful lot of toxing. Otherwise, you won't feel the benefit.

Just drinking some water now and again clearly not being sufficient, today's detox business – which includes diets, tablets and drinks said to flush out toxins – is said to be worth tens of millions of pounds. Which, as Carol '*Detox for Life*' Vorderman will tell you, is big numbers. Cabbage soup? She must be parping like an old van with no exhaust pipe.

Anyway, the Medicines and Healthcare Regulatory Agency recently questioned the claims of a range of detoxing products. Tracey Brown, director of Sense About Science, said of detox products: 'They waste money and sow confusion about how our bodies, nutrition and chemistry work.' Human nutrition expert Professor Martin Wiseman said detox fads were an 'example of the capacity of people to believe in and pay for magic despite the lack of any sound evidence'. Apparently, the main effect of Gillian McKeith's 24-Hour Detox sachets was as a laxative. Maybe it was another fiendish McKeith plan to get her mitts on more of our shits.

Buy this detox fox. In a box. With some hollyhocks. Which is a mallow, a type of flowering plant. Or is that just stupid?

What about a detox ox?

Dictionary services for text messaging

Dictionaries: not exactly in the spirit of the texting age. If these mobile dictionary services are meant as an enticement to stick strictly to the rules of the language, they conspicuously are not working.

Or maybe they're there to inspire greater linguistic flourishes when working out where to meet up and who has been doing what to whom. In which case, maybe we could fit other great reference tomes on to our mobile phones – like dictionaries of quotations for when the time has come to stand on the shoulders of the giants of erudition.

'I believe it was aphorist and clergyman Charles Caleb Colton who first said, 'Wen u hav nutn 2 say, say nutn. :)'

'Gr8'

Diet apples

Scientists testing the hypothesis that the diet industry 'is not nearly mental enough left to its own devices' have developed apples with almost half the amount of sugar found in standard, outrageous apples.

By tweaking the level of the natural sweetener sorbitol, the boffins at the Davis campus of the University of California have brought forth the so-called 'mutant apples'. Mmm, mutant apples – why, they're as homely and hearty as mutant apple pie.

Definitely, though, to lose a bit of weight, if there's anything you want to be cutting back on or finding a lo-cal option for, it's apples. In fact, you might want to cut them out altogether, what with apples being well known for fucking up your health generally.

Also, diet apples: that's never going to fly with the male populace. It's hard enough getting men to eat apples in the first place. Unless you want to take the bloke-Coke route and market them as Apple Zero – perhaps with a cartoon showing the apples' sugar content ripped out from the heart of the apples and then trampled into the dust by an American footballer wearing armour. Perhaps yelling: 'Frat party!'

Pete Doherty blood paintings

Romantic rock rebel and poet Pete Doherty speaks to his generation. And what he mainly says is: 'Give me some money so I can go and buy some crack with it. I'm literally crackers – for crack!'

In one interview, Petey D showed how chic using crack makes you by climbing aboard the motorbike in his hotel room and making motorbike noises. 'Vrooom!' he said, then, 'Vrooooom!' He probably shouldn't be encouraged to ride motorbikes, though. What with being on crack.

When Doherty was imprisoned for his various cracky crimes, newspapers ran extracts from his prison diaries: 'I'm an innocent man. Wiggy only goes and gives me a stretch in chokey! Oh, my stars, the curdled days of toil and distress – lay me down my rivers of blue chalk and tears. And that.'

Doherty's inchoate ramblings were due to be published in 2007 as *The Albion Diaries*; 'Albion', of course, being one of his big ideas – the name of a ship sailing to a utopia called Arcadia, a place without rules or authority. And there will be lots of free sweets on the boat and jelly and ice-cream and lashings of ginger beer! And crack.

Doherty has famously broken down the historic barrier between musician and fan. Sometimes, he does this by removing blood from fans' veins with which he then produces useless paintings for his website. In response to pictures of him seeming to inject an unconscious girl with heroin, he revealed that he was only taking blood from the girl's arm for another painting – kind of the blood painter's equivalent of nipping down to WH Smith's for some more watercolours. He wrote on his website: 'The photos are stolen from my flat so . . . upsetting and personally catastrophic . . . how rude, secondly it's a staged shot and what a fucking liberty to suggest I'd bang up a sleeping lass.'

Yes, how rude. Says the man who went down for burgling his best friend's flat. Of course, removing someone's blood while they lie on the floor for a blood painting is the height of modern etiquette.

Doherty has famously built back up the historic barrier between musician and fan by failing to turn up to many of his own gigs. Asked about this by the *NME*, he explained: 'Yeah? In what sense did I miss gigs? Missed them as in fondly missing them? I didn't miss any fucking gigs.'

When the *NME* pointed out that he'd 'missed' them in the sense of 'not turning up', Doherty countered: 'And who did? Who did? Who did turn up? Let them show their faces. What do they want, blood?'

Well, we know he's got some.

But maybe there is hope. During a 2005 *NME* interview, he refused to speak to the journalist until he gave him money to score drugs. He then jumped on the *NME* hack and tickled him and coercively removed his jacket because he fancied it, then suggested the journalist's drink had been spiked with acid, then boasted about headbutting someone.

By July 2006, he just wanted to tell the *NME* about his exciting new direction. So he's moving away from drab mumbling of dull nonsense over listless strumming to . . . rap. ('Purple's rapping now. He does his thing, the purple man.')

So, rap, then. Oh, and – wait for it – reggae. So we can presumably expect, any moment now, a Jah Rastafari reworking of Tony Hancock's 'The Blood Donor': 'I'm having a right old Cockernee Knees-Up in a cage on a stage / A pint? Why, that's almost an armful . . . Jah!'

Dubai

I've seen the future and it works! Well, with the help of slave labour it works, anyway.

Through a combination of ambition, sunshine, not levying tax and old-fashioned lunacy, Dubai has turned itself into the fantasy-world holiday destination of the age, offering ample parking, shopping and money-laundering opportunities on the side. There are underwater hotels, the world's tallest building, and the whole thing is being run off slave labour. It's what

Vegas would be like if it had any kind of gumption at all. I mean, have you seen all the amazing things going on over there? It's almost like, only 800 miles away from the chaos in Iraq, there's this awesome, glittering haven that's . . . well, it's chaos too – but mighty fine chaos.

The new opportunities and cheap flights are attracting people of all descriptions: 15 million of them visited Dubai in 2005, of which the largest single group were the Brits (650,000 of them). Richard Branson has an island there; Gordon Ramsay has opened a new restaurant; Michael Owen and David Beckham have villas; Jim Davidson now lives there. This dusty, quite deserty garden of earthly delights has become our closest terrestrial equivalent to those casino-planet pitstops the Starship *Enterprise* was forever stopping off at in the original *Star Trek*; a place where all species can kick back and where Captain Kirk's eye will be caught by a woman with big hair and blue skin before the façade cracks to reveal the kingdom's dark secret . . .

In Dubai, being big is big. The most famous landmark is the sail-shaped Burj al-Arab hotel, the world's only self-styled *seven*-star hotel built on its own man-made island with a helipad on the 28th floor. Everything is covered in gold. It's the last word in luxury. (I once saw Anthea Turner and Grant Bovey staying there for a show on Channel 4, which should give you an idea of quite how clean it is.)

When finished, the five-billion-dollar Dubailand theme park will be the world's biggest, bigger even than Manhattan. There's the world's biggest mall, commonly called The Mall, soon to be supplanted by an even bigger mall inside the world's upcoming tallest building, the Burj Dubai. The world's largest indoor ski resort will be supplanted by another, which will feature a revolving mountain (great news for all those who see a mountain and think: 'Hmm, if only it revolved').

Not having much real coastline, Dubai has built more: the man-made island shaped like palm fronds, called The Palms, adds another 120 kilometres. Soon to arrive will be an archipelago of 300 man-made islands, roughly reflecting a map of the world, called The World. This World is a funny old world: Rod Stewart has reportedly already bought up Britain; and there's no Israel.

For many, this energetic display is a demonstration that only when you cut the brake-cable does capitalism get really good. 'In the next ten years,' reckons free-market website Liberty, 'Dubai look-a-likes will spring up around the world like variations on a theme . . . it's either imitate Dubai, or become a petting zoo for those who do.'

So how does it all happen? Well, through a kind of magic: an ancient form of magic called serfdom. Workers (largely Muslims from the Indian subcontinent) hand over their passports, work twelve-hour days and live eight to a room, then send home their wages to families they don't see for years at a time. Work is supposed to stop whenever temperatures top 100°F, which they do often, but that never seems to happen. This is because of one of the truly magic aspects of the Magic Kingdom: whenever it exceeds 100°, there is officially 'no temperature', so work continues. 'Hot, you say? I grant you, it might *feel* hot. But to be off the scale would require a scale to be off. And today, there is simply no temperature, scaldingly hot or otherwise. Even though we are, as you say, sweating like a pair of bastards.'

But look, they're happy! Oh no, sorry, they're not. Like slaves throughout the ages, the construction workers in Dubai are often very unhappy. Puzzled by a recent wave of strikes, interior ministry official Lieutenant-Colonel Rashid Bakhit Al Jumairi declared: 'The workers are demanding overtime pay, better medical care and humane treatment from their foremen . . . But they agreed to their employment conditions when they signed.'

Poor workers enslaved by the forces of kitsch: it's very much the future! 'Can I have my passport back so I can see my family again?'

'No! You must finish building this water park made from gold . . .'

Of late, there has been a spate of workers committing suicide by walking into traffic. (If their deaths are deemed to be accidents, their families back home receive their pay packets.) In Dubai, even suicide isn't really suicide. That's postmodernism for you, to match the 60-floor apartment blocks in the shape of Big Ben, the Eiffel Tower and the Leaning Tower of Pisa.

Then there's Flower City, which aims to take over the international flower trade from Amsterdam. (Dubai City also apes the Dutch capital by playing host to hordes of prostitutes.)

Or there's the underwater hotel, Hydropolis, with its watertight rooms offering views into the ocean (views, presumably, of Pakistani builders making more man-made islands). I've seen the future! It's kind of like Dickens but with more hotels for people who really like late-70s James Bond films. (Incidentally, with everything being built on sand, any rise in sea level could see many more hotel complexes suddenly being 'underwater', but that's a worry for another day.)

Then there's Beef City, which will sell all the beef in the world and will be in the shape of a cow. Every five minutes, it booms: 'Where's the beef? In here! That's where the beef is! In here! In Beef City! Where do you think the beef's going to be? Somewhere else?'

And there's The Stairs: a spiral staircase that leads out of the stratosphere and will eventually reach up to the moon.

Then there's The Shoe: a shoe-shaped hotel where people are free to wear expensive shoes – or not! (Shoes available.)

The Dog: the world's biggest dog hotel.

The Iron: don't know what that one is.

E

Noel Edmonds' relationship with the cosmos

Noel Edmonds needs to be on television. When he is not on television, the cosmos is actively out of kilter. This is why the cosmos was so desperate for him to get back on television. The cosmos has great affection for Noel Edmonds. Perhaps it grew up watching *Swap Shop*.

As we now know, the cosmos is responsible for resurrecting Noel Edmonds from the TV dead. His adherence to cosmic ordering has changed his life from one in which he wasn't on television to one in which he is on television – almost every day. It's the latter he prefers, most definitely.

The method, garnered from the bestselling self-help manual, *The Cosmic Ordering Service: A Guide to Realising Your Dreams* by German writer Bärbel Mohr, is a little like ringing up for a takeaway. But this is ringing up the cosmos for a take-away. And it's not just good for a nice green curry or those hot Thai salads with beef. It's good for houses, too. From his six wishes, the cosmos first gave Noel a holiday home in the South of France. 'I got it two months early,' he said. (He paid for the house, obviously.)

Two months later, he was again serviced by the cosmos: his order for a 'challenge' was answered when a TV executive called him asking him to front *Deal or No Deal*. 'Spooky,' he reckoned.

Bärbel Mohr claims she gained her dream job, the ideal

man, money, health and, finally, a castle. Key phrases she advises adopting include: 'There is no evil! You are perfect, just as you are' and 'The most loving person is the person who is self-centred'. You can see why Noel Edmonds, who always seems like one of the most 'loving' people imaginable, finds this philosophy appealing.

Since adopting its methods, Edmonds has appeared on television with stars and rain clouds on his hands and has become a rabid proselytiser for the belief system. In a recent interview, he said: 'You'll think I've gone away with the fairies – but it's fantastic.'

And he now has a taste for all things spiritual: 'I have faith. I don't know what shape it is. I feel uncomfortable to think it's purely Church of England, and I'd like to learn more about Islam.' (Noel Edmonds learning about Islam. Could this be the cosmos telling him to save the Middle East? Let's hope so.)

I've always wanted a castle, too. Although I wouldn't want the cosmos to spring one on me unawares. I'd want some preparation time before being in receipt of a castle. I'd get some meat in. Probably oxen, and calf.

8th Habit, The

Seven habits must surely be enough, even for the highly effective? Certainly they were highly effective enough to make Stephen Covey a highly effective billionaire with many highly effective dollars.

But following the initial 1989 list in *Seven Habits of Highly Effective People*, he discovered another one. And so, in 2004, he published *The 8th Habit: From Effectiveness to Greatness*. This doesn't inspire confidence. Say I wanted to become highly effective myself, how could I be sure they won't find a ninth habit, or maybe even a 10th?

I'm not even up to speed with the first seven habits of highly effective people (although I imagine it's things like getting up early and never finding yourself on a Tuesday evening at closing time with someone saying, 'Let's go on somewhere else'). But start adding further habits, and very soon you are verily swimming in 'habits'.

And now we've crossed the Rubicon, where will it stop? This adding of habits could become habit-forming. He might start introducing, say, complicated ways to cook fish. Or ceroc.

Energy drinks

These days, being given 'wings' is not enough. Today's young folk sleep around 20% less than their parents' generation, while being 64% more badass, which means they need 750% more tartrazine, sugar, caffeine and lurid food dye.

Rockstar energy drink – 'Party like a rockstar' – plays on rock stars' legendary love of energy drinks. Sometimes they party on energy drinks to the point where they choke on 'their own' energy drink vomit.

Another group with much activity to cram into their busy days are pimps. Their favoured energy drink is Pimp Juice, which does not contain juice. They also probably take cocaine.

Entourages

Imagine, if you can, being a member of Donatella Versace's entourage. Is it the height of *sophis de sophis*? Or do you fear the night, the dark, hollow times where you believe that you do not even exist? Come on! Faux-royal grotesques are a total hoot!

As we all know by now, from the VH1 documentaries or just from the ether, entourages are great fun. Diddy has a permanent video diarist and on-call writer for off-the-cuff speechifying. Mariah needs people to hold her cups, to waft cigarette smoke away from her environment, and also to waft the air when she blows off. Shania apparently goes around with grooms for her horses and two sniffer-dogs (plus handlers) who sweep concert halls for explosives. (Who could be arsed to blow up Shania Twain? Who?)

Then we can drool over the fabbo gunplay between rival rap packs who, with ineffable willingness, shoot each other's legs off for their main man. Like the incident resulting from 50 Cent deciding to kick The Game out of his own G-Unit entourage. When you're out of an entourage, you're out: not a bit in and a bit out. Out. So outside Hot 97 in Greenwich Village, a member of The Game's entourage – he, of course, had his own entourage by this point – was shot three times in a confrontation with 50 Cent's new entourage. Another of 50's crew got really confused and sadly shot his own arms off.

All this is clearly guns-a-totin' fun, but all these Western pretenders have so much to learn. They have nothing – *nothing* – on North Korean player/dictator Kim Jong-Il. That guy is so boss! Since his sharking days under his father's rule in the 1970s, he's accumulated a truly world-beating entourage, including a multinational team of personal chefs. While 'his people' starved – North Korea endured a famine – he imported ovens and two Milanese cooks to prepare his favourite dish: pizza. Extra capers? You bet.

'What do you mean, only one visit to the salad cart? With these words, my friend, YOU WILL DIE.'

Kim even imported American professional wrestlers, at a cost of 15 million dollars, for entertainment purposes. And he's spent the last few decades stocking his 'Pleasure Brigade' with the prettiest women in the country. The brigade is divided into several groups, each of which is composed of three teams: a 'satisfaction team', which performs sexual services; a 'happiness team', which provides massage; and a 'dancing and singing team', which, well, sings and dances.

In 1978, when he decided he wanted to build a native film industry, he simply kidnapped the South Korean film director Shin Sang-ok and his actress wife Choe Eun-hui. Kim forced the director to make 20 propaganda films, and sent him to prison for re-education classes when he tried to escape.

We can but hope that, in years to come, capricious, famine-ignoring velour-tracksuit-wearing dictatorial kook Kim Jong-Il might decide that he needs his own velour-tracksuit-wearing hip-hop/fashion mogul and spirit away Diddy. Maybe Donatella, too. And Mariah. For them, what's the difference? This is the promised land of lifts in your shoes, and a penchant for foreign liquor.

Perhaps Kim will choose to kidnap all the other entourages to make one super-entourage. Then he could construct the biggest VIP club in the world: a crazy cosmos of mirrors and 80s pop hits and small armaments. Each sub-entourage will sip the right brand of champagne and swagger and view each other warily – possibly all in separate roped-off areas, as logistically difficult as that would be – before it suddenly kicks off good and proper over a rice-based dispute and they all end up shooting each other's legs off.

Poor Kim. As if he hasn't got enough on his hands, what with trying to acquire a functioning nuclear arsenal.

Estate agents 'going to war' for their customers

If your estate agent seems slightly edgy, it is perhaps no wonder. They are foot-soldiers in perpetual combat. We realised this when a BBC undercover reporter working at Foxton's discovered that owner Jon Hunt's mantra was: 'Our clients expect us to go to war for them!'

Maybe this is why they feel the need to parade around their chosen patch like Field Marshal Haig, if Field Marshal Haig was always fiddling with his flies.

In this new Long War, under-performers are heckled and prime deal-makers are rewarded with champagne and fifty pounds. Foxton's actually hold regular rallies where each local member of staff's photo is flashed up on a screen and their sales figures are announced: winners are whooped, losers are booed. Then they sing 'Land of Hope and Glory'. I'm not making this up (it was all in the BBC documentary). Successful gazumping and over-valuing sees you paraded around the offices on comrades' shoulders and fanned with big FOR SALE boards. (Okay, I did make up that bit.)

But estate agents going to war is stupid. Estate agents are, after all, only meant to be agents in the 'go-between' sense of the term. Not in the 'CIA/KGB' sense of the term. Or do they actually hang around St James's Park talking about the ducks giving head on a Thursday?

If estate agents did go to war, perhaps they could smarmily hand out business cards saying: 'Mike Barker BREATHES TALKS KNOWS LIVES war. He is the LORD of WAR – but NOT like that dreadful film with Nicolas Cage in it. MUCH better than that. He's more like The Dogs of War. He might actually be better than The Dogs of War.'

Ethical living

'It is during our darkest moments that we must focus to see the light' – Aristotle (Onassis)

Throughout our history, we have wrestled with the complex web of emotions and reason and social relations and aspirations and power and freedom that define us. Thinkers and activists alike have debated who we are, what we are and how we should be – from Aristotle's belief that virtuous behaviour is inherent to us and would see us flourish as ideal, happy human beings, to Kant's assertions that we should obey immutable moral rules – categorical imperatives to be good; to Marx's ideas that we can't understand humans without considering their social context – that for humans to flourish as Aristotle had foreseen, there can be no slaves, no aristocratic society like Aristotle's, no classes. Plato, Ayer, Nietzsche. Liberals, Christians, Muslims, Marxists, Jonathan Porritt – all of them addressing two questions: 'How should I live, what actions ought I to perform?' and 'What sort of person should I be?' In essence: can we be good? How should we be moral? What is right?

And all of them could not see the truths that were staring them in the face and which now we hold to be self-evident. What sort of actions ought I to perform? Buying Fairtrade coffee, hemp Frisbees and 'Give Peas a Chance' organic baby-gros. What sort of person should I be? Smug.

The salvation of humanity lies through the judicious purchase of ethical goods. You can gen up on all the new products in special magazines while you fire one out on your compost toilet. Britons spent £25.8 billion on ethical goods and services in 2005, up 15% on the previous year. You can even buy stuff you don't want or need – it all helps.

Let us now take a moment for reflection and self-congratulation – crack open some Fairtrade Sauvignon Blanc and enjoy our Ethical Rightness Awards for the Ethically Right (Not Wrong).

1. The eco-clutter couple. Pete May and partner Nicola, one of the authors of *Save Cash and Save the Planet*, cut down on waste being dumped in toxic landfills by, in large part, keeping their own and other people's rubbish in the confines of their own actual house: piles of Tetra Paks and padded envelopes patiently await recycling that WILL NEVER HAPPEN. The subject of a major broadsheet photo feature, the couple do at least prove that ethical living need not mean having to go without stuff. As long as it comes out of a skip. They keep chickens, and have made an 'eco-four poster' by attaching bits of twig to their bed. Their garden seats are made of reclaimed logs, there's old orange peel on the boiler because 'it smells nice', a 'lavender harvest from our garden is drying in the fireplace', there are 'free-range stick insects . . . roam[ing] the kitchen', and 'segments of indigenous hedgerow' are growing *inside* their fucking house. This is caring for the environment by taking it home with you, like a goldfish from the fair; going organic by turning your house into a living organism. Possibly they mistranslated Aristotle's notion of the flourishing human being living 'the good life' as meaning 'living like you're in *The Good Life*'.

2. The residents of BedZED. The Beddington Zero Energy Development in Sutton, south London, is the world's first eco housing estate: the dwellings have solar panels; the materials are renewable; there are dual flushes; allotments; all of that. The occupants are true pioneers – taking self-regard to hitherto uncharted levels. One told *Time Out*: 'You are saving the planet just by living here.' Another told the *Observer*: 'I live

with a clear conscience and I haven't had to give up a single thing.' What they have done: lived in a house. What they have not done: solved the Israel-Palestine question; explained *The Da Vinci Code*; made wine out of water (drinking your own water doesn't count).

3 The ethical earl. Fred Lambton, the future Earl of Durham, advertised his Ethical Network website with a 20-foot Union flag banner on the side of his massive London house. 'BOY-COTT SUPERMARKETS', it said, 'THEY ARE KILLING BRITAIN'. A massive 20ft Union Jack? That wasn't doing wonders for the visual environment. So the council made him take it down. Fascists! Oh no, hang on. Fred's thinking about going into politics. Really, your Lordship, please don't bother.

4. Jeremy Paxton is the '46-year-old former water-skiing champion, publishing tycoon and, now, eco-millionaire' behind Lower Mill, a gated eco-retreat for the truly minted at Somerfold Keynes in the Cotswolds. According to the *Sunday Times*, Sol Campbell has commissioned a 12-million-pound glass-and-limestone mansion on the site; John Travolta has also expressed an interest – attracted by nearby Kemble Airfield, where he can land his eco-private jet, the Scientologising freak. Paxton himself is passionate enough about the environment to fly everywhere in his Hughes 500 Combat helicopter, 'even once to pick up Gloucester Old Spot sausages at the local farm shop'. No one is allowed to use the estate unless they buy a house there, with prices starting at £400,000 and going into millions. Local residents, who 'have not been invited in for a peek', let alone for a free go in the 5 million-pound eco-spa, complain of residents 'oozing out in their Chelsea tractors'. Lower Mill even features 'designer

allotments', where, says Paxton, 'We do the work, then you can do an hour's weeding and take your Brussels sprouts home.' Cool: sort of like the pretend farm at Versailles so beloved of Marie Antoinette. Let them eat organic veg!

5. Hugh Sawyer. At the time of writing, Hugh Sawyer was camping out in the woods in Oxfordshire – sleeping under a piece of tarpaulin stretched over a frame made of tree branches, cooking on an open fire, freezing his eco-nuts off. He was commuting daily by train to his job in London, where he works at Sotheby's. Hugh said: 'Once I arrive [at work] I pick up my suit – I have hanging space in the office – and use the showers. My desk drawers have been taken over by clothing and personal equipment. I'm also slowly taking over a filing cabinet – no one's said anything yet.' Why does he do this? To raise money for the Woodland Trust (hoping to raise a whopping £8,000 in a year) and also because 'I guess, having spent my formative years with trees, I have empathy for them'. Hugh explains his typical day: 'It's nice to have the woods to go back to – especially when there's a lot going on at work . . . I get into bed around 10 and only leave the fire burning if it's really cold – otherwise it's a waste . . . I try to cook something good once or twice a week. The meal I'm most proud of was my Christmas dinner: venison in an earth oven . . . It was beautiful. But on a normal night I might have soup or sandwiches. I've been ill a couple of times from not cooking meat properly, and being careless with filtering water from the stream. I also had bronchitis. But it's an adventure . . . I often end up in the woods with suits hanging from the trees.' He lives in the woods. He works in London, but he lives in the woods. In Oxford. He lives in the woods.

You don't have to live in the woods – although, clearly, that would help. Just buy as much ethical stuff as you can carry. But remember: self-regard is free, and doesn't harm the environment. You can get through as much of that as you like.

But is it enough? Sadly, the answer is: balls, no. The top five big polluting companies in the UK produce more CO_2 than all the traffic on all the roads. Individuals can, of course, make a small difference – yes, use farmers' markets if you can afford to; don't be wasteful; recycle . . . It's all to the good. But it's dwarfed by the day-in, day-out destruction casually wreaked by industry. So anyone who thinks living la vida eco makes them a saviour is off their organic nut.

It's like looking at the coming Apocalypse and saying: 'I didn't do it. It wasn't me.' Yes, like a prissier, more self-regarding, eco- version of Shaggy. Like Shaggy with plant pots made out of old Ecover bottles.

And, do you know, I think he did do it on the bathroom floor. It *was* him. He was guilty as hell.

'Everyone's doing it – except you!' culture

The school playground has long revolved around the question: have you done it yet? By adulthood, the answer is generally 'yes', so magazines have to invent new questions by changing the 'it' from 'had sex' to 'had sex with three or more ladyboy geishas in a hot-tub?' If the answer is 'no', you're pretty much still a virgin.

Basically, it's time to get jiggy with the 'new sex rules'. (What do you mean, you don't find 'rules' sexy?) Women's magazines like New Woman open up this awesome new bedquake by offering coverlines about 'Kinky survey results' revealing 'The daring new sex <u>everyone</u> else is having! Lose your morals on p. 94 now'. <u>Everyone</u>, that is, except you.

Some journalists are now single-mindedly dedicated to reporting back from the hot-sex frontline: they're like the Diplomatic and Home Affairs Correspondent . . . of Bits. For her 'Sleeping Around' column in the *Independent*, Catherine Townsend offloads her weekly experiences as a hot sexualiser experiencing everything with everyone, from sulky stock-broker to sulky wannabe novelist. Her lusty liaisons are short on communication – 'We never talked much . . .' – but they always end in 'hours of very intense sex' (sex with Townsend is invariably 'very intense' – like driving a speedboat accompanied by a pressure cooker and a leopard).

To prove they have what it takes too, men's magazines send reporters into the underbelly of this new sexy sex-beast. *Arena*'s Steve Beale reported back on his visit to a dominatrix. Afterwards, he felt 'grounded'. Of being whipped with a riding crop and having molten wax poured on his back, he claimed: 'It hurts.'

Now, whatever anyone wishes to do sexually, I personally couldn't give a flying fuck (hey, you could even have a flying fuck). But I do wonder if <u>everyone</u> is <u>constantly</u> pushing the boundaries in the same way as the *New Woman* reader who, when responding to their Kinky Sex Survey, revealed her 'hottest sex ever' was – no word of a lie – 'being spanked by a dwarf while tied up'. Come on! <u>Everyone</u> else is being spanked by a dwarf while tied up! What? You haven't tried that yet? I thought <u>everyone</u> had done it by now. Oh well.

I've no idea why she was showing off anyway. Spanking is not where it's at with dwarf sex this week. She hadn't even watched a leather-clad Russian oligarch nosh off a blind Asian crack-dwarf while herself manually pleasuring a stoat. <u>Everyone</u>'s done that.

F
—

Fairtrade Towns

With over a hundred Fairtrade Towns in the UK – including Birmingham, Norwich, Edinburgh, Exeter, Newcastle, Liverpool and various London boroughs (Fairtrade Ken has launched a bid to become a Fairtrade City) – the concept is sweeping the nation like a caffeinated hurricane of trade justice.

I can't stress enough the sheer scale of this phenomenon. The waves of thwarted workers' revolutions all over Europe after the First World War; the national liberation movements that swept the colonial world after the Second . . . They have NOTHING on this.

This is the Long March to Islington. That's what this is. Led by Chairman Now.

How does it work? Well, brace yourself, because you may – *may* – die. It is this: for a town (or city) to be awarded Fairtrade Town status . . . the local councillors must drink Fairtrade tea and coffee.

I will say that again: the local councillors must drink Fairtrade tea and coffee.

Or, more precisely: 'The local council must pass a resolution supporting Fairtrade, and serve Fairtrade coffee and tea at its meetings and in offices and canteens.' That's offices *and* canteens.*

Fairtrade is all about. As Lenny Henry says: 'When you reach for your wallet, you're reaching out to help someone.' Well, not really, you're actually reaching for some coffee. Which you were going to do anyway. So it's not much of a sacrifice, all told. Certainly not so much that you need to be pictured in the *Observer Food Monthly* with a Brazil nut up your nostril by way of congratulation.

It's not exactly Oskar Schindler levels of heroism we're talking about here. So maybe, just maybe, we really, really, really don't need any more broadsheet-supplement self-love-fests about it generally at all in fact.

By the way, if you do go on a Long March to Islington looking for a liberal paradise full of woolly progressives earnestly discussing the future of the left, you'll be pretty disappointed. It's more about thoroughly charmless career- and property-obsessed types who come over like they'd happily practise eugenics. Funnily enough, the 'N' in N1 stands for 'Nazi'.

Oh, sorry: I've just been told it stands for 'North'.

* Becoming a Fairtrade Church is *much* harder. As well as the tea and coffee, you must 'Move forward on using other Fairtrade products (such as sugar, biscuits, fruit).' Obviously, though, you are still free to argue that Africans mustn't be allowed to use condoms.

Filming gigs on phones

You are at the gig. You don't need to film it. You can DOWNLOAD CLIPS LIVE RIGHT NOW – with your eyes and your ears. It is literally right in front of you. They really should put up some signs: NO PHONE-CAMERA TOSSERS! NO! NO! NO! AND ALWAYS! NO!

Food halls

Dishes from the four corners of the world! Left half-eaten, on paper plates, stacked up, on Formica tables.

The food hall, or food court: the most monstrous part of the already desperate shopping centre 'experience'. It's like a horrible accident at an MSG factory.

And always, as well as the usual suspects, there are outlets that you never see anywhere outside of food halls. Singapore Sam Express. Quizno's Sub. What is that? Who is this Quizno? What is this for? Who are these people? WHAT DO THEY WANT FROM ME?

Football pundits

At the 2006 World Cup, Martin O'Neill took the *Mumbling-Idiot Football Pundit Rulebook* and ripped it to bits – as befits a man who drinks petrol for fun and spent his downtime stalking the studio like an avenging justice, casually breaking stuff and seething with barely suppressed bestial rage at an ignorant, heartless world.

O'Nails, officially the world's hardest man, rocked the *Match of the Day* universe by seeking to pass on genuine knowledge and insight. He also eschewed the cardinal rule of exhibiting a general, false bonhomie; instead he seemed actively to despise his colleagues.

The former Celtic and now Aston Villa manager was never happier than when taking former England captain Alan Shearer to pieces on live TV. Toying with the ex-Toon striker as the gods are wont to do with men, O'Nails said Shearer's name had 'cropped up' at his recent interview for the job of England manager. 'Have you worked with

Shearer?' asked the FA. 'Would you consider doing so?'

'I said no. Now that I have [worked with you], the answer would still be no.'

At half-time during the Germany–Portugal play-off for third place, O'Neill recounted Hollywood screenwriter William Goldman's famous remark that 'nobody knows anything'. Not seeking to alienate viewers, he was careful to explain exactly who Goldman was – mentioning his most famous screenplay, *Butch Cassidy and the Sundance Kid*.

Lineker and the two Alans looked a little shellshocked. Shearer said the story was as boring as the game's first half. O'Neill shot back with the veiled but tragically unfinished: 'Well, maybe you should spend more time watching films and less . . .'

When Ian Wright interrupted O'Nails as he was explaining the finer points of a Holland v Serbia & Montenegro game with, 'So, you like to talk about S&M? Eh? Eh?', O'Neill looked a small step away from chinning him.

As a manager, you could imagine him stamping his authority on the dressing room by freaking out the players – by standing up in front of the chalkboard and arguing . . . with himself. 'You want to spend more time watching football and less time shouting at yourself . . . Yeah? Well, fuck you.' And so on.

Where was I? Oh, yes – with the exception of O'Nails, pundits are generally idiots. Football punditry is a world where Peter Schmeichel, asked to explain why a Blackburn Rovers player received two yellow cards but was not sent off, will oblige by repeatedly shouting throughout the action replay: 'Look at that! Look at that!' Or former England striker Mick Channon can make it through the entire 1986 World Cup finals without once correctly pronouncing the name of England's current star striker, Gary Line-acre.

The same standards applied to other areas of media punditry would have financial reporters on *Newsnight* saying: 'The Bank of England, though, you've got to say, they're a different class. They've got everything. Interest rates. Pace. Lots of money. Sensational.' Or authors turning up half-cut on *Start the Week* and saying: 'Books? Yeah.' (Actually, in the case of *Start the Week*, that would be an improvement.)

Ian Wright, for instance, loves England like only a nutter loves England. He made his name as a pundit during ITV's coverage of the 1998 World Cup, where he spent England's rollercoaster second-round defeat to Argentina sulking (1–0 Argentina); jumping up and down while grinning (1–1); jumping up and down while shouting randomly generated vowels (1–2); standing with both hands wedged firmly into his armpits, refusing to speak (2–2); sticking his bottom lip out like a six-year-old (England defeated on penalties).

His greatest moment at the Beeb was his reaction to England's first defeat in 473 years to Northern Ireland. Asked for the in-depth analysis he was paid to give, he just said: 'I don't want to talk about it.'

In Germany, he was rarely used for games not involving England. Presumably as he'd only say things like: 'You'll have to ask someone else because I don't give one. Come on England!'

Alan Hansen's analysis, meanwhile, can always be distilled thus: 'They've got pace, power, desire, pace, desire, passion, drive, pace, passion, power, pace, drive, pace, power and power. And power. And pace . . . And power.'

Funnyman presenter Gary Lineker ('We've got the big three in action tonight: West Brom, Norwich and Palace!') was probably just relieved that, with the World Cup not having handles, this was at least one tournament where he doesn't look like the trophy.

Over on ITV, we had Andy Townsend and Ally McCoist perched behind a lectern on the touchline sporting the finest suits Ciro Cittero have to offer. Viewers had to keep reminding themselves it wasn't the adverts and had nothing to do with homeowner loans.

After one disappointing Spanish display, Townsend was asked whether Spain's complicated ethnic politics may have contributed to the team's failure to gel. It was irrelevant, he said: 'The coach should sort it out.' Ruud Gullit suggested it was 'a bit more complicated than that'. 'The coach should sort it out,' repeated Townsend – conjuring up images of Spanish coach Luis Aragones, perhaps aided by the ITV Sport team, launching a Truth and Reconciliation process for the Franco dictatorship.

Maybe they could get Everton Giant Peter Reid in to help? Reid celebrated England's 2002 World Cup defeat of Argentina with some refreshing cold drinks. However, unlike everyone else enjoying the carnival atmosphere that morning, he was booked to appear later that evening as an expert pundit on *Match of the Day*. He was nothing if not honest as he slumped on the edge of the sofa: 'I've had a few drinks,' he admitted. "Scuse me if I slur m'words.' Sadly, he clammed up for the entire hour of broadcast, only coming to life right at the end when asked for his opinion of Brazil. 'Sorry, were you talking to me? I've missed my cue again, haven't I?'

Free CD gunk

What is it? Where do they get it from? Is it bat-sperm? Is it hellspawn? Is it mined by infants? What is it?

Free magazines

The ones you have to pay for are bad enough. But then there's all the free magazines – on trains and aeroplanes, in shops, coming through your door, from trade unions, from insurance companies.

Supermarket magazines never say things like 'Of course, you'll want to get the vegetables for this recipe at the market, where they're much cheaper'; or 'If we're honest, most of our competitors have a much better selection of wines than us. We tend to just get the stuff with the biggest mark-ups or see if it's got a pretty label. Sorry about that.' That's possibly because they're less about being informative than about trying to sell you their stuff. Hence, I guess, the age-old adage: there's no such thing as a free magazine.

Who could really say their life was meaningless before *Sorted!* – 'the Post Office magazine'? Among features like 'What Does Your Car Say About You?' and 'Handy Andy's How Not to Have a DIY Disaster' there are articles on how the Post Office kept going in the Blitz and exhortations to send more parcels. There's even 'For the Record', a two-page photo spread of celebrities' reminiscing about the Post Office. 'I always go into my local Post Office and come away with all sorts,' says Joanna Lumley, actress. Who can argue with endorsements like that, or this one from Fiona Bruce, presenter: 'I get letters from all kinds of people, and I reply to a lot of them'?

Then there is encouragement just to post more stuff generally. It's desperate. It's not just pointless; it's clingy. They might as well throw themselves onto the dirty pavement at your feet and *beg* you to buy more stamps: 'Please! Even a second class. Don't leave me. DON'T YOU FUCKING DARE LEAVE ME!'

As for the *Norwich Union* magazine, I found the big spread

on the aftermath of the Boscastle flood just tasteless – like they were trying to get something back after all the payouts. 'Well, it's not like we haven't got all the details. And the photos . . .'

'Funky' portraits of celebrities by 'hip local artists'

This 'local artist' presumably thought long and hard about how best to express their feelings about the concepts of subject and object in the 21st century. And then decided to trace a photo of Johnny Rotten onto a canvas, colour it in garishly and charge about £150 in the nearest 'local art shop' and/or bar-cantina-vibe-hole.

Then do Bob Marley. Then John Travolta and Sam Jackson pointing their pistols at blokey on the couch (they're about to shoot him to death!). Then Keith Flint. Then Caine as Carter and Fucking Yet Again It's Fucking Bloody Bastard Tossing Fucking Scarface.

Who the fuck thinks a crap sub-Warhol portrait of Keith Flint will set off their living room?

What both art-maker and art-buyer should realise is that this is not like Warhol. It's Athena with oils.

Of course, Warhol wasn't like Athena. That was different. For some reason.

David Furnish getting tough on crime

I want to love David Furnish – he's a professional hanger-on who loves indie, which is cool. But then he must start with all the talking.

When *ES* magazine asked him, 'What would you do if you were mayor [of London] for the day?', he replied: 'I would take a much harder line on crime.'

How hard a line he might take was left undisclosed. Maybe Mayor Furnish would stalk the streets of London in body-armour, tracking down drug-dealers and giving them a taste of justice with his cold .38. I now always imagine David Furnish laughing ferociously into the night sky as he aims a flamethrower at the villainous vermin of the streets – perhaps muttering: 'How's this for a candle in the wind, you fucks?' But maybe that's just me.

G

George Galloway, unfair pillorying of

George Galloway has been the victim of woeful aspersion and mighty depreciation. He has been sore detracted with muck-raking, mudslinging obloquy and scandal. The mockers have mocked their mock of mockery like mocking mocksters of mock. There has been calumny and also smear. But leotard me no more leotard. I say: ENOUGH!

For, as Galloway himself was keen to point out in an interview in the *Oldie*, he always, *always* gives of his best. 'So if you're asked to be a cat, be the best cat you can.' So he licked at Rula Lenska's hands like a submissive, like he was her lick-spittle, licking? What of it? He gave it a good go.

And who – what sort of curmudgeon – cannot draw pleasure from an evening watching 'Gorgeous' George Galloway in his jim-jams, puffing on a stogie while Jodie Marsh chats about fisting? *Who?*

He was only doing his best. If you're going to take a dislike to Preston, do your best. Don't just mumble some mealy-mouthed nonsense about his silly little ska tunes. Call him a 'plutocrat'. You know, like Stalin. Oh no, hang on, Galloway called the collapse of Stalinism 'the greatest catastrophe of my life'. Which must make Preston worse than Stalin. Preston out of the Ordinary Boys is worse than Stalin. Preston out of woeful mod-ska also-rans the Ordinary Boys – they of the execrable 'Boys Will Be Boys' and the jumping up and the jumping down – is worse than Stalin. Now, *that's* making an effort.

And if you want to denounce Iraqi trade unionists, do your best. Others may see people who risked their lives opposing the murderous Ba'ath regime – brave, principled people who are now being murdered by Islamist/Ba'athist insurgents – as enemies of religious reaction. No matter. You should focus on the small minority who supported the war, and denounce them all as 'quislings'. What of it? If you're going to take issue, take issue. Really get stuck in there.

And if you simply must have a go at Galloway, do your best. Don't go on about the cat thing – it doesn't matter. Don't criticise his low attendance at the Commons – he's quite justified in saying that the impact he can make there is limited. Don't keep making vague accusations of financial impropriety you can't prove. That's just stupid – and, ironically, it's making him rich on the libel winnings.

You would probably want to focus mainly on his support for despotic regimes. And don't just lazily accuse him of toadying up to the indefatigable Saddam Hussein. Do it properly: point out that he toadied up to *all* the Husseins. Including Uday, the man Egyptian President Hosni Mubarak labelled a 'psychopath'. (Well, he had just seen him murder his father's personal valet at the dinner table: first beating him repeatedly with a cane, then finishing him off with an electric carving knife.)

Here is George chatting to Uday at a meet and greet in Iraq:

GALLOWAY: 'Your Excellency, very, very nice to see you again.'

HUSSEIN: (*replying in English*) 'Nice to see you.'

GALLOWAY: 'It's almost one year since we met. How are you?'

HUSSEIN: 'You seem in very good health.'

GALLOWAY: 'I lost weight, I'm very happy about that.'

HUSSEIN: (*replying in Arabic*) 'Yes, I see you've lost some weight, so I think it's better.'

GALLOWAY: 'It's good, but unfortunately I'm losing my hair also.'

HUSSEIN: 'Yes, I've noticed, especially on the left side. But I'm one step ahead of you, I've quit cigars, you are still smoking.'

GALLOWAY: 'People of good taste either used to be, or still are, smokers of Havanas.'

HUSSEIN: 'That's why we have opened this subject so we can call you to quit smoking.'

GALLOWAY: 'I'd like you to know that we are with you until the end.'

He was as well. So you shouldn't accuse of him of lacking stamina or being disloyal.

Ginster's Buffet Bars

The Ginster's Buffet Bar purports to be a bar of buffet, a buffet in a bar, but it's nothing but a bar of cheap lies.

Unless, somewhere out there, there are people being heartily satisfied with a buffet whose sole foodstuff is coleslaw mixed with creamed cheese.

It should be obvious that any catering company offering buffet services along these lines would leave their clients feeling desperately short-changed, and would not survive long in what is, as I am sure you are aware, a highly competitive market.

So buffets aren't real buffets – and delis aren't real delis. En route to my summer holidays, the airline's 'Deli in the Sky' menu promised some 'gourmet' sandwiches specially 'created' by 'celebrity chef Brian Turner' (or, more familiarly, 'The Absolute Arsehead Off *Ready Steady Cook* Brian Turner').

On this particular day, the choice of 'gourmet' sandwiches was between BLT and cheese and pickle. I had the latter. It was shit.

I'm not saying Ginster's could or should put everything in there that you would expect to find at an adequate buffet. All I'm actually saying is: if you don't know what words mean, DON'T FUCKING USE THEM.

Or you could get a dictionary.

Zac Goldsmith

Great news: we've got Zac on board! Following the lead of Cameron's Tories, we too have realised the need for some wafer-thin green credentials. So, great news: we've got Zac on board! *Is It Just Me, or Have We Got Zac on Board?* That's what this book should have been called.

Handsome, dashing, good-looking and very, very, very rich, he's the playboy gambler with the cruel, weird father who shouted, 'OUT! OUT! OUT!' into David Mellor's face like a pissed Trot student after standing against him in the 1997 election. Honestly, he's so exciting, I almost feel like writing a series of novels about him – like Horatio Hornblower, but campaigning against leaving the lights on rather than against

Napoleon. (Although I bet Napoleon was a leaving-the-lights-on kind of guy anyway.)

Of course, *Ecologist* editor Zac is less an actual person, more a big sign saying, 'We care about your future'. For this reason, David Cameron has got Zac to head up his new environment and quality-of-life policy group. Of course, the Tory Party has historically regarded the environment as something to cover in tarmac and then privatise. But people can change and, luckily, this renowned environmental campaigner would not simply let himself be used as a tokenistic figurehead for that lot. He's better than that. Just look at him!

Oh no, hang on. That's exactly what he would do. But then, Goldsmith's environmentalism is not really of a stripe to make the Tory heartland shudder and shake. In a recent *Times* piece, he was asked how he thought we should do our bit. 'It's not about living like a monk,' he assured us. 'The single most important thing is to buy local food.'

Bloody wow! How easy is that? No wonder Cameron's such a fan: when it comes to saving the planet from environmental collapse, the absolute number-one priority, the single most important factor, above everything else, is visiting a farmers' market.* I thought things were scarier than that; I thought the Earth was melting and WE WERE ALL GOING TO FUCKING DIE. But clearly I was wrong. We just need to buy courgettes with the soil still on them.

*Oh, and also not letting the kids eat junk, as expressed by Zac's ex-model wife Sheherazade in a gushing portrait in a glossy newspaper supplement: 'I'm not fanatical. One of the children might occasionally eat a KitKat at a party.' Only one of the children, mind – let's not go crazy. Couldn't they have a finger each?

Good and evil as demonstrated in the marketing of automotive transport

Now, more than ever, we need a firm moral compass to guide us through our treacherous age. Let us be thankful, then, for car ads.

It might not have escaped your notice that many of the ads are car ads. And you might well admire the way many cars embody very distinct moral attributes. Some cars are repositories of goodness that make you feel honest, real and true – like getting emotional about the memory of *Brokeback Mountain* while sitting in a hedge.

Other cars, very different cars, make you feel dark, cruel and sleazy, like you're eating a dirty burger for breakfast in preparation for a day's gunrunning.

Very much in the former camp, the new Nissan Note understands that having kids is the greatest adventure in the world (it's not, though – skydiving is: it's over quicker, and people don't clam up when you talk about it). Billboards show this vehicle of virtue speeding through the French countryside with a kite flying behind in the clear blue skies. It's wholesome, pure and pure, like Chris Martin, fresh from having a bath, smelling a fragrant meadow at dawn.

Alternatively, if the idea of going on holiday with children makes you feel nauseous, there's Joss Ackland's doom-laden voiceover and 'Antichrist Superstar' Marilyn Manson creaking out the Eurythmics' 'Sweet Dreams' (it's an ironic cover – it's not about having sweet dreams at all!) as the new Fiat Punto bursts through some weird, gloopy glass walls in a spooky nocturnal cityscape. The subtle message is: you'd better be one sick puppy to drive this baby. This Fiat Punto.

Or you might prefer something more in keeping with Cameron's Britain. 'Go Beyond', says Land-Rover. Appreciate nature, the hills, the dales, the misty moors . . . by driving across a misty moor, in a Land-Rover! Because the Land-Rover is the only off-road vehicle that naturally occurs in nature. Land-Rovers are actively beneficent – like sharing cherries with an Eskimo would be good. Maybe the Eskimo has never had cherries before, and you'll laugh and laugh and laugh.

Or you might prefer to fuck that shit up. In which case, here comes the Predator Jeep – less a vehicle, more an abattoir on wheels. The epitome of public enemy. Recent billboard posters showed a pair of these dark beasts standing with quite alarming amounts of menace in some shadowy, rubbish-strewn arches in the dead of night. This image appeals perfectly to everyone who wants their vehicle to carry really quite strong connotations of assault. It's rather upsetting. So, you know . . . *cool*!

With its 'beyond the clouds' campaign, Volvo claimed, somewhat controversially, to be 'For Life' – which is very sweet of them. As though anyone would claim to be 'For Lingering, Painful Death'! Oh no, hang on: here's Audi. TV ads for the RS4 portrayed the new model as a black widow spider bleakly devouring rival cars. Explains Bill Scott, Audi's business director at creative agency BBH: 'The car was described as a predatory animal, one that shows no sympathy, no mercy . . . Our brief to the creative team was "RS4: sinister Vorsprung durch Technik".' As the Germans say.

So the choice is clear: you can drive a car that's truly at one with the cosmos, that will make you feel like the Buddha on a mellow tip. Or you can drive the trenchcoat Mafia's crack-mobile. At least until these two eternal opposing forces come crashing together in a final titanic struggle that will see the skies rent asunder, the ground shake and the seas get decid-edly choppy.

At this point, the lamb will lie down with the lion. The shepherd will lie down with his flock. It will rain cats and it will rain also dogs. The beetles will lie down with the monkeys. The Green will lie down with The Black. Everyone is lying down. Brm brm.

Goodfellas pizza

If you served pizza like that to some real 'goodfellas', you could reasonably expect to get 'whacked'.

H

Teri Hatcher, philosopher

As Bertrand Russell once noted: 'Philosophy bakes no bread.' This is true: philosophy is no baker. And bread has never been especially beneficial to philosophy. But that all changed when one modern philosopher was struck by inspiration while thinking about bread. Toasted bread. Toast, in fact.

The philosopher in question was, of course, Teri Hatcher, philosopher, whose subsequent treatise *Burnt Toast: And Other Philosophies of Life* expanded upon her belief that, when presented with burnt toast, women often eat it rather than throwing it away and starting again. The thing is, it's not just about toast – the toast is a metaphor, you see. For all poorly prepared breakfasts. Not that Teri Hatcher seems to ever eat breakfast, what with her looking so thin and all. Or, indeed, elevenses.

Anyway, what follows is a kind of aphoristic free-for-all reminiscent of the work of Friedrich Nietzsche. For instance: 'When my waters broke with Emerson, I was in the middle of cooking dinner. I called the doctor who told me to come straight to the hospital. I asked her if I had time to blow dry my hair. She said, "What?"'

And: 'When I hung up the phone I burst into tears. That motherfucker. I opened myself up and what did I get? Scorched. I rallied a couple of girlfriends for burn-victim treatment.'

And: 'When we're kids, our instincts are raw and untempered by all the pros and cons and second-guessing that take over our adult lives. But we suffer the consequences. I kept the cat. Kitty was her name.'

Fairly soon, you realise that the desperation is no act, that Hatcher really is that desperate – for truth! Among other things.

I wonder what Eva Longoria's great philosophical investigation will reveal. She's certainly due her own 'eureka' moment sometime soon. What with all that sitting around in the bath.

Hedge-fund boys

In a get-rich-quick world, hedge-fund boys get rich the quickest. How they spend their cash influences whole lower stratospheres of vacuous consumption. Currently, 'hedge-fund boys prefer to splash their cash ordering cocktails for thousands of pounds a glass' at bars with names like Umbaba. 'Umbaba, Umbaba, that's how it goes,' they sing, à la Oliver Twist.

If professional watchers of the super-rich are to be believed, these 'lords of havoc' (the *New Statesman*) drive the tastiest motors, eat at the fastest restaurants, swim in the wettest pools and stalk London and New York like Knights of the Bastard Table. The *Sunday Telegraph* estimated that in 2005, around 200 to 300 UK hedge-fund managers carved up $4.2 billion of pure profit between them. In 2005, according to the US *Institutional Investor Magazine*, the top 25 hedge-fund managers earned an average of $251 million each. The amount of money the world's hedge-funders handle could be as much as $1.5 trillion.

So how do they do it? Well, it's tricky. Even people who understand economics do not understand hedge-funds. These secretive, privately owned investment companies are massive – if they were a country, they would be the eighth-biggest on the planet. But it would be a country you could not visit or even see: hedge-funds, of which there are reckoned to be 8,000 in the world, mostly based in the US, 'fly under the radar' (CNN) and cannot be regulated – mainly because regulators don't understand what's going on; even though hedge-funds may be responsible for over half the daily turnover of shares on the London Stock Market alone. After looking into the matter, the Financial Services Authority, Britain's regulatory body, said: 'Chuff this for a game of soldiers.' It's very much like *Deal or No Deal*: people claim to know what's going on, and superficially there would appear to be some logic, but actually they're making it up as they go along.

I've looked into it and have to say it sounds a lot like internet gambling for the super-rich. Investors must place a minimum of a million dollars into a fund; at enormous risk, the fund managers take these tax-haven stashes and place stakes on anything and everything – FTSE100 companies, commodities, options, stocks in developing countries, anything that might shoot up in price or can be made to . . . Often they will take the tax-haven dosh and borrow against it – that is, borrowing money in order to gamble it; which is exactly the sort of responsible activity that should remain unregulated. When the hedge-funders lose their shirts (one Japanese fund lost $300 million in a week), it's okay because they've got more shirts. But often, other losers – like Colombia or Egypt (both of which saw their stock markets slump after the hedge-funders parked their mobile casinos in them) – don't have any more shirts. Which makes riding with hedge-funders quite a bare-knuckle ride, with no shirt on.

In 2006, the 'hedgehogs' came into the light with Hedgestock, a festival at Knebworth that mixed bands and utterly incomprehensible business seminars ('Incubator Alligator? – sowing the seeds, but do they stay for a cigarette?'). It even had its own jingle, which sounded like the worst thing ever. To the tune of 'Sex Bomb', it went: 'Hedgestock, Hedgestock, Groovy Hedgestock, a little bit of business and a whole lot of rock. . .' And you thought Glastonbury had gone 'a bit corporate'.

Contrary to initial feelings of disappointment, the fact that this event was headlined by The Who was actually quite fitting. In their pomp, The Who would enter town, take over a hotel, drive a Rolls-Royce into a swimming pool, stick bombs down the toilets, smash up the furniture and nail every piece of wood to the ceiling. Then, when things looked like getting sticky, they'd move on, leaving others to clean up their mess. For 'hotels', merely read 'emerging economies'. Perhaps replacing 'I'm a Boy' with 'I'm a Hedge-Fund Boy'.

Anyway, these festivals, which are also victory parades over the assimilation of the counter-culture, could really take off. You could have one specially for analysts, called Analstock. And one for stockbrokers, called Stockstock. And, of course, the V Festival.

Helpdesks

After being shunted between four different clueless cretins, after an epoch of holding on at 35p a minute, being subjected to what must be the world's only extant T'Pau CD, your psyche oscillating between impotence and rage, there is a voice, a connection, a lifeline . . .

'Okay, I've found a website about it.'

So, I'm paying you two kings' ransoms plus a small fortune and a pretty penny to browse around software company websites, ambling towards some kind of non-resolution that I could just as easily have been stumbling across myself on the very same software company websites if I were not sitting here listening to your insensate minion ooze bewilderment down my fucking telephone.

I DON'T THINK YOU EVEN *WANT* TO HELP.

Hip holidays

'From the cliff tops of Mykonos,' the *Guardian* informs us, 'to the beaches of Mallorca, a quiet revolution is under way . . .'

That's right. Revolution is in the air. But it isn't very loud. Can you hear it blowin' in the zephyr-like breeze? Was that it? Not sure. It's a whisper. But it's growing louder. Soon it will be a muffled roar.

'Today's savvy travellers demand cutting-edge design, lavish spas, infinity pools, sunrise yoga classes and sunset chill-out sessions with big name DJs.'

Everyone is uniting and demanding more. More hipness. From their holidays.

Well, not everyone. Only those willing to seek out 'the sort of luxury that sheikhs, millionaire playboys and royals take for granted' and who slavishly stay ahead of the herd: the 'Burberry bikinis or throngs of ex-pats' who are, as the name implies, basically just animals.

So where to begin? According to a 2006 'Travel Trends' piece in *The Times*, Shanghai is now the 'ultimate hip urban hangout' for 'Gucci-loving City types'. Alaska is hot stuff with 'wannabe 007s with egos to flush, Armani snowsuits and £170,000 a week to burn'. (007 wannabes?) The Indian state of Uttaranchal is 'set to take over from Nepal for moneyed, trend-conscious spiritual types taking a break from their busy–busy lives'. Hip holidaymakers are the leaders of the Gucci-loving, wannabe-007, trend-conscious spiritual pack.

When these guys hit the scene, really quite old places magically become the new somewhere else. 'Miami is the new New York,' reckons *Condé Nast Traveller* (New York being, of course, the new York – only without the ace Viking museum and so therefore not as good). Where's the new Barcelona? It's a place called Lisbon. It's going to be big. And where to hang in this hotspot? Definitely the Lux nightclub and sister restaurant Bica do Sapato (in part backed by John Malkovich). According to a promotion in *Wallpaper**, it's 'the place to join Lisbon's beautiful people, as they lounge on vintage Knoll, Mies van der Rohe and Saarinen furniture'. That's what I always miss on holiday: Bauhaus furniture.

This form of travel writing may seem new, but it's actually in the great tradition of Marco Polo, the legendary medieval Italian trader whose *Travels* detailed his literally groundbreaking exploration of Central Asia, passing through scalding deserts, desolate steppes and precipitous mountains to become the first Westerner to encounter China, then under the rule of the Mongol emperor Kublai Khan. On returning, his tales were so bizarre that many believed them to be fabrications:

'Chan-Ghain-Fu is a city of the province of Manji, the inhabitants of which are idolaters, subjects of the Great Khan, and use his paper money. They gain their living by trade and manufacture, and are wealthy. They weave tissues of silk and gold. This playground for the rich and the well-connected was recently blessed by Philippe Starck's diva-defining new venture. Marble, gilt and deep-red velvet feature throughout, adding to the drama of it all and creating a very decadent space.

'The province of Tholoman lies towards the east, and its inhabitants . . . burn the bodies of their dead; and the bones that are not reduced to ashes, they put into wooden boxes, and carry to the mountains, where they conceal them in caverns of the rocks, in order that no wild animal may disturb them. As the sun goes down, the big-name DJs speed things up – I particularly marvelled at Julesy – and exotic cocktails are served into the night. Saucy sophistication to a tee!

'In a western direction from Painfu there is a large and handsome fortress named Thaigin, which is said to have been built, at a remote period, by a king who was called the Golden King. The sun-kissed terraces are great for power-lunching or just people-watching; plus there's the best lifestyle gym in the region. The must-have treatment here is the full-body lava mask. I've been there. And, unless I'm very much mistaken, you have not. Me. Not you.'

Historical reconstructions

So you've devoted two years of your life to a prestige documentary series about Auschwitz. You've got hitherto unseen photographs, interviews with survivors, shedloads of CGI and a narrator with more authority than Charlton Heston. But there's still something missing. What if viewers think you're making it all up? It could happen. You've been reading all about this Irving guy.

So, obviously, you hire some actors to dress up in German uniforms and stand in a field (possibly in Poland) pointing meaningfully at a map. Ah, so *that's* what Nazis looked like. Cheers for that. Because I thought they just wore pinafores and cardies. That silly walk! It's mad!

The makers of the recent documentary *Munich: Mossad's Revenge* had the cunning wheeze of juxtaposing contemporary footage of Palestinian terrorist suspects assassinated by the Israeli secret service with reconstructions featuring actors who looked nothing like them. Unless you were pissed, squinting at them through tracing paper. Which is not something you do often. Any more.

During one revenge job, future Israeli prime minister Ehud Barak was obliged to dress as a woman to get close to his target. To illustrate that this *really happened*, the docudrama-makers recreated the event using the world's shittest transvestite, thus giving the impression that Mossad entrusted the biggest, riskiest operation in its obsessive mission to track down and eliminate its sworn enemies to Lily Savage.*

*We have been asked to make it absolutely clear that, to the best of our knowledge, Lily Savage has never worked for Mossad – neither as an agent nor as an agent of influence. Although they did try luring her away from ITV on at least one occasion.

Hitler, people calling each other

The Bush administration loves comparing people to Hitler. Iran's president, Mahmoud Ahmadinejad, is apparently considered a 'new Hitler'. Donald Rumsfeld compares everyone to Hitler. Abu Musab al-Zarqawi in hiding was like 'Hitler in his bunker'. Saddam Hussein has joined the pantheon of failed, brutal dictators, 'alongside Hitler'.

Even Venezuelan 'peoples' hero' Hugo Chavez was like Hitler because 'he's a person who was elected legally — just as Adolf Hitler was elected legally'. (The presumed implication: because George Bush was not elected legally in 2000, he is therefore unlike Hitler.)

In retaliation, Chavez compared Bush to . . . can you guess? That's right, to Harold Lloyd: 'He's always hanging off clocks, like a goddamn fool.' Not really; it was Hitler. And he added: 'Mr Tony Blair is the main ally of Hitler.' (So who does that make him: Eva Braun?)

Chavez didn't call hideous Zimbabwean despot Robert Mugabe 'Hitler', though. Instead, this ally of workers everywhere said: 'He is my friend. Have you met him?' Of his various crimes against humanity? 'We all make mistakes.' Yes, but ours generally involve losing our keys, and far less slaughtering of the innocents and starving and impoverishing an entire population.

Perhaps feeling slightly left out, Mugabe compared *himself* to Hitler (no, really), only more so: 'Hitler tenfold'. Because he too wanted 'justice for his own people'. Yes, that was Hitler alright: justice, justice, justice.

Changing tack slightly, Mugabe also compared Bush and Blair to Hitler and Mussolini. But can Blair really be like Mussolini when he has already been compared to Hitler by the countryside marchers? 'Hitler 1936. Blair 2002,' claimed one banner. (Hitler famously hated the countryside too: 'Blood and soil? Basically, it smells of shit and I do not like it.')

North Korea called George W. Bush both an 'imbecile' and a 'tyrant that puts Hitler in the shade'. So, he is Hitler, but in a Barrymore/Freddie Starr sort of a way. But not – NOT – as good as Chaplin in *The Great Dictator*.

Noam Chomsky is 'the world's leading intellectual'.

Intellectuals are paid to see things differently, and Chomsky certainly succeeds on this score. His latest work, *Failed States* (yes, he means America), holds that the US has been whipped into a state of 'demonic' scariness to rival National Socialism. Don't forget that '[Goebbels] boasted that "he would use American advertising methods" to "sell National Socialism" much as business seeks to sell "chocolate, toothpaste, and patent medicines".' He forgets that it was rare for Hitler's popularity ratings to fall to 32% (unlike Bush's). In fact, they usually hovered nearer the 100% mark. Certainly I would have thought it would be intellectual not to play fast and loose with the definition of 'fascism'; but maybe I just don't have the requisite number of degrees in conspiracy theory studies.

Bush and Blair, of course, never compare themselves to Hitler. They prefer comparisons with Winston Churchill, who was on the other side . . . and won. During the Iraq War, Blair apparently had to be restrained from turning his Downing Street office into a replica of Churchill's war bunker in the Second World War (perhaps forcibly, who knows?). 'We wouldn't let him,' said close political adviser Sally Morgan. 'It would have looked awful. He really would have liked a sand-pit with tanks.'

I would like to offer a corrective on this point. Yes, it would have been awful. But it would also have been very, very funny.

And it could have enabled Blair to face down the critics attacking his 'bunker mentality' with some of that trademark gall: 'I would say to you this: I *do* have a bunker mentality. I'm sitting in a bunker right now. What do you expect? I'm sitting in a bunker.'

Amanda Holden not doing a delivery-room webcast

Like you, I was riveted by the whole 'Amanda Holden having a baby' saga.

Her delight at being pregnant; her playing of classical music to the bump; her general feelings of love for her fiancé; details of how and where she conceived (on a carpet, apparently); loving Abba – all of that . . . The pictures of her looking radiant after the announcement; looking radiant just before the birth; looking radiant just after the birth, with the baby, 'feeling fantastic'; looking radiant nine weeks on, *avec* child, at a charity function . . . I followed it all, and it wasn't even difficult as all I had to do was open a newspaper occasionally and there she was, up the stick, blooming.

It was because I found myself so fascinated that I have always rejected my initial feelings that it was almost like she had a team of publicists working day and night to place stories about the amazing event at every available opportunity, working the phones like a call centre on crack, stopping just short of taking out billboard ads at major road junctions employing the slogan: 'Look! Yes, you! At me!'

But I can't help feeling mildly let down. Just a bit. Why no despatch from the delivery room? Nothing tacky, obviously. Just a quick word from La Holden, during a quiet moment, to reassure us all that, yes, she was still famous. Just a brief chat, Ms H staring into the webcam with those cold, dead eyes of hers, to reassure us all by saying: 'Don't worry, there will not be another series of *Mad About Alice* or that stupid thing in Africa, the name of which escapes me.'

Hollyoaks hunks

All that gel does at least make them more flammable.

So the chances of a *Hollyoaks* hunks inferno is slightly increased.

It's still fairly unlikely, though, to be honest.

Horoscope consumerism

Taureans smarting from a tough 2006 may find it's because they're bull-headed tightwads who failed to snap up a £4,450 De Beers ring at the start of the year.

According to *Grazia*'s exhaustive six-page feature 'What's in store for YOU this year?' by astrologer Peter Watson, the De Beers ring was a 'key buy' for those sharing that star sign – along with Janet Reger bloomers and camisole (£290) and some Dune sandals (a welcome snip at £45).

According to this particular analysis of the universe, Taurus loves buying stuff. As does Pisces. As, indeed, does the rest of the night sky. Leos needed an £890 luggage set from Rupert Sanderson. Because they tend to be the sort of people who pack their luggage into suitcases. Librans are implored to shell out £8,625 for an Ebel watch. Presumably to tell them when it's time to buy some more stuff.

Still, what appears indisputable from all this is that nowadays even space wants you to consume your frickin' nuts off. Cosmic!

Horseracing tips

When it boils down to it, what you're being asked to do here is take financial advice off a gambler. Is that wise? These are people prone to investing large sums of their own money on chance events, and then jumping up and down exhorting horses to 'run quicker, you fecking horse, you', so they are not necessarily the model of an independent financial adviser.

Tipsters are obsessed with 'value'. The first aspect of this is looking for an event priced higher than its actual likelihood. So, if you can find a horse priced at 12-1 when really it should be 8-1, bet on it, quick. Never mind if it has much chance of winning – just remember that, if it does, you'll have four times as much money as you should have! Barman – drinks for all my friends. It probably won't win, though.

Of course, the theory is that some value bets come off, so over time a few big winners will cancel out your losses: the odds are greater than the probability, so in theory it has to even itself out in your favour. This may or may not happen, but for it to apply you'd have to bet on every over-priced event, which would certainly keep you busy. And that's what value is all about.

Except it's also about avoiding bad value. What this means is, in a race most likely to be won by one clear favourite – which thus is trading at very low odds – you look for a horse with better odds to bet on: the weight of money being slapped on the big, strong, fast horse that is probably going to win is making the price 'too short' to be worthwhile. And the low price of the favourite makes the price of all the other, not so fast horses greater. It's an attractive proposition: your new selection might be trading at, say, 14-1; so you'll win 14 times as much back. Barman – drinks for all my friends. Except they're advising you to bet on it 'just in case' it wins. Which, in all likelihood, it won't. Probably the strong favourite will. Or it might get beaten by a 'live one', only not the 'live' one you bet on, which turned out to be more asleep than alive for most of the race.

Tipsters will often refer to making a selection for a particular race as 'solving the puzzle'. But while a puzzle has a fixed end – the picture on the box of a jigsaw puzzle, for instance – the only fixed point in a horse race is the finishing post. Which horse will run past it first, however, is open to quite a few variables. The horse only has to clip a fence, have an off day or get a bit tired out and your jigsaw puzzle's flying up in the air in as many pieces as your torn-to-shreds and discarded betting slip.

So if it's a puzzle, it's a 4D puzzle that constantly shapeshifts, the selection of roses becoming a painting of the Houses of Parliament viewed from the South Bank with tugboat; then one of the pieces falls over and gets shot through the back of the neck inside a little tent.

Of course, the real problem facing tipsters is that they have to make a call for each and every race. In closely fought races, or if they just haven't got much idea who will win, tipsters will use words such as 'might' and 'could', as in 'could go close'. This is code for: 'Well, you never fucking know. The jockey's wearing blue, and that's my lucky colour. How many days to the Solstice? Bollocks.'

It would perhaps be better to suggest you stick a pin in the racecard, or say: 'Don't bet on this race, it's a bugger, bet on another one. If I were you, I'd get some contacts in the trade who are going to run a mustard first-timer at Wincanton at 50s. That's what I do, although obviously I'm not sharing that information with you. Not even if you ring my seven-quid-a-minute premium-rate tips line for the requisite half an hour of waffle before I finally deign to tell you that the hot favourite in the 3.20 at Brighton is probably going to romp it, which you already knew anyway.'

Little wonder, then, that at the end of 2005 pundits were sweating even more than usual over the *Racing Post*'s tipsters' table, which rates each tipster's best bets of the day (their nap) for how much you would win (or lose) if you put a pound on each of their naps. Because that year, for the first time, the *Post* included in the table what would have happened if you'd just popped your money on the favourite in each race – that is, completely dispensed with form, statistics and, of course, tipsters. Come December, you'd have been better off blindly doing this than following all but two of the 51 tipsters in the league – and best of luck guessing in advance which two that might be. By the end of the season, only nine of the 51 had returned a profit.

And who could have predicted a chance event such as that?

'How I got my body back'

'I didn't eat anything.'

Inconvenient truths

Al Gore's heart-warming global-warming documentary *An Inconvenient Truth* is a rotting bag of recycled compost. Okay, it's a film. We are told this talking-the-talk movie has been breaking US box-office records (although it's not clear which ones: possibly those for documentaries made by former vice-presidents). Of course, Gore's record on caring about the environment is second to none. It goes right back to the 80s. (He actually invented it, right before coming up with the internet and roller-blading.)

And since his failed presidential bid in 2000, Gore has been campaigning ceaselessly on behalf of the environment, urging everyone to reduce their carbon footprint before it's too late. In fact, there has only been one itsy-bitsy, blink-and-you'd-miss-it, tiny interregnum in Big Al's near-lifelong campaign for the environment: the years 1992 to 2000. During this short eight-year period, he was far quieter about the environment. So quiet that even those in the front row of the cinema auditorium, excellently positioned with regard to the surround-sound speakers, would be reduced to lip-reading lips that were not actually moving.

Oddly, this coincides almost exactly – no, completely exactly – with the time he was vice-president of the God Bless the United States of A – in the Clinton administration that did slightly less than fuck all about reducing America's gargantuan carbon footprint.

Shame he took this particular period off from the environmentalism. Because he might have proved quite useful then.

Crikey! These inconvenient truths get everywhere, don't they?

Indian restaurants with irregular plates

Octagonal ceramics and chicken dopiaza do not mix. Like the earthy tones on the walls and herb/ spice name ('Cardamom', 'Coriander', 'Bayleaf'), it all signifies just one thing: smaller portions yet larger prices than you get at Indian restaurants with round plates.

If your local pub suddenly announces itself as a funky 'bar and kitchen', meanwhile, look out for square plates. There must be a sinister New Britain cooking college somewhere churning out millions of young chefs whose entire repertoire is monkfish and/or lamb shanks, served with the ubiquitous jus.

They seem to have some kind of Masonic code, possibly to tip each other off, which boils down to: square plates – we're going to rob you blind. Square plates? Piss on them!

Actually, don't do that.

Innocent

Fruit? Why not? So the smoothies I'm not going to take issue with. It's the matey marketing that gets the apples falling off my tree in anger. Who is this mindless chatter aimed at? Did they spot a big gap in the market by noticing that crying out for additive-free crushed fruit concoctions were armies of total fuckwits? 'These fuckwits: they're vitamin mad, I'm telling you . . .'

It's like they're talking to babies. Innocent promise to never use 'weird stuff in our drinks. And we promise never to cheat at cards.' We're crazy guys, it says, but also we're crazy guys who don't fuck you over with chemicals when you fork out the best part of two quid for a small fruit drink; so we're pretty great people all round. 'Summer's here and we thought we'd give you nice stuff.' This whole tack is so twee it would make Heidi retch her berry smoothie all down her front, staining her one frock, which her grandad or whoever he is would then have to wash in a stream. And he's got logs to chop and all sorts.

These are the sort of people who call food 'grub' and can't do anything without winking. Who winks? These bastards. No one else. They probably have 'Naughty person on board' stickers in their cars too. And these wacky, all-natural funsters are not even hippies. The crazy Innocent founders are ex-corporate types now turning over £75 million a year. So probably if you took them up on the offer to pop round to Fruit Towers ('Do pop by if you're ever in the area'), they might well not be there. They might be skiing. Not that you would take them up on it, obviously. ('Just swing by. Pop along any time. To a factory.' 'Yeah, cool. Is it a disused factory with a huge soundsystem in it?' 'No.' 'I might not bother.')

Say you did bother, though, perhaps tipping up at Fruit Towers with a few beers hoping they've got a widescreen TV, I can't help wondering what sort of welcome you would actually get. Are they inviting us to pop in like some people ask 'How are you?' – that is, not really meaning it? Who can say? There's only one way to find out, and that isn't happening – not now, not ever.

You can even join the 'Innocent family' on their website – which has at least one thing going for it; come Christmas time, they're never going to be short of cranberries. Although they would get stupidly over-excited about the jokes out of the crackers. But do you really want to be in a family with people whose delivery vans are either made to look like cows or have fake grass all over them: 'When we're not busy making nice drinks, there's nothing we like better than doing up our vans and making them look sort of innocent. Naturally, this means that we now have a herd of cow vans and a couple of DGVs ("dancing grass vans" to the man on the street).'

Here's an idea: just deliver your drinks, quietly, in normal vans, then fuck off home. If I want a fruit smoothie, I'll buy one. And that's it. I've got a family. I have friends. If I didn't, I'd even stoop to, say, joining a church before I'd organise my life around people who crush up fruit.

Interactive bus stops

Bus stops with screens set into billboard advertisements – usually for new films – with a button for you to press to select clips and miscellaneous info to watch as you stand about, slowly wasting away in the breeze. Now sprouting up throughout London, interactive bus stops will be arriving everywhere soon – possibly in threes.

I'm not sure I want to be standing at a bus stop watching clips from *Sin City* of avenging psychopath-with-a-heart Marv reaping righteous justice on the twisted and depraved of Basin City that done his Goldie wrong. It doesn't feel right.

In fact, there's only one thing that I want to interact with my bus stop – and it's got a big number '7' on the front of it.

It's raining today.

Internet cafes

Particularly those with threadbare psychedelic carpets that do international calls in decrepit chipboard booths with no soundproofing, run by a money-grabbing misbegotten who probably owns half of Sandy Lane in Barbados purely from the profits he makes on printing charges, full of preppy Americans doing pretend higher-education courses sending long, banal emails home before realising that there are other preppy Americans in the room and sharing their inane platitudes loudly and at length while you are innocently trying to send abusive emails to cabinet ministers using fake Hotmail accounts and you only went in there because your shitty broadband has screwed up yet again and you have no alternative to come back here even though the last time you went in they charged you 20 quid to send a fax and you told the usurer behind the counter that you'd never patronise their stinking digital shit-farm ever again.

Some of them are nicer than that, though.

iPod fashion

The iPod has been venerated in many extraordinary ways. iPods have inspired books, like GQ editor Dylan Jones's epic novel sequence *A Dance to the Music of My Lovely iPod of Time*. They have inspired songs, like the U2/Pavarotti collaboration 'Funky iPod (Funky iPod)'.

They have even inspired a panegyric from David Cameron, who recently declared: 'Unlike Gordon Brown, I actually understand all the complicated functions on my iPod. He doesn't even know how to use the party shuffle. The Jock twat.'*

Maybe slightly less extraordinary, but potentially more disturbing, in that it's actually real, is iPod fashion. That phrase exists. It is a phrase which exists. The mere phrase 'iPod fashion' – which exists – should make you shudder.

There's Karl Lagerfeld's rectangular gilded purse – roughly the size of 'a bread bin', oddly enough – which is lined with multicoloured cloth and incorporates a pocket for holding up to a dozen iPods. Or some crusty rolls, I suppose. (Incidentally, Karl Lagerfeld now owns 70 iPods . . . the newly thin German freak.)

Gucci recently introduced an iPod Sling, a 200-dollar carrying case with leather trim and silver clasps. Colours include Namba ('shines golden colour in direct sunlight'), Chocolate ('rich and dark, almost good enough to eat') and Deadly Nightshade Returns ('subtle and elegant').

There are even iPod pants – pants with a pocket for your iPod ('Party on with iPod pants').

There's also a swath of new sleeves and hoods, with one internet reviewer deciding of the foofpod, that, 'Overall, it's a recommended sleeve for the iPod if you want to get away from the "skins" scene.'

Jesus Christ, there's a 'skins' *scene*? I need to lie down.

*The speech continued: 'And I was into the Arctic Monkeys way before he was. I told all my mates about them on MySpace when they brought out "Fake Tales of San Francisco".'

iPod popes

The Pope has got an iPod, hip hip hip hooray, the Pope has got an iPod and he's coming out to play.

Yes, the Pope has got an iPod. Of course he has.

A Vatican spokesperson said: 'He is very pleased with the iPod. The Holy Father likes to unwind listening to it and is of the opinion that this sort of technology is the future.'

He's up all night, you know, illegally downloading Gregorian chanting.

iPod wages

The iPod city of Longhua has 10 factories making iPod components for Apple.

Workers can sleep a hundred to a room and earn 27 dollars a month. It would cost them half a year's salary to buy an iPod Nano. Their wages are low even by Chinese standards. At another iPod city outside Shanghai, 50,000 workers are enclosed in a barbed-wire compound the size of eight football pitches.

Yue, a worker in Longhua, said: 'We have to work overtime and can only go back to the dorm when our boss gives us permission. After working 15 hours, we are so tired. It's like being in the army. They make us stand still for hours – if we move we are made to stand still for longer. The boys have to do push-ups.

'And if we make the black ones, we have to listen to the preloaded U2 tunes. It is terrible.'

(She didn't say the last bit.)

It's a Royal Clearout!

Viscount Linley has always been the most intriguing minor royal. Firstly, he's called Linley, which no one is. Secondly, his first name appears to be Viscount, which is the name of a biscuit.

But you do have to feel sorry for him. In June 2006 Viscount Linley was forced to sell off possessions left to him by his mother Princess Margaret in order to pay death duties.

Oh, hang on. That's 'forced' as in he's broke because he only owns the two swanky furniture shops selling his own line of desks at six grand a pop and armchairs for a mere £2,885 each.

And that's 'his mother's possessions' as in most of them were paid for by the state or were gifts from the Empire/Commonwealth. So they weren't her possessions at all and in fact belonged to me (and all the other taxpayers).

Linley got £13,200 for a George V gold menu-card holder carrying Margaret's initials (yep, that'd be mine); the same amount for George VI's personal set of playing cards; and £102,000 for his Cartier gem-set cigarette lighter, which he presumably used to light fags I paid for during stressful moments gambling my money over a game of those cards I seem to have bought him. My Fabergé clock netted Linley and his sister Lady Sarah Chatto £1.24 million. They even trousered £2,400 for a trio of 1960s disposable plastic umbrellas. The final tally was a whopping £13,658,728.

You could say he was trying to sell everything that wasn't nailed down. Except he did try and sell something that was nailed down. Linley was all set to auction a set of railings around his mother's (that is, my) garden at Kensington Palace. But the white iron balustrading was withdrawn from the auction, where they were expected to fetch between £8,000 and £15,000, when it became clear that, as part of Kensington Palace, which is a 'scheduled monument', dismantling the railings would have needed consent from English Heritage and the Department for Culture, Media and Sport. Linley decided instead – somewhat magnanimously – to 'donate the railings to the nation'. The nation could be forgiven for not getting overly excited about this, though, as they are in an area of the building not open to the public. So the nation will only be able to enjoy its magnificent bequest by craning out of an upstairs window of a palace they would have to pay to enter.

Personally, I blame daytime TV. If the Royals had proper jobs, they wouldn't be sat round at home all day watching *Cash in the Attic*. Maybe they could do one called *Stealing My Cash*.

'It's what John would have wanted'

John Lennon appears to have spent the 1970s alternately baking bread; getting the English out of Ireland by putting tampons on his head; playing those mind games; not living with straights who told him he was king; getting shitted on drugs and wanking himself off practically all the time at every hour of the day and night (I read that in a book).

This sounds like a tremendous way to spend a decade, particularly if you could fairly have been described as 'very busy' during the preceding decade. But no. It seems that what he should have been doing was whoring his name out for any conceivable bit of tat. Handily, his death, while it had its obvious downside, liberated others to do this for him.

Real Lennon products include crockery for children, sunglasses, figurines, plates, watches, Nike Converse Peace trainers featuring lyrics from 'Imagine', innumerable piss demos ('Cold Turkey' sounding like a bad busker in an echoey Tube corridor in which it is somehow raining; revealing studio dialogue such as 'Can you turn my headphones up a bit? No, up. Not quite that much. Yeah, that's it'); and an airport. The Liverpool John Lennon Airport slogan? 'Above us only sky'. Well, it's better than 'Help!'

When news recently arrived that flyglobespan would in 2007 commence daily flights from John Lennon Airport to New York, Yoko Ono said: 'How fitting that there will soon be flights from John Lennon Airport to New York. As you all know, John had a tremendous fondness for both of these cities. He would have been delighted that now there will be a direct flight between these two historic cities – across the Universe, so to speak. Best wishes from me to you. Yoko.'

Of course, John Lennon would have loved the reasonably priced transatlantic flight revolution (he loved revolutions). If only the flights had been cheaper when he was alive, he would have been nipping back to Liverpool all the time.

Given these shimmering oceans of product, the scope for further diversifying the brand might be considered limited. But still, here follows a list of proposed Lennon merchandise which we humbly submit for Ms Ono's consideration . . .

- Bed-In bedding
- Bag-ism bags
- 'Come Together' love beads
- 'The Dream Is Over' alarm clock
- 'Mean Mr Mustard' mustard
- A nine millionth re-release of 'Imagine' to coincide with random events of cosmological/political/religious/cultural importance

- 'Mother' Mother's Day cards featuring the inner message: 'MOTHAAH DON'T GOOOOOOOOOO OOOOOO!!!!!'
- 'DADDY COME HOME!' get-well-soon cards for hospitalised fathers
- John's 'It Won't Be Long' longjohns
- A walrus

ITV Play

ITV Play's *The Mint* is on for up to four hours during the night, with viewers urged to call in, at 60p a pop, for a chance of winning a cash prize. All they need to do is answer a simple teaser such as 'Who was a smooth operator? Was it a) Sade or b) The Stone Roses?' or decipher a 'word snake' that looks to have been copied out of old editions of *Junior Puzzler* magazine. So far, so so. The innovation is to play each question for about one whole hour, with presenters Brian Dowling and Beverley French gabbling unscripted piss dotted with the phrases 'call in' and 'win' – filling the interminable spaces in which ITV rack up those 60ps.

French looks like the terrifying women who stand behind make-up counters in department stores – a bit like someone who has just had a *This Morning* makeover, then another *This Morning* makeover straight over the top of the first one. Even her name sounds like a makeover: 'Yeah, I'm having a Beverley French'. An alumni of Granada's Men & Motors channel, French is a professional Mancunian, but with a slightly strange, high-pitched accent. Imagine a glam Daphne from *Frasier* trying to skank you for 60p every two to three seconds – for four hours – and you'll just about get there.

Dowling can look a bit strained and shell-shocked. Like a usually bubbly individual with a hangover at a wedding, struggling to keep up the bonhomie because they feel they should and everyone's expecting it, even though their heart isn't really in it. He just repeats himself (and Beverley) in a hyperactive camp way. If anything happens – which it doesn't – he describes it in detail in a hyperactive camp way. He appears not to understand what is happening even when something happens.

You can see his point when someone gets through to fill in the blank in 'Water —————' (bear in mind that, if they made 10 attempts to get through, they have already spent six quid by now) and gives the answer 'mayonnaise'.

Water mayonnaise? Really – how is Brian supposed to understand this?

As far as ITV is concerned, *The Mint* is the shape of shit to come, which is possibly why they show it on ITV1 simultaneously with its airing on ITV Play. Either that or it's just for the money. They claim *The Mint* is a brave pioneer in the world of 'participation' TV – where you, the viewer, can get 'live and interactive' with the content. This translates as: there is no content. They've just taken the premium-phoneline element from various hit shows and removed the actual programme bit. And quadrupled the length.

No wonder Brian gets so philosophical and reflective with us. 'We're just like puppets,' he said in a rare moment of profundity, 'dancing on their strings. We don't know the answers.'

Certainly that's how I felt about things at the time Brian, yes.

J

Michael Jackson fans

There was the lady who released doves into the air in response to the liberating verdict, while the man beside her shouted, 'Praise be!' to the skies.

And the lady who cooked raccoons over a log fire to pass around to her hungry comrades.

The fan who, as every 'not guilty' verdict was announced, sawed off one of his own toes to express his gratitude – sadly, but also joyously, running out of toes before the verdicts had ended.

The family from Arkansas who re-enacted crucial moments from Jackson's life – the *Motown 25* show, the baby-shaking incident, the Martin Bashir interview, the morphy video for 'Black and White'.

The SCID-suffering boy in the bubble whose mother was convinced that some tooth enamel from his hero would cure him of his strange, sad condition.

The South Dakotan death-cult who all sported white gloves and reinterpreted 'Man in the Mirror' in the style of Nine Inch Nails.

The Catholic priest who added a fifth gospel to the New Testament – 'The Gospel According to Michael' – featuring Jesus continually explaining to his disciples that he is 'bad, but bad meaning good'.

Whenever Michael Jackson fans gather in one place to give thanks and praise, you can guarantee some serious End of Days shit will be going down. Some appeared almost ecstatic that their idol was up for child molestation again. It's nice to have a reason to get dressed up, isn't it? 'Hi, sweetie, they're trying to kill Michael again by saying he's into kiddy-fiddling, showing them porn and getting them drunk and all that kind of crap! Tell work I'm not coming in – it's the End of Days!'

JK and Joel

Two nutty funsters who have spread across Radio 1 like a nutty fun plague. When their show was expanded, Radio 1 controller Andy Parfitt said: 'JK and Joel are Radio 1 talents. They've got engaging personalities and a real sense of fun.' It's hard to disagree with this statement. Except for the words 'talents', 'engaging', 'personalities', 'real' and 'fun'.

Rules for life, then: if JK and Joel say something, it's wrong. If they say a word, never use that word again. If they even use a letter, try to avoid that letter for a while. If you know anyone who vaguely reminds you of either of them, I'm sorry but it really is time for that friendship to end. These are, after all, two grown men – both around 30 – whom the world seems to have completely passed by: you almost wonder if they have lived their whole lives in a cupboard watching episodes of *Hollyoaks*.

I once heard them loudly praise former Radio 1 *Chart Show* presenter Mark Goodier as a 'legend'. Imagine a world where you are a mere munchkin at the feet of 'legends' like Mark

Goodier. They would presumably also worship at the altar of long-lost Radio 1 'funster' Adrian Juste. In fact, they could well be part of a secret army dedicated to bringing the 'comedy king' back to the airwaves and, as a result, possibly bring about a clash of civilisations.

Then, amid all the senseless slaughter, they could cite the principle of a Juste war.

Justifying train/bus station concourse mark-ups

'Because we can' would at least be honest. Or: 'Because we know you'll never get your shit together to buy it beforehand (except when you visit your mum and she makes you sandwiches)'. Usually, though, they mutter something about the high rents.

The thing is, that's kind of their problem. I really don't want to be getting into the finer points of Burger King's accounts. It's not the level on which I see us interacting. But you seem to manage to charge the same in Dumfries and Newport as you do on Oxford Street, so where's the beef (no pun intended)? The rents on Oxford Street will be higher than those at Leeds station, and the outlet on Oxford Street is massive whereas the Leeds station one is quite small, which must effect some considerable savings in rent, surely?

Just be honest about it. That's all I ask.

And Journey's Friend? Journey's *Friend*? If I got to the station and had neglected to pick up a bottle of water and a Twix on the way, I should have thought a friend – a *true* friend – would not look to profit by selling them to me – *selling* them! – at a handsome premium.

A friend – someone who really cared about me – would *give* me the Twix.

I know I can be difficult. Can't we all? There was that incident. Okay. But I'm loyal. I'll stand by you. But you? *YOU?*

You're a user! I hate you!

K

The Kaiser Chiefs

The Kaiser Chiefs always act like they can't believe their luck. And they are right not to believe their luck. Their massive success is, frankly, unbelievable. Ricky Wilson, rock hero as balloon-animal party entertainer, famously said he would 'wank a tramp for fame'. This was meant as a typically affable, self-deprecating joke. Although, now that he has achieved his fame, we should maybe consider conducting an experiment into what he might do to hold on to that fame. I reckon it won't be pretty. The Kaiser Chiefs actually rolled up stinking of desperation, like a junkie child actor trying to get a peas advert. So, now they've had a taste, God knows what they'd be capable of.

Of course, everyone's middle-of-the-road nowadays. Even New Wave guitar-tykes who sing 'state of the nation' songs about riots. From occupying the cutting-edge of Western social advancement (in terms of sex, class, race, peace, the big stuff), albeit often not that seriously, many bands now seem to find the cutting-edge a bit, well, sharp. And, unfortunately, quite edgy.

The Kaiser Chiefs were apparently mildly perturbed to hear that the local police played 'I Predict A Riot' before heading out on Friday nights. But this is hardly in the same league as Reagan appropriating Springsteen's 'Born In The

USA'. There wasn't any message there to rewrite. Anyway, it's surely the Kaisers to a tee: *X-Factor* indie, ideal for helping psych up coppers for a night out belting bingers. It's only a bit of fun.

Of course, The Kaiser Chiefs are just one of the New Wave of Careerist Bands Whose Careerism Makes Them Nowhere Near Interesting Enough To Sustain A Career. It's often all in the name. The Kooks sound quite kooky. They're bloody not, though. They're just called The Kooks. This doesn't mean that 'Britain's new favourite band' (the *NME*) have to be remotely 'kooky'. It's only words.

The Futureheads, meanwhile, sound all futuristic. They're not, though. Unless your idea of sounding like the future involves bands sounding exactly like they did in 1979. They should be called The Pastheads. This is wormhole rock, studiously aping music that was already slightly too studious to begin with. And it's been going on for bloody ever. In full swing at least since 2001, when New York bands Radio 4 and The Rapture decided okay bands like The Gang of Four and XTC were actually the best bands of all time. The *only* bands, in fact. So by now, this post-punk revival has lasted longer not just than the original post-punk, but longer than punk, post-punk and the bit that came after post-punk put together. Now *that's* entropy!

The Ordinary Boys sound ordinary. And, to be fair, they are. Lukewarm retreads of other people's music and lyrics (to the extent of just wholesale quoting of lyrics, phrases and song-titles) are always going to be pretty 'ordinary'. Yet they claim to be both Ordinary and fairly extraordinary all at the same time. Preston was once asked: 'Preston what?' He said: 'Just Preston. Like Madonna.' Preston what, indeed. He also claimed his songs are 'British satire', which they are in a way, but not the one he intended. Referring to his appearance on *Celebrity Big Brother*, he said it was okay for a 'punk' because 'the line between alternative and mainstream is so blurred'. Yes, it is sort of punk-rock of the mainstream to embrace the alternative. It's kind of what the mainstream does, though. Then the alternative has to be something else. Otherwise it's not the alternative. So maybe you should consider renaming your light entertainment troupe The Redundant Boys.

You can sort of understand the critics not exposing the bands for what they are. They've got their future lad-mag careers to think about. But other bands don't even slag them off. Come on – get effing and jeffing. Here's a couple of insults to get you started: 'You journeymen merchants of ear-cack are happy to be lauded as "artists" and avatars of a generation, yet you churn out the aural equivalent of gaudy, cart-strewn landscapes that even the makers of chocolate boxes would consider a "bit hackneyed" – and would eat your own hair if you thought it would get you on the Friday Fucking Night Project.' 'You're shit – and you know who you are.' 'Ricky Wilson is an arrant disgrace who is ideally equipped to play Buttons in a panto at the end of a pier that is not connected to any land.' And don't even get me started on the The Hat One. Other than to say that any sexually frustrated tramps out there might want to form an orderly queue.

Kamikaze gentrification projects

'Hi there, I'm James and this is my place,' says ex-public-schoolboy bar-owner James, gesturing around his refurbed pub in an edgy, actually quite 'vibey' part of town.

He might have renamed it something like The Progress, in the hope of pushing things further along the gentrification route. This chichi drinking hole is symbolic of how the area will undoubtedly become the next estate-agent hotspot and those boarded-up shops and crackdens will soon be delis and tanning salons. He read about this whole postcode being up-and-coming somewhere or other. It's all going to be fine.

He's got the sofas. He's polished the floors. He's got three three-star rooms upstairs. He's got no customers.

But they will come. The new gentry are on their way. Right now. Any moment, they'll burst in, order some pints of Staropramen and choose which type of mash to have with their sausages. The monkfish is on ice.

Actually, they should probably be here by now. Hope they come soon. Starting to get a bit scared. What with all the crack-heads everywhere. And the night is closing in. Oh no, not the night.

That's when all the beasties come out to play . . . What was that noise?

Six months later, here's James, jumpy, clutching a blue corner-shop carrier-bag of chocolate bars, crushing a Galaxy into his pale, spotty face – 'suicide Tuesday' taking on a new meaning from the long-lost happy comedown sessions at other people's bars.

Mummy! Mummy! Can you get my room ready? I'm coming home . . .

Keystone terror interrogators

The very word 'terror' is enough to strike terror into the heart of most people. Personally, I'm very much against 'terror'. I hate it. You could even describe me as being 'anti-terror'.

But, without wishing to seem needlessly controversial, I do wish the UK/US governments would stick to doing the 'anti-terror' in a way that didn't jettison human rights. Or diminish global standards on what constitutes torture. Or ignore likely big leads (like concerns expressed to police by Martin Gilbertson that the 7/7 bombers were up to some serious bomb planning). Or lose rucksacks containing suspects' details on the streets of south-east London. (What were they doing? Scoring an eighth on the way home from work?) Or ask questions so stupid that they would make a stupid person ask: 'What exactly the fuck do you think you are doing?'

Holed up in Guantanamo, one of the Tipton Three, Shafiq Rasul, was repeatedly asked: 'If I wanted to get hold of surface-to-air missiles in Tipton, where would I go?' Before being interned without trial for three years, Shafiq had worked at Currys, so maybe they saw a possible connection there. That's Currys, the high-street electrical store: 'Always cutting prices . . . on surface-to-air missiles!' (We're joking, of course – to our knowledge, Currys has never stocked surface-to-air missiles.)

Also in Guantanamo, Moazzem Begg was questioned about the US sniper John Mohammed (sentenced for shooting 11 people in Washington in 2002), because he was called Mohammed, which is Muslim. He was also shown pictures of the Pope taken from his computer's hard-drive and questioned about his apparent assassination plans. Begg was initially confused by these pictures, until he remembered that all computers' 'Temporary Internet Files' folders store all of the images from any visited website. So a visit to the BBC news website, say, might lead to your computer storing all sorts of pictures from the home page that you hadn't even paid any attention to at the time. (The interrogators also presented him with a picture of a camel spider and asked him for an explanation, although they did not accuse him of planning to kill it.) The Catholic major told him: 'If anything happens to the Pope, I swear I'll break every finger in your hands.'

On other occasions, Begg was asked to identify someone from a picture of the back of their head, or an arm, or a leg, and asked: 'Do you recognise this?' To which he might reasonably have responded: 'Hmm ... tricky one, this ... (decisively) Montgomerie! Yup, it's Monty; Colin Montgomerie, the golfer . . .' before realising he wasn't after all on *Question of Sport*.

Prior to being released, one of the Forest Gate brothers – arrested in June 2006 in a massive police raid after a tip-off regarding a non-appearing 'chemical jacket' – Mohammed Abdul Kahar was continually asked about his membership of a series of terrorist organisations, culminating with the question: 'Are you a member of the Ku Klux Klan?' He replied: 'Damn it! You've got me. I'm a white supremacist. I thought I had the perfect alibi – what with not being white and all.'

It was perhaps doubly rude of officers to question Mohammed Abdul Kahar in this way, what with having just shot him.

At the time of writing, none of these people has been charged with any terror-related crime. But even if they had been, it's hard to see how a viable comeback against extremism could ever involve asking really stupid questions.

Incidentally, according to Begg's account of his incarceration, the British MI5 officers reacted to their US allies' brutality with the patrician care of John Cleese's Robin Hood in *Time Bandits*: 'I say, are you absolutely sure that's all necessary?'

Which is at least a pertinent question.

Ben Kingsley, Sir

Sir Ben Kingsley has been woefully misunderstood. When he was billed on the posters for *Lucky Number Slevin* as 'Sir Ben Kingsley', he was accused of being 'barmy' by Lord Puttnam and of talking 'pretentious bollocks' by Roger Moore. (*Lucky Number Slevin* wasn't lucky, by the way, it was shit.)

Sir Ben Kingsley shot back, telling the *Sunday Telegraph* that he was 'shocked' by the producers' 'faux pas'. His case was sadly weakened because he was quoted as accepting the knighthood by saying: 'There is no Mr Ben Kingsley any more. Being a Sir brings with it responsibility.' And an old document sent to all crew on his previous movie *Mrs Harris* read: 'We received a call from Ben Kingsley's agent ... Please address him as "Sir Ben" if you find yourself in his presence.'

It puts one in mind of his most celebrated role, that of Mahatma Gandhi. Except, for all the humility, the grace and the kickstarting of campaigns of civil disobedience. As Gandhi famously said: 'I want an M&M-filled trailer the size of Jupiter. Right here. Right. Fucking. NOW!'

Krispy Kreme doughnuts

Are suddenly EVERYWHERE. With concessions at Tescos, Harrods, Kempton races, shopping centres, etc., etc., etc., etc., you have to ask: how come the sudden doughnut hegemony?

What's with this sudden appearance of forward troop positions for an invading green, red and white-liveried doughnut vending army?

It can only be a matter of time before Krispy Kreme start opening concessions inside other Krispy Kreme concessions. And that will be rings within rings, and then where will we be?

Jeremy Kyle

'Look at me. Look at me. Look at me!'

I don't want to look at you.

L

Learning to live with global warming

During the summer months, Britain could erect a great big sign saying, 'FRYING NOW'. Quite aware that our hair is burning, we have now officially *got it* regarding climate change and we look to our leaders for guidance and encouragement to modify our lifestyles accordingly. 'It can be done! It can be done!' is what we want to hear.

Responding to this challenge, David Cameron took a cheap flight to the Arctic and erected a husky on his roof. The government did less than that: when asked of any occasion whatsoever when Margaret Beckett's Department of the Environment had triumphed over their Trade and Industry/Treasury counterparts, her advisers reportedly looked at their feet. Blair has since called reducing UK air travel through taxation 'unrealistic'. So that's it, then. Saving the planet: 'It can't be done! It can't be done!'

So it's probably all for the best if we just cut our hot cloth accordingly. This is the newest message from business, the right, New Labour, Clarkson (everyone in power, basically): we should all start learning to live with global warming. Let's face it, we can't really do anything, so we just need to be flexible enough to cope with sunshine that might scorch our faces off. It's easier by far. Come on: we've lived with cheap flights for, ooh, at least five years. We can't go back now.

Adapt and improve, while sweating profusely: it's the 21st-century way. A fact many of the world's animal species seem woefully unwilling to appreciate. Using mid-range climate predictions, researchers reckon that by 2050 between 15 and 37% of all species will be heading towards obsolescence, leading some to hail a forthcoming mass extinction event similar to that which wiped out the dinosaurs.

Maybe they're hamming it up a bit. You know what these dinosaur guys are like. We've all seen *Jurassic Park*. And so what if we are facing another mass extinction event? Even then, it's not all doom and gloom. After the fourth mass extinction 251 million years ago, following the worst crisis to affect life on Earth (probably caused by a giant volcanic eruption in what became modern-day Siberia), the only land animal of any size to survive was the lystrosaurus, largely thanks to dumb luck. This creature was probably fairly hideous – imagine a pig crossed with a lizard – but it proved flexible in the face of new challenges. So there you go.

But, hey, let's look on the bright side. You know what we've got that the great crested newt and polar bears haven't? Sun cream. You'd better believe it.

Left/liberal apologists for Islamic fundamentalists

There are some ground rules that need establishing here: blowing oneself up in a shopping centre to forward a medieval theocracy involving the suppression of women and the stoning of gays is a bad thing, isn't it? I think we can all agree on that one.

Ah, apparently not. By some crazy twist of logic,

reactionary bigots who seek to plunge the world into religious darkness can become freedom fighters – a 'deformed' liberation movement; the ANC by other means. If you don't like US imperialism (and, hey, even the Pentagon seems to be wavering on that one these days), you must be okay – even if what you do like is slaughtering people standing at bus stops because of their religion. So we end up with anti-war demonstrations where purportedly socialist paper-sellers mingle with thoroughly fundamentalist Hizb ut-Tahrir, chatting, their stalls standing next to each other.

There's George Galloway, of course (see **George Galloway, Unfair pillorying of**). Meanwhile, Ken Livingstone (yes, the 'Red' one) has warmly welcomed reactionary bigot Sheikh Yusuf al-Qaradawi to London. (al-Qaradawi supports the execution of all males who engage in homosexual acts and 'personally supports' female circumcision. Of suicide bombers, he says, 'For us, Muslim martyrdom is not the end of things but the beginning of the most wonderful of things.') Tariq Ali has set himself up as one of the world's premier cheerleaders for the bigots dominating the insurgency in Iraq, casting them as anti-imperialist warriors and saying: 'The resistance in Iraq is not, as Israeli and Western propagandists like to argue, a case of Islam gone mad. It is . . . a direct consequence of the occupation.'

It's a funny sort of business when you consider that, historically, the British left has failed even to develop a united campaign against racism. You'd have thought that, broadly speaking, the entire left wing in British politics is not going to have such amazing differences of opinion about racism (they'd all be against it, which is a good start) that could not be contained in a single campaign. But recent decades have seen a profusion of mutually antagonistic, left-inspired anti-racist organisations – many, ironically, sporting the words 'Coalition', 'Unity' or 'United'. Yet the differences between these various battling groups are minuscule when compared with their differences to, say, the Muslim Association of Britain, who are major partners in the Stop the War campaign. The MAB's leadership has sympathies for the Jamaat-i-Islami in Pakistan and Bangladesh, and the Muslim Brotherhood in Egypt – both of which firmly believe in the creation of an Islamic state and the establishment of Sharia law. A left that can ally with religious reactionaries but can't ally with itself might want to sit down for a bit of a think.

Critics of this abject moral and intellectual collapse are often accused of 'Islamophobia'. But this isn't about Islam per se. What we are talking about is Islamic fundamentalism – a fanatical politico-religious ideology that would outlaw homosexuality, kill trade unionists, institute medieval, religious feudalism . . . sort of like fascism, only less modern.

So, all things considered, if ever the worldwide Caliphate is established, it seems like a few people will be in for a nasty shock:

THE MEDIEVALISTS: Ah, honoured gentlemen. If you'd be so kind as to file into this football stadium . . .

KEN LIVINGSTONE: Turned out nice again. I'm into buses, you know. In here, you say?

THE MEDIEVALISTS: Yes, please, and if you can hurry it up. We've got a load of stonings still to do – and we'd just like to slaughter you all.

KEN LIVINGSTONE: Lovely. I like buses, you know.

TARIQ ALI: What? You're going to what?

GEORGE GALLOWAY: They're going to slaughter us. It's

nothing to worry about. It's customary among such peoples. Cigar?

TARIQ ALI: Don't they know who I am? You really should have mentioned this before.

THE MEDIEVALISTS: We did.

TARIQ ALI: Oh.

KEN LIVINGSTONE: Yes. Now I come to think about it, they did give some signals in this direction. I like buses, you know.

TARIQ ALI: Well, I think it's rude. I'm going to write a big piece in the *Guardian* about it.

THE MEDIEVALISTS: We've burned it down.

TARIQ ALI: The *Independent*?

THE MEDIEVALISTS: Yeah, that too. We didn't like the new tabloid format. Only joking – it was for being infidel.

Lemsip

Of all the cold-and-flu-relief citrus-flavoured powdered drinks, only Lemsip would need spokesperson Reckitt Benckiser (who exists) to declare: 'It is fair to say that it doesn't cause poetry in most people.'

Lemsip is scientific, not versificatory. Science with a capital 'Science'. Even the blackcurrant ones. The heavyweight nature of the bestselling concoction is reflected in its various sub-brand names: Lemsip Fist, Agent Lemon and the all-new Lemsip Bird Flu Fuck You. I'm scared of it, and I'm not even the sniffles.

Oh, hang on, it's just some crushed-up paracetamol that tastes a bit lemony. It perks you up slightly, but then so do most things that contain caffeine.

What you need to make your own 'Lemsip':

- Paracetamol
- Hot water
- Packet of Refreshers

Nevertheless, Lemsip can be extremely dangerous, intoxicating and even addictive, as Poet Laureate Andrew Motion has found.

The poet told the *Daily Telegraph* he 'uses' the potent drug every day to help him write. It gives him the sensation of having 'a mild illness', which is good for the fine poetics, apparently. 'I've been doing it for years and it's become habitual,' he said. Every day, he chases the lemon. 'It's my Lemsip-inspired trance, and I can only say thank heavens it's not laudanum or absinthe,' said Motion.

Indeed. If only Pete Doherty had kept to Lemsip. He might then have been able to speak in sentences and write lines that scan, such as the finely honed stanzas of Motion masterworks 'She Will Rock You' and 'The Prince Has Got a New Hat'.

Here is Motion's poem 'I Wonder if the Queen Does Lemsip?'

I wonder if the Queen does Lemsip?
She's good, mind
The Queen

I like her
A lot

Becher's Brook?
I'll say.

Would you?

I would.

(But then I'm fucked up on Lemsip.)

© A Motion (Hur hur, it says 'a motion'. His name's 'a motion'.)

Lord Levy's impressions

During the furore of Lord Levy's arrest in the Labour loans-for-peerages scandal, *Channel 4 News* scooped all other news sources in dropping this major, remarkable revelation: Levy was prone to ringing up journalists claiming to be various leading politicians, whom he would then impersonate.

And you thought he just sat round in his Totteridge mansion holding dinner parties and waiting for Tony to swing by for a game of tennis. (Which always, in my mind, conjures up the image of Blair arriving one day, in his tennis shorts, arms of his white jumper tied round his neck, racquet casually tossed over his shoulder . . . and Levy being out, and Blair waiting on the doorstep for an hour before giving up and going home for his tea. Maybe it's just me?)

In the spirit of investigative journalism, we have obtained these exclusive transcripts:

LORD LEVY: Hello, it is me, John Prescott, with all the pies.
JOURNALIST: Oh, hello, Lord Levy.
LORD LEVY: No. It's me, Big John. Anyone for croquet? That's my catchphrase.
JOURNALIST: I'm not going to give you any money.
LORD LEVY: Oh.

***

LORD LEVY: Ooh, Betty – the cat done a woopsie on the carpet. Titter ye not. Ooh, I don't really know.

***

LORD LEVY: Hello, it is me, Alistair Darling.

JOURNALIST: Who?

LORD LEVY: You know. Alistair Darling. Out of the Cabinet.

JOURNALIST: No, I don't think so.

LORD LEVY: Come on! I've been in there since '97. I'm the one when you see the pictures of the Cabinet you go, 'Look – Alistair Darling is still in the Cabinet. I never knew!' And I – hello? hello? Are you still there? Hang on, I'll do my Ruth Kelly. Damn those gays! That's what she says. She's the Minister for Equality, you know.

Richard Littlejohn, gays constantly sharking after

Richard Littlejohn is quite hard done by. I don't just mean the way he looks – that face and so on. People can be really very rude about him. These people go around saying the million-pounds-a-year *Mail* columnist is 'just a greasy homophobic shithouse'. They say he's the sort of unmitigated nasty person who could suggest we should be pleased if refugees drown on their way to Britain. The sort of heartless fuck who could say of the Rwandan genocide and the terrorised people fleeing it: 'Does anyone really give a monkey's about what happens in Rwanda? If the Mbongo tribe wants to wipe out the Mbingo tribe then as far as I am concerned that is entirely a matter for them', not caring about the gross associations of the word 'monkey's' or maybe even actively enjoying them. 'What a cunt.' That is what these people say.

But what is clear from Mr Littlejohn's articles (he often expounds on the matter), and what might go some way to explaining his advanced level of anxiety and social fear, is that he is under constant pressure from gay people – or, if you will, 'proselytising homosexuals and lesbians' who are often to be found 'recruiting outside schoolgates'. The country is being increasingly gripped by an all-pervasive, creeping, fully gay conspiracy, chock full of men whose only wish is to give Richard Littlejohn a good bumming.

It's 'poovery'. They want, quite literally, to touch his *little john*.

Maybe it's more than one gay man at a time – big chaps, with tattoos, perhaps five or six of them – perhaps even covered in sensual oils, caressing and massaging Littlejohn, fingers and tongues seeking out hitherto unknown pleasure spots, teasing his anus, rolling him over under a pulsating sea of supple male flesh. We just don't know.

Dick? He's having none if it. Maybe if all these 'homosexualists' gave him some space he'd calm down a bit and stop being such a fucker. We just don't know. But, please, for now, give the man a break and refrain from constantly trying to put his erect penis in your mouth.

Lost
Lost interest.

Luggage on the catwalk

We've had the 'it bag' for female bag connoisseurs. Chloé's brass padlocked Paddington bag sold out worldwide before a single one had reached the shops (well, they stopped your marmalade sandwiches from getting stolen).

According to *Telegraph* fashion director Hilary Alexander, 'Like thousands of women and girls, I have developed something of a handbag fetish over the past decade. When I travel, I think nothing of cramming at least five bags into my suitcase.' This means, sadly, that she is mental.

Now the latest accessories for everyone to enjoy is luggage. Suitcases and stuff. First Miuccia Prada sent her models down the catwalk lugging suitcases behind them. At a recent Milan menswear show, Valentino fitted a jetset couple pushing an airport trolley bearing a signature red luggage set. Apparently, models could be seen zigzagging faulty luggage trolleys crazily around the catwalk shouting to imaginary accomplices: 'I'm telling you, it said Gate 19 was back that way! Where are you going?' And: 'I told you there wouldn't be a toilet up here; you *always* do this.'

Apparently luggage provides men with the chance to join in the accessories fun that women have been having for years without risking their masculinity. Insiders claim, 'The key is for [men] to look as if they're travelling.'

Luggage that makes you look as if you're travelling. It's the new thing! It's a new bag!

Lunchtime boob jobs

All the fun of shopping. But shopping for tits! How fun is that?

The phrase 'lunchtime boob jobs' sounds particularly furtive and risqué – after all, lunchtimes can be boring, once you've paid in that cheque and flicked through the magazines in Smith's. So why not take the opportunity to undergo some major surgery?

The nifty lunchtime boob job op was first publicised in February 2006 by Cheshire's MediSpa Clinic because, said owner Carl Lewis: 'Professional women haven't got time to spend lying in hospital.' Lying around in hospital waiting to recover from operations? That's for losers. Tits to that.

The first wave undergoing this lightning incision included a Cheshire student who was afterwards trotted out for the media's delectation. Why did this perfectly attractive young woman feel the need to big-up her breasts? 'We live in a visual culture and my confidence was really affected,' she explained. 'My mum said they were saggy . . . The surgeon told me it looked as though I had breast-fed two children.'

The operation was partly a 21st birthday present from her parents; the remainder came from her student loan. Apparently, despite being awake, she was on such a high that she didn't feel any pain or anything, although it did start to smart when the anaesthetic wore off (that would be the 'serious operation' aspect kicking in). Still, apparently, she was out shopping a couple of days later.

'You only live once, so you might as well,' she said. 'I would like to try being a TV presenter if I got the chance.'

Not all plastic professionals hailed such efforts to seize the day. David Whitby, consultant plastic surgeon and member of the British Association of Aesthetic Plastic Surgeons (yes – the acronym is BAAPS), reckoned heading home straight from the operating theatre increased the patient's blood pressure and risk of bleeding. 'I would have hesitation in thinking that is the ideal scenario,' he mused.

Nevertheless, big boobs are, well, big. In 2005, according to BAAPS (they're called BAAPS!), the market for elective cosmetic surgery grew by 35%.

And it's not just women: men are having new pecs inserted as a kind of unsweaty workout. But as they are now also high on grooming products and mainlining Botox, maybe it's time the chaps went the whole hog. Certainly the idea that you can squeeze it into a lunch hour that would otherwise be spent browsing in Currys.Digital will be attractive.

So come on. Be a man! Get yourself some tits.

M

Markets' reaction, the

Whenever a new terrorist catastrophe hits a major Western city, the first thought on every citizen's mind is: 'Hmm, I wonder how my shares are doing. Oh, that's right, I don't have any. Still, I wonder how other people's shares are doing . . .'

This is why, following the 7/7 London bombings, news networks speedily escorted viewers and listeners away from the sites of the atrocities and towards the City of London to discover how 'the markets' might be affected. And what did our market reaction correspondents tell us? Stocks remained 'resilient' throughout trading. Thank God.

Showing touching concern for their War on Terror comrades, America's Fox News even discussed how to capitalise on all the murder and maiming. Washington managing editor Brit Hume told host Shepard Smith (great name, Shepard) on air: 'Just on a personal basis, when I heard there had been this attack and I saw the futures this morning, which were really in the tank, I thought, "Hmmm, time to buy." Others may have thought that as well. But you never know about the markets.'

Those markets, eh? What are they like!? You just never know. If we dare tangle with their mysterious workings, they'll be liable to strike down upon us with great vengeance and furious anger. They're like Dennis Hopper meets

Krakatoa – on crack! One flick of the tail and, seriously man, we're all goners. If only these terrorists knew what they were messing with . . . well, then they'd be sorry.

To be fair, Hume did get some flak for positing 7/7 as a great day for bargain-hunting. But maybe using the instability to make a killing is actually a noble way of doing our duty. After 9/11, one media stock commentator – James B. Stewart of *SmartMoney* magazine – even urged readers to follow his example and buy shares 'both as a sound investment and as an act of patriotism'.

Momentarily halt the quick-buck rollercoaster? You might as well piss on the Stars 'n' Stripes. More weirdly still, some readers responded that Stewart wasn't being sufficiently self-ish to be a true American. Surely, he later paraphrased, 'something as abstract and emotional as patriotism was heresy, and that the sole basis should be a rational calculation of economic self-interest. Anything less, they argued, under-mined the markets' efficiency and in that sense was actually unpatriotic.' To which the only rational response is: 'Aarrgh!! Aaargghhh!!!!' And probably: 'Aaaaaaaaaaaaaaaaargghhh!!!!'

The message for those with capital to burn is clear: in the event of the next horrific attack on a major Western city, don't flinch from making merry. Don't you dare. To display even a tiny chink of respect or humanity might anger the markets. They'll think we're going pink. Then they'll fuck us. They'll fuck us all to hell. Then we'll really be fucked. Not like we are now. More fucked.

As flies to wanton boys, are we to the markets. (I exagger-ate, of course.)

Bob Marley tat

I believe it was the great Tony Parsons who identified the author of 'One Love' and 'Exodus' as the ultimate signifier of multicultural Britain: 'There are now a hell of a lot of us who have Bob Marley records,' he wrote perceptively in his column in the *Sun*.

But Marley is more than that. He is a symbol of resistance. Particularly for middle-class white boys who have always enjoyed pretending to dig him. In the old days, this used to require some effort, such as growing some dreadlocks by not washing your hair. (Admittedly, not washing your hair doesn't require that much effort, but it does indicate a certain stiffness of resolve.)

These days, you can see clean-cut Aryans sitting on trains playing games on their mobile phones wearing Bob Marley T-shirts and toting a Bob Marley bag. A human being could not physically look less like they were feeling some Rastaman vibrations or were dedicated to the downfall of Babylon.

You look like Prince William. You ARE fucking Babylon.

Mashed potato as iconic style item

New Britain eateries can get wanky and overwrought about many things, but nothing brings them out in rashes of excitement like mash. Root vegetables – usually, but not always, potato – mashed. With a masher.

The hip diner needs mash options for his or her mash dish. Places like hip Manchester diner Hugo Mash ('Man of action, man of mash') pride themselves on their mash options, including 'honey roasted parsnip and garlic mash, fennel mash or simply hugomash'.

One good thing to have with mash is – get this! – sausage. Sausage and mash: try running that combo round your lips for size. I know! Sounds delicious, doesn't it? Where did some of these mash-happy eateries get that 12-quid-a-plate idea from? Where?

New Britain is literally crammed full of food gurus telling us that things that have traditionally been seen as rather proley are really, you know, okay. Nigel Slater was recently seen on television tucking in to a Mr Whippy ice cream: 'It's very common, but like a lot of common things – snigger – it's actually rather good . . .'

Wow, did you hear what Nigel said? It's okay to like Mr Whippy now!

Now we just need our instructions from on high re: Mr Softee. Command us, Nigel.

Misery memoirs

There's not nearly enough misery in the world, is there? Every time you turn on the news, it's nothing but sunshine and every-one laughing and people dancing with puppies and attractive old people. Sickening. If only there were some way of escaping into a world where children are made to live in the washing machine and eat nothing but sanitary products and cigarettes.

Thank jiminy, then, for misery memoirs. Which one do you fancy? Dave Pelzer's *A Child Called It* has someone being forced naked onto a hot stove. But then *Ugly* by Constance Briscoe has bleach-swallowing. You're spoiled for choice: *For Crying Out Loud: One Woman's Story of Hope and Courage*; *Friday's Child: What Has She Done That Is So Terrible?*; *The Little Prisoner: How a Childhood Was Stolen and a Trust Betrayed*. Excellent.

Some people really love their misery. Consider this Amazon customer review of Pelzer's *My Story* trilogy: 'these stories will leave you sickened shocked sad crying happy thankful every feeling you could feel you get when you are reading these stories they grip you from start to end'. Other misery fans are more demanding: 'in "a child called it" his mother did horrible things to him such as made him eat his own sick! but the others don't seem to be as interesting.' It's so easy to play the sick-eating card too early, isn't it?

In 2003, a reformed drug addict called James Frey wrote a memoir called *A Million Little Pieces*, full of can-you-handle-it-punk accounts of his junkie hell, rendered in short, punchy, macho paragraphs.

Just.

Like.

Fucking.

HEROIN!

This.

Oprah Winfrey, who really likes misery memoirs, loved *A Million Little Pieces* and had Frey on her show so she could tell him how moved she was. Naturally, it became a bestseller. But then the Smoking Gun website uncovered documents proving that Frey had made bits up, so it wasn't entirely real after all. There was misery in there, to feast on, but it wasn't the genuine misery suffered by another human being that people felt they were paying for when they bought into the whole thing.

Oprah invited Frey back onto the show and proceeded to tell him that he had let himself down, he had let the whole nation down and, most heinously, he had let Oprah down. He did, it must be said, look genuinely miserable.

Maybe he'll write a memoir about it. He could call it *My Oprah Sick-Eating HEROIN Pieces*.

Piers Morgan

Piers Morgan is the would-be Muhammad Ali of disgraced tabloid ex-editors, forever talking a good fight about being the greatest disgraced tabloid ex-editor of them all. Here he is on Jeremy Clarkson after their feud descended into actual fisticuffs at the *Press Gazette* awards: 'Clarkson is such a little squirt. If there is any repetition of that behaviour I shall make him go down like a sack of spuds.' (Clarkson had punched Morgan in the head several times.)

Following some long-running nastiness with Cherie Blair, during which she questioned his 'moral compass', he told her: 'We both know our feud was down to sexual tension.' Yes, that's right. I'm sure she's just like all the rest of us: on the sight of Morgan's face, we simply can't keep the sexual tension down.

Sadly, relations were seemingly never cemented and Morgan is now feeling sour again. Indeed, according to David Cameron (interviewed in *GQ*), Morgan asked if he could climb aboard the C-Train to help savage Blair and New Labour, telling the Tory leader: 'Put me in a cage, and feed me on red meat, and I'll 'ave 'em. I hate 'em.'

Of course, Morgan's last flesh-fuelled efforts to bring down the government ended with his being sacked after failing adequately to check the authenticity of fake photographs of prisoner abuse in Iraq. So Number 10 is probably not shaking at the thought of him slavering to get at them. 'No, spare us the fake pictures, Piers! We can't take any more!' they might not say.

But, despite all, Piers Morgan is 'still the greatest!' I'm looking forward to him naming the round in which he's going to take down Ian Hislop, another rival whom he has previously dubbed a 'moon-faced little midget' and wanted to smear so much that he publicly offered money for dirt: 'Now you see me, now you don't. Ian thinks he will, but I know he won't! His *Private Eye* ain't gonna do no good when I start to dance! I'm gonna dance, Ian, I'm gonna dance! I'll be floating like a pig and snorting like a labrador. I'm so fast that last night I printed some pictures before checking whether they were real! It's hard to be humble, when you're as great as I am.'

Then he started a newspaper for kids.

Multiple-choice Christian Education schemes

The Accelerated Christian Education (ACE) scheme, already widespread in the States, is now used by about 50 independent schools in Britain and is being welcomed into the fold by all sorts on the growing education/faith interface.

Why not test your knowledge against a sample question from ACE's geography exam:

1. The circumference of the Earth at the equator is 24901.55 miles. Given this fact, what force should we let into our lives to save ourselves from eternal damnation?

   a) devils
   b) devils
   c) devils
   d) devils
   e) devils
   f) Jesus
   g) devils
   h) devils

The ACE syllabus involves learning 'facts' by rote to retell 'facts' in multiple-choice and fill-in-the-blanks tests. All discussion or dissent is discouraged as pupils sit in stony silence at individual desks with high dividers and work through booklets that all begin with Christian homilies. ACE students are not quite placed in a box into which voices periodically bellow, 'Are you feeling the spirit of THE LORD!?' but it's not far off.

Admittedly, multiple-choice Christian Education schemes are often successfully completed by students who are otherwise unable to find their way educationally. However, this is, at least in part, because answering multiple-choice questions is easy-peasy lemon-squeezy. Particularly when one of the answers is always 'Jesus'.

University academics have found that successful ACE students – even those scoring 95% in National Christian Schools Certificate (NCSC) exams – often show no conception of independent thought; in a very real sense, it was never an option. But really, is this such a massive problem? These schools turn out orderly children with 'ethos' to spare. Seriously, if hardcore Christians want to take over everything, what's the big problem? You know, apart from their urge to burn J.K. Rowling as a witch. But then, she's had it good for too long.

The ACE website shows pictures of children sitting in Dilbert-style cubicles alongside computers and dinky little American flags – which conjures the not entirely accidental idea of children learning in cubicles for The Man Upstairs (God) to acquaint them with a lifetime of working in cubicles for The Man.

Interestingly, corporate life in the US is now awash with a new breed of perma-grinning Christian professionals – people whom journalist Barbara Ehrenreich dubbed 'the new ideal Christianized, "just in time", white collar employee – disposable when temporarily unneeded and always willing to return with a smile'.

Certainly, one privately educated Christian seems to find such faith-based intelligence a great solace. Interviewed on More4's *Iraq: The Reckoning*, Professor George Joffe, a leading academic expert on the region, recalled being invited to No. 10 before the Iraq War to advise on the possible consequences of invading the region. Warning about the seemingly inevitable fallout resulting from Saddam's removal, he predicted the sectarian hatred, the Ba'athist-led insurgency, and so on.

Tony Blair simply responded: 'But he's evil, isn't he?'

In ACE terms, this question would presumably be phrased:

1. Is Saddam Hussein evil?
    a) Yes, he is evil.
    b) No, he is not evil.

Answer: The correct answer is a) Yes, he is evil!

Right. That's sorted, then. Let us now proceed directly to the wailing and the gnashing of the teeth.

Museum tat

Surrealist pioneer Georges Bataille said 'a museum is like the lung of a great city: every Sunday the throng flows in, like blood, and leaves it fresh and purified . . . [a] torrent of people visibly animated with a desire to be at one with the celestial apparitions with which their eyes are still ravished'.

He forgot to mention how absolutely thrilled they are with their novelty apron and ruler.

German green-anarcho installation provocateur Joseph Beuys, subject of a recent Tate Modern show, was known for huge installations involving stuffed huskies or petrified trees, and vitrines containing everything swept up from the street after a vast workers' demonstration. Beuys would hold teach-ins where, standing in the middle of the crowd, he would frantically scribble all his and their thoughts onto a huge blackboard as they attempted to pack and unpack the world around them.

At its Beuys exhibition, Tate Modern sold . . . very small blackboards. About A6 size – a quarter the size of A4; the sort you might stick on the wall in your kitchen or next to the phone – maybe representing our ability to forget the things we really need. Still, at least you can get involved – although, of course, where Beuys's blackboards were full of inspired dialectical thought-storms, these will probably just say: 'milk, beans (2), lager, curry paste, glue, crisis, mother, mother, mother, mother, I'm dying.' (That's actually quite good; you should exhibit that.)

On sale at the 'Modernism' blockbuster at the Victoria and Albert Museum – as well as the pencils, the T-shirts, the canvas shopping bags, the mugs and Mussolini's bust – were, naturally, branded Utopia shampoo and soap. Presumably, the ravished-eyed throng coursing out onto the Brompton Road had conversations along the lines of: 'That really made me think about the social dimensions of design, and how it's possible to construct human environments in a human way rather than just slap up a load of shops and offices to turn a fast buck.'

'Yeah? I might have a shower later. With my new soap. That's my Utopia right there, so swivel . . .'

It's only a matter of time before art galleries and museums rearrange their space in line with their new priorities, using most of it for a giant shop with row after row – battalions – of fridge magnets. A small area near the exit displays a few bits and pieces of art they happen to have lying around. Actually, the Royal Academy of Art is virtually there, planning a shop in the City of London that's just that: all shop, no art. (Maybe they should call it the Royal Academy of Shop.)

Kit Grover is a leading designer of customised museum merchandise for Tate Modern and the National Gallery whose creations include the Gilbert and George Rubik's cube, art-themed fridge magnets aping *Hello!* magazine and, for Tate Modern's 'Surrealism' show, a huge crystal paperweight containing a photographic image of an eye. Which is sort of surreal, but not in a way that offers liberation from bourgeois mundanity.

'My crusade is to identify what someone would want to buy after they've had an intense experience,' said Grover.

But surely buying is the most intense experience of all. Not buying is no experience whatsoever. The idea that a gallery is the sort of place where people might think more generally whether just going around buying stuff all the time is much cop is a patent absurdity; and people who have historically suggested otherwise – like artists – are, in essence, just twats.

Incidentally, the Mussolini bust was modelled on Renato Bertelli's 1933 strange, revolving sculpture *Head of Mussolini: Continuous Profile*. It therefore has nothing to do with Il Duce's tits. Although, of course, he was very proud of his tits. You can tell that from the way he walked.

N

Nazi hate pop

Modern-day fascists have such poor taste in music. Anyone would think they have poor judgement generally. All that bad metal; all that *shouting*. You'd think they'd want to unwind after rupturing their rectums with all the Nazism: the marching, the bellowing ignorance, all those close-typed leaflets they hand out. But no: it's frenetic thumping and gruff slogans about white supremacy. Angry Aryans? I ask you!

One striking departure from fat, bald blokes screaming is Prussian Blue – a girl group who are a sort of Nazi version of the Olsen Twins. But where the Olsens appeal to fans of anodyne family fun, Prussian Blue appeal to fans of Aryan racial hegemony. Group members Lamb and Lynx Gaede are two blonde, blue-eyed 14-year-olds from Bakersfield, California, who wear mini-skirts and T-shirts with yellow smiley-faces on them (ah, cute), but the yellow smiley-faces are actually Hitler (oh, not so cute), complete with moustache and distinctive hair-do. (I'm not making this up!) It's like Girl Power, but it's White Girl Power.

'We are proud of being white,' says Lynx – unsurprising given that their shows incorporate *Sieg Heil* salutes and that one song, 'Sacrifice', is dedicated to Hitler's deputy Rudolf Hess (a 'man of peace who wouldn't give up').

Other top tracks are 'Road to Valhalla' and 'Aryan Man,

Awake'. Lyrics include: 'Strike force! White survival. Strike force! Yeah.' Gig itineraries sometimes feature Holocaust-denial festivals. (How would one of those 'festivals' pan out? 'I don't believe the Holocaust happened.' 'Neither do I.' 'Let's get a beer.' 'Okay.' 'Is David Irving coming this year?' 'No, he's in chokey.' 'Shame.')

Erich Gliebe, operator of notorious race-hate label Resistance Records, which releases Prussian Blue's efforts, believes young performers like Lynx and Lamb will expand the base of white nationalism. He said: 'Eleven and 12 years old, I think that's the perfect age to start grooming kids and instil in them a strong racial identity.'

Lamb and Lynx were 'groomed' by their mother April, who home-schools them using 1950s textbooks, and by their grandfather. He has a swastika on his belt buckle, on the side of his pick-up truck and registered as his cattle brand with the Bureau of Livestock Identification. (So he definitely likes swastikas. And presumably Nazi cattle.)

Lynx said: 'We want to keep being white. We want our people to stay white . . . We think our race is different to other races in positive ways and that we've done more for civilisation.'

We must wonder, though, exactly what benefit civilisation will garner from two barely pubescent girls gyrating in front of mostly male white supremacists. The target market of this pop group would appear to be Nazi paedophiles. Which even a fascist must appreciate is, in PR terms, a double-edged sword.

Nazi paedophiles: what are they like, eh?

Nazi porn

When BNP leader on Barking and Dagenham Council Richard Barnbrook was outed as the maker of a gay porn movie, the former teacher maintained: 'It was an art film.'

Apparently *HMS Discovery: A Love Story*, which Barnbrook made as a student, contains scenes of 'flagellation, men undressing and frolicking in a river and a naked man . . . performing a sex act on another'. There is 'full frontal nudity', and also 'fondling'.

Despite co-writing and featuring in the film, Barnbrook has denied penning the erotic poetry recited in the gay bongo flick, which includes the lines: 'It bares you like a foreskin's folds' and 'Open-mouthed, I shall dream of altar boys.'

Not having seen *HMS Discovery: A Love Story*, I don't know the 'sex act' in question or the role played by Barnbrook, but it's easy to see how this could cause confusion within BNP ranks. I was definitely under the impression that the party was meant to be anti-gay. And if, in *HMS Discovery*, Barnbrook is the man involved in a 'sex act' with another man, well, that's not going to look very anti-gay.

If, for example, he's being pumped up the jacksy and loving it, that wouldn't scream 'anti-gay' to me. He might be screaming, but what he would be screaming are basically howls of ecstasy at the good seeing-to he's having. So the message could at best be described as 'mixed'.

Nazi wine

Marketed with the slogan 'Drink for Britain with the BNP', the party's own-brand wine – available at £8.29 a bottle from its website – features a fetching picture of leader Nick Griffin on the label. Well, it makes a change from an etching of grapevines on a hillside – albeit not a pleasant one.

But just when BNP supporters thought they had solved their gift-buying dilemmas for the undiscerning drinkers in their families, a problem occurred: because the British National Party's wine is not British.

It might be bottled by Cornish Moorland Wines, but the grapes come from Chile and Canada – both of which are very much Abroad.

Also, although I really don't want to get into advising the BNP on how to handle their PR, they really missed a trick here. The wine is red. Not white – like the super-race. Red – like communism. You want to do a white wine, you big sillies. You could call it White Supremacy.

Apparently, the BNP wine doesn't even taste very nice. So burgeoning fascists should, for now, stick to getting drunk on Aryan bloodlust.

New bins

Can't you see? The public says, 'No to new bins!' Wherever you go, the windows of Great Britain display this same strongly negative position. Will the authorities never understand?

No to the tyranny of big, plastic, wheelie bastards!

On the messageboard of Woking Council's website, 'Paul' says of the new bins policy: 'This is simply not serious and has not been thought out.' 'Anonymous' has 'driven through a couple of the areas' testing new bins: 'What an eye sore!'

'Knaphiller' declares: 'I am totally against wheelie bins in Knaphill. If they try to force their use here, I will personally canvass against our local councillor on this subject at the next local election. And advise others to do the same.'

Meanwhile, in Brighton, there are no prizes for guessing where Beautiful Brighton website user 'nonewbins' stands on the issue. With regard to the new bins, he or she is not in favour.

nonewbins says: 'I fought bitterly prior to the bins' arrival, knowing that once they arrived that was probably the end. Today it seems they will ratify the lies and deceit they have continually pumped out to force the bins on the rest of Brighton. Is it ANY surprise that their totally fictitious statistics [in a poll claiming to show general satisfaction with the new bins] were going to result in anything other than it appearing a glorious success. It is comparable to a Saddam election where he gained 98% of the vote . . . the only surprise being that [anti-new bins campaigner] Tony Davies isn't currently being tortured into proclaiming his own love for the bins by the Secret Police in [Chair of the Environment Committee] Gill Mitchell's basement.'

'Maybe to new bins'? Bollocks.

'I'm coming round to the whole new bins thing'? I'm bloody not.

The answer is 'No, no, no . . . No and again no.' To new bins. And, by implication, yes to the old ones.

New towers

But 'Yes to new towers'. That's what we need. Or maybe a new wheel. Either way, if we build it, they will come. Not in a rude sense. In a bread and circuses sense.

Following the success of the London Eye, city fathers

throughout the land are realising that the best way of serving their citizens is to build white, elephant-shaped attractions which, as the name applies, will attract . . . Well, who, exactly? People who really like going up and down in lifts?

Or maybe it's a good way of getting our disenfranchised youth to respect adult things. Faced with something so impressive, they will probably gather at the bottom and simply spend hours staring in awe.

The planned 60-million-pound Birmingham Pinnacle, for instance, will boast theme-park-style thrill rides, a restaurant/bar and an observation deck. From the top, you can observe the dismantling of Longbridge. And Hooters up near that piazza at the top of the town centre.

Andrew Carter, leader of Leeds City Council, revealed that city's intentions to build a major new construction. Although, with Leeds being a city build upon hills, staring down at it is not a rare privilege. You can do that by looking out of the window.

It's all kind of a bold attempt to turn town-planning into the architectural equivalent of the cock-rock guitar solo: ostentatious, extraneous, wholly unnecessary and, most of all, proudly erect. If councillors don't accept this double-concept-album, widdly-widdly new direction, they could be left behind.

Unlike Portsmouth, whose sail-shaped Spinnaker Tower was a grand Millennium project that was meant to turn the town into the South Coast equivalent of Dubai. Unfortunately, it was five years late and residents had to foot the 11-million-plus overspend. Its 2005 opening day was marred when the external glass lift jammed a hundred feet in the air, trapping the council's project manager, David Greenhalgh.

On returning to the ground, Greenhalgh said: 'I didn't want

it to happen, I hoped it wouldn't have happened. We thought we'd deployed all the resources we could to make sure it didn't happen. But unfortunately it did, so we're very upset . . .'

He added: 'I would say a big sorry to the people of Portsmouth.' (The people of Portsmouth replied: 'That's okay, we thought it was quite funny.')

You know why councillors want these constructions? They want to meet in the middle of the night and hold going-up-and-down-in-the-lift parties. Then they will quietly hold a roller-disco around the piazza as the sun comes up, listening to *Saturday Night Fever* and Sister Sledge through wireless headphones, high-fiving each other as they swoop past.

See them deny it if they can.

NHS computers

The disappearance of patient records, cancelled operations, delays in outpatient appointments: just some of the greater efficiencies wrought by the NHS's new £6.2bn IT system, which are causing trusts across the country to withdraw from the scheme in horror.

At the time of writing, the government had revised the probable final cost of the network's installation to £20 billion – and it still didn't work properly. Computer specialists – who know more about computers than the government – said the figure would probably rise to £30 billion.

Just imagine what chaos might have ensued if the £30 billion project had been entrusted to the public sector? Thankfully, the £30 billion IT scheme was rushed through by the government, who are spending £30 billion on it, to showcase how dynamic private enterprise beats public every time. It's about 'what works'. Even if it doesn't.

£30 billion? You could pay for an awful lot of inefficiency with that. Let nurses make paper aeroplanes out of those funny cardboard hats they wear. Maybe even just burn the money to provide heat for elderly patients? Why not? If we're just chucking it about anyway?

Of course, how the private sector tends to 'save' money is to reduce wages, lay people off and cut services to the bone. When you add in company profits and dividends to shareholders, and the fact that in PFI projects (where private consortiums borrow money to build facilities that the NHS then leases back from them) we taxpayers also chip in on the loans' interest payments, private provision actually costs more – . . . for less actual healthcare.

PFI was, of course, a Tory invention. Its architect, Kenneth Clarke, later called it a 'terrible idea' (in part because the private sector has to borrow money at much higher rates than the public sector) before breezing off to market fags to kiddies. But, crucially, when Labour came to power in 1997, no PFI contracts had actually yet been signed. So they could have said, 'Knickers to that.' But they ploughed on so no one could question how pro-market they were. If anyone did question how pro-market they were, they could – in all good faith – answer: 'Very.'

Former Health Secretary Alan Milburn liked to talk of PFI being the largest hospital-building programme in the NHS's history. He neglected to shout so loudly about the services being simultaneously cut or closed. As health expert Allyson Pollock says in her book *NHS plc*, PFI was paid for by 'major cuts in clinical budgets and the largest service closure programme in the NHS's history'. Which is a different way of looking at things.

So yes, it's about 'what works', particularly what works for private healthcare middlemen able to play golf in Dubai on our tax money. Because they're people too. The three founders of iSoft, the company behind the NHS computer, made £41 million, £30 million and £10 million respectively from selling shares in the company, which, at the time of writing, had just been made the subject of an investigation by the Financial Services Authority over irregularities in its accounts. Alan Milburn, of course, went on to take a 30-grand-a-year consultancy from private healthcare investors Bridgepoint. He might consider having the words 'NO' and 'SHAME' tattooed on his forehead.

According to *The Times*, NHS expenditure on management consultants increased by 23% to £3 billion in 2005. Presumably this army of shysters could work out exactly how much money is siphoned off from the public purse to private companies. If they had a computer that worked.

NHS drafting errors

In June 2006 the government accidentally revealed a plan to privatise £64 billion worth of NHS services when an advert inviting tenders appeared in an official EU journal before any announcement of the policy had been made.

The Health Department's commercial directorate placed the advertisement inviting companies to begin 'a competitive dialogue' about how they could take over the purchasing of healthcare for millions of NHS patients. After a small fuss, the junior health minister, Lord Warner, withdrew the advert because it had 'a drafting error'. They didn't mean to part-privatise the NHS. It was a typo.

The advert's invitation to provide management, health and support services across primary care trusts suggests that the NHS as we have known it is being wheeled to the morgue as we speak. Certainly, in any meaningful sense, it's hard to feel like you own your NHS if you have, quite definitely, sold it to someone else. Or maybe this is a new tactic for deflecting claims that the NHS is no longer 'safe in our hands' . . . by putting it into someone else's hands. It can't be unsafe in your hands if it's not actually in your hands, now, can it? 'Hands off our NHS? They're not on the NHS! Aren't we clever?'

A new advert appeared in July 2006. It was drafted differently, but it still proposed to privatise the same services. The trade union Unison said there was 'very, very little difference' from the first one. Maybe Lord Warner will withdraw it again, once he realises that, for the second time on the trot, his silly aides have mistakenly attempted to part-privatise large chunks of the NHS. D'oh!

Those NHS guys, though. Mad! I don't know about you, but I can't wait for the next series of *NHS Managers Do the Craziest Things*. Come on ITV!

Rio Ferdinand could present it.

'Not like everybody else' advertising

We must not be like everybody else. We must be different. Original. And special. And we must always, *always* expect more. How do we know this? Because that's what the advertisers tell us.

'Try Something Different' suggest Sainsbury's and Jamie Oliver. 'Most of us are asleep most of the time,' he explains over footage of droney dozers. 'Even when we shop, we're sleep-shopping.' WAKE UP! Use your imagination. Stop being a droney consumer. Go to Sainsbury's and buy some supermarket produce! But slightly different supermarket produce! It's an inspiring, almost Blakean, message: I will now go to Sainsbury's in a heightened, almost visionary state. That's right: I will take shitloads of drugs.

'Be Original' implore Levi's. We need to go 'moon-bathing', claim the ads, showing a buffed, shirtless, Levi's-wearing man balancing precariously on a moonlit rooftop. They make it look quite the thing. But if we do actually go 'moon-bathing', surely we are not being 'original'. We are being 'unoriginal'. It's like jumping in the fire because a bigger boy told you to, except it's climbing around on the roof at night because Levi's told you to. Which is potentially deranged. 'What, Officer? But the jeans people told me to do it!'

When IBM used the Kinks' proto-punk anthem 'I'm Not Like Everybody Else', they subverted meaning with an audacity that would make a French philosopher gasp. The song fronted the computer giant's 'What Makes You Special?' campaign, which conveyed the idea that IBM was in fact an anarchist collective specifically there to cater for disaffected wildcards. Except that, in the ads, everyone was singing the anti-conformity song in perfect unison – like corporate Stepford androids. The levels of irony became so richly confusing that I started spinning out and needed talking to with patience and care – to be reassured that I am, at least in some senses, like everybody else.

'Expect More' say Matalan. And that's just taking the piss.

O

Oscar parties

So many parties, so little talent. There's Barry Diller's pre-Oscar luncheon, CAA agent Bryan Lourd's day-before shindig, the Weinstein Company's Saturday bash, the Governor's Ball, *In Style*'s viewing party at Republic and – of course – the *Vanity Fair* soirée at Morton's.

They all sound amazing, except for the fact that you are not allowed to get pissed ('You just want to have a celebratory glow,' says one insider), there's never enough room ('There's never enough room,' says another insider), and if you're not either a mogul or someone involved in a nominated film, no one will be that interested in talking to you. Says yet another insider: 'If you're not one of those people, you're always looking around wondering, "Who do I know, who do I talk to, why am I here?"'

Of course, the party to be seen at is always Elton John's party. Everyone simply had to get into Elton's party. If you weren't at Elton's party, you don't want to know about Elton's party. You will choke. You'll just die. You *had* to be there. Nobody who was there can even bear to tell others who weren't there how good it was: that's how good it was. Actually, an insider did spill the beans: 'It was lovely, lots of margaritas.' What time was the party? Margarita time.

I do not understand this. How is Elton John, now, in the

21st century, still the celebrity hub around which whole other galaxies of vain, vacuous fluff revolves? He had some hits in the 70s. Then there was 'Nikita'. He loves Watford FC. And what else? Is it a Diana thing? What?

This is supposed to be Hollywood. You know, the shining city on the hill; homeless runaways being lured into the porn industry; 'It was just the pictures that got small'; complicated young people with a whole set of personalities . . . Have they not seen those photos of Captain Fantastic in the duck outfit? The Post Office adverts?

To me, it's not screaming Rita Hayworth.

Over-sharing

'My husband thinks I'm sexy, which is great. He still loves me and fancies me. It's all about the boobies with him. Lots of booby-feeling goes on . . . He's a real booby man.'

So revealed Lorraine Kelly. And she didn't stop there. Here she is on her husband's penis: 'What a winkie it is. I'm very happy. I have no complaints in that department.'

From the amount of information the daytime goddess regularly divulges, you would think the showbiz interviewers shine torches in her face and show her pictures of her kidnapped firstborn. There is no evidence of that, yet she has also confessed to trying amyl nitrate, and to having outdoor sex in the wilds of Scotland with her 'winkie-boy' husband. I, for one, will now find it hard to visit the Highlands for fear of Lorraine Kelly, off her face on poppers, getting loose and jiggy in the heather. And I love the Highlands.

Or Trinny Woodall revealing the contents of her handbag on live telly and showing us the packet of baby wipes because, oh God, she can't stand having a 'dirty hole'. Bloody hell!

Then one episode of *The F-Word* had a whole feature about Giles Coren's sperm count. Sorry, this really shouldn't need spelling out, but Giles Coren's spunk is not a fitting subject for a food programme.

Over-stimulated children

Are your children mural artists? No. So do not encourage them to draw on the fucking walls. If they must display an artistic bent, simply supply them with a piece of paper. Or a canvas. Try to find a happy medium between fucking them up – you may not mean to, but you do – and letting them trash other people's houses. No one wants a miniature rampant id crashing round their house, drawing on it.

According to many reports, children are increasingly brought up to believe they are the last in line of the Ming Dynasty. The Commons Education Select Committee has learned of middle-class parents creating a new generation of 'brat bullies'. The National Association of Head Teachers said some children were falling asleep at their desks because their parents failed to send them to bed at a reasonable time.

Some parents are unwilling to curb their children's desires, believing this would stifle their creativity. These worshipped little gods 'expect all the teachers and other kids to kow-tow to them. If they don't, they start to bully the other children.'

Still, at least brat bullies' dads aren't hard. Ghastly wankers, yes. But definitely not hard.

Although they are possibly not as wanky as those parents who write columns about being crap parents. 'I can't stand all those yummy mummies, they make me feel so worthless – I'm more of a slummy mummy! I was late for the school play because I was putting on my lippy for three hours. I'm so worthless! But I'm sort of rock 'n' roll too. Blah blah blah blah blah blah blah!' That sort of thing.

P

Panda diplomacy

In this ever-changing world in which we live, communication is more important than ever. Which is why all efforts to step up diplomacy are now so imperative. The pandas are on board. Are you?

In January 2006 the deputy secretary of state assigned to manage US relations with China, Robert Zoellick, entered the seemingly cuddly, but actually rather prickly, world of panda diplomacy.

Asked to meet a prize cub, he acknowledged to reporters that he and his aides had pondered any message the image might convey. They had discussed the various inferences that could be drawn from several panda poses before agreeing to 'take Jing Jing on his lap'.

We too share doubts about what message this pose might convey. 'You want to know how the panda felt?' Zoellick asked reporters. 'Very soft.'

In fact, panda diplomacy is among the more treacherous forms of diplomacy. In 2005 Taiwan was offered two pandas by the Chinese Communist Party. The panda diplomacy, in this case, was backed by hundreds of missiles pointed at Taiwan across the 100-mile channel which separates the island from China. So accepting the pandas meant subconsciously acquiescing to Chinese domination: 'Look, pandas! Accept

Chinese rule. Aren't they cute? What did I just say? Oh, nothing. Accept Beijing's divine diktat. Aaah, pandas . . .'

When Taiwan understandably hesitated, the *China Daily* newspaper painted President Chen as 'bellicose' in his opposition to the 'peaceful pandas'. The editorial ran: 'Stubborn as he is, Chen has to face the reality: he may be able to block the entry of the panda couple but he cannot stop the Taiwanese people's love for the pandas.'

Frustrated with some of the media's coverage, Jan Jyh-horng, secretary general of Taiwan's Mainland Affairs Council, argued that 'pandas are not communists'.

That is true. Pandas tend to fall into one of two camps: they are either instinctively in favour of bringing about greater redistribution of wealth by reform of the capitalist system from within; or they advocate a simple life based on anarchist collectives, which admittedly is communistic, but certainly not in any sense akin to Stalinist-style 'communism'. How do I know this? I asked one.

Want to know how it felt? Very soft.

Pap pics of celeb kids with their faces blocked out

Here's Zoe Ball in the *Mirror* on a jetski with her little son Woody. But look, we respect his privacy, so we've made his face all squarey so he looks like a victim of crime. But he's holding his thumbs aloft, so he must be all right. Look at the caption: 'Thumbs up – shows he's happy.' See?

But should his thumbs have been pixellated too? You don't want his face growing up perfectly well adjusted while his thumbs turn into really weird digits, all warped by the strains of celebrity. Have the boy's thumbs not the right to privacy?

Or maybe I'm missing something and celebrities just have children with really blurred faces.

Past Times

A shop about old stuff. But all the stuff's new and that means it's new old stuff, and that's just fucked up.

Past Times themes everything in a strange, pick 'n' mix historical way. Collections include Victorian, Art Deco, Medieval and even Post Modern (that's Beatles mugs and Mongolian wool pouffes, rather than Umberto Eco hipflasks). The Medieval stuff includes things like the 'Depart for the Chase' wall hanging, depicting 'a richly dressed nobleman on a fine white horse out hunting with his falcons. Tabs for pole hanging (pole not supplied).' Bring back hanging? They're not saying that, but they are saying bring back medieval wall hanging.

So it's a mixed bag, with the main rule being: it must be new stuff that looks like old stuff, and as far as possible be made out of polyresin, a mysterious synthetic material that Past Times boffins may well have devised themselves. I don't actually know.

Recommended 'gifts for her' include the Lesley Anne Ivory musical waterglobe: 'This glass and polyresin waterglobe is based on a painting by the celebrated cat artist, Lesley Anne Ivory. It plays Beethoven's "Moonlight Sonata".' At last this piece's muted melancholia finds its rightful home: as the soundtrack to a plastic cat in a snowstorm.

One 'gift for him', meanwhile, is the Battle of Bannockburn

hand-decorated chess set (yours for £149.95). The Scots are led by Robert the Bruce, who was 'famously heartened by the tenacious spider to persist in his struggle against the English'. The English are represented by Edward II, who ended up 'deposed, imprisoned and horrifically killed at the behest of his wife'. Murder by means of red-hot poker stuck where the sun never shines: now that's your authentic Past right there. In full, red-hot effect. And who wouldn't want to live somewhere like that?

A major Past Times speciality is 18th-century stuff. Not stuff from the 18th century – which is pricey – but replicas of stuff from the period that really enjoyed replicating classical antiquity. So this stuff has been modified and refined *twice*, and must therefore have attained the kind of perfection unknown to those in ancient Greece/Rome/Etruria. In fact, when Plato spoke of another plane where everything existed only in its ideal form, he was probably thinking of somewhere like Past Times. The ancient Greeks hadn't even *heard* of polyresin.*

All told, you get the impression that this is the sort of conservative-retro-items shop old people would run if old people were all on crack. A polyresin Mucha wall sconce in the shape of a woman with her hair and her light and airy robe billowing in the wind? That's old people tooting rock, that is. Past Times? High Times more like. Metaphorically, obviously. I am patently not stating that Past Times is run by old people on crack: they'd never open on time. Although it might be, for all I know. But I hope not: crack is a terrible addiction that would wreak havoc at any time of life.

*Polyresin wasn't even dreamt about until the Renaissance, when Leonardo da Vinci drew a picture of what it might look like, should he be able to make it, which he could not. Leonardo was always doing shit like that. He 'invented' the helicopter in the same sense that I 'invented' DVD-playing electric shoes – that is, he's got a jotting on a beermat somewhere, if only he could find it.

Pay off Your Mortgage in Two Years

With house prices now being set by absinthe-crazed madmen throwing dice at each other, people are taking out 35-, 40-, even 45-year mortgages. But you can do it in two.

Saving pennies makes pounds, so if you save a lot of pennies, well, there you go, you've paid off your mortgage. It's all about tightening your belt here and there. To the point where your waist measurement is the same as your shoe size.

Money-saving tips in the book of the programme by René Carayol include stopping smoking (they all add up, and are bad for you anyway), not buying coffee (instead, go to places where they give you free coffee) and, if you must buy things, getting them on the internet (it's slightly cheaper!). Be careful, though. One top tip warns: 'If foraging or looking for food in the wild, make sure you properly identify safe foodstuffs.' So try to avoid toadstools and deadly nightshade if you can. The road to early mortgage repayment is full of victims who, rather than shedding the dark cloak of mortgage, had their stomach pumped after munching the wrong kind of toadstool.

But even this is amateur child's play to the King of the Saving of the Pennies, financial writer Cliff D'Arcy. If saving pennies were a sparky young lady with excellent conversation, he would be her Mr D'Arcy, Cliff D'Arcy. He's the sort of guy who thinks lying down in a darkened room is wasteful.

In July 2006 Mr D'Arcy announced in a promotional email sent out by popular financial website the Motley Fool that he was about to embark on a period of 'Extreme Budgeting': 'In January of this year, my discretionary spending came to less than £15, which is a new personal best . . . [Now] I plan to steer clear of alcohol, cigarettes, drinks and snacks, fast food and takeaways, with my only treat being a weekend newspaper or two . . . I appreciate that extreme budgeting isn't everyone's cup of tea, because it is a tough test of willpower.'

Speaking of tea, Mr D'Arcy signed off: 'I'm off to have a nice cup of tea, which is my only vice during my (financial) detox month!' Presumably reusing the bag for the twentieth time. Possibly a Value bag that came in a food parcel from the Red Cross.

Putting aside minor worries that money is just a chimerical, abstract way of exchanging goods, services and human effort, and that this might be an utter waste of miserable time which involves actively hegemonising yourself with the mores of Mammon, we have created our own 'Very Extreme Indeed and Certainly More Extreme Than the Motley Fool's, Which Isn't Extreme at All . . . In Fact They Are Just Pussies: I Could Pay off My Mortgage in Three Months, No Bother – What Do You Think of That Then, René? Budget'.

Take all of the measures we have listed here and you could be saving – quite literally – in the region of two or even three hundred pounds EVERY SINGLE YEAR:

1. Swap credit-card and utility companies to get the best deals. Switch companies anything up to four or even five times a day. By really staying alert you can save well over a whole entire pound each and every week. Some people might argue that if you expended the same amount of effort working, you would make considerably more, but screw them. They don't know.

2. Don't piss your money up against a wall. I get tired of end-lessly telling people that if they keep going to pubs, buying beer and generally enjoying themselves, that they will inevitably have less money than they might otherwise have

had. Why can't they just suck on the juicy beermats provided at the bar? Money's going in one end and getting pissed out the other. Unless you can find me someone who will pay for piss, I'm not interested. And you won't. Because that doesn't happen. A piss merchant, buying and selling piss – it's a fucking stupid idea. (If you do ever come across somewhere with a piss merchant, let me know.)

3. You should always – *always* – only use financial products you've never heard of. If you've heard of an ISA, you need a cash ISA. If you've heard of a cash ISA, you need a mini-cash ISA. If you've heard of a mini-cash ISA, you need to call the Bank de Bank, Zurich, and ask for Juan. Say you need 'a dirty one'. The codeword is 'flaps'. You'll also be wanting a PEP, a PAP, the PUP and a PARP. Don't forget to claim your allowances for those either, like some sort of twat.

4. Boil up some grass to make grassy stew. Eat stuff out of bins.

5. Sell your toenails on eBay (what are they actually *for*, anyway?).

6. Never. Ever. Do. Anything. Ever. At all.

7. Help me.

8. Kill yourself. There's no surer way to spend less than being dead. As a bonus, any insurance policies you hold will be paying out like a fruit machine with three triple bars on hold – not that we'd know about that, not risking our precious pennies on such atrocious fripperies. Irony is free – so treat

yourself to a highly poignant death by smashing your brains open against the window of your bank. (If you bank online – which I would advise; there are some great deals out there – just go to the nearest branch of the bank of which your online account supplier is a subsidiary.) Now, for insurance reasons, it needs to look like an accident. You'll need a big run-up to get enough force to kill yourself, so start from the other side of the road while looking down the street and smiling and waving into the distance, as if you have just seen an old friend or acquaintance and have become distracted. Just keep running until you hit the bank and hopefully die. Remember to run very fast or you won't get enough force to kill yourself. No one wants to come round outside NatWest with blood from their own head smeared down the windows. Also remember, in the days leading up to killing yourself, that you can save money by not eating anything or turning on any lights.

Allison Pearson

I don't know why she does it.

People in bear costumes on motorbikes advertising stuff

Happens more than you might imagine.

Sean Pertwee voiceovers

Sean Pertwee appears as a voiceover artist on everything ever, despite the single, one and only voice he ever manages to come out with being a Middle England 'hello, ladies' come-on better suited to one of those plausible chancers who defraud vulnerable women in '70s sitcoms.

Surely directors could at least attempt to move him off this track slightly: 'Sorry, Sean, you're trying to explain the race to the moon. Not get fruity with a colleague on a training week-end at a Northampton hotel. Less sauce, more seriousnessness.'

Or: 'For fuck's sake, Sean, this is a programme about seals. You're not trying to pull the seals. These seals, Sean, do not care to "share a little drinky" with you or anybody else. Seals do not booze. The lady seals' husbands understand them perfectly well and so therefore have no need of your consoling company. Your dad was good in *Worzel Gummidge* but you're an animal, Pertwee, an animal.'

Pictures of clubbers

As in, people gurning at the camera used to illustrate listings and/or articles about clubs. You'd think that if people were off their faces, they might consider staying away from the camera lens, what with being off your face not usually considered to be a good look for your face. But no.

It's been a staple now for about 20 years: loads of faces, off their faces. Holding onto their mate, waving a fag about, throwing their hands in the air. Why the fuck would anyone want to see this picture? We weren't there. We probably don't wish we had been there. If I am going to see pictures of people fucked out of their minds in a nightclub, please have the decency to make them members of the royal family. Or high-ranking television personalities.

On the odd occasion that I buy *Dazed & Confused* by accident – which, by the way, claims to be a journal of 'ideas' – the photos in the back of some hip schmoozathon or other always, ALWAYS include the same hairy, mutton-chopped Japanese man holding a beer bottle. It doesn't seem to matter where the party is – London, New York, wherever. He really gets around.

I don't know what that's about.

Stephen Poliakoff's London

Said Robert Lindsay of working on *Gideon's Daughter* and *Friends and Crocodiles*: 'You think of Dennis Potter, Tom Stoppard, Alan Bleasdale and Stephen Poliakoff; he's one of a select band of writers who have elevated TV drama to an artform.'

'In an age of wall-to-wall popcorn drama, reality TV and soap opera,' declared *The Times* on the occasion of the eminent TV dramatist's BBC4 season, 'Poliakoff stands alone as the last genuine auteur in the medium of TV, given the room to express his vision.'

Poliakoff does often succeed in his stated aim of making 'something people remember'. Certain scenes from *Gideon's Daughter* are etched onto my brain like a recurring nightmare. A recurring nightmare that shouts, 'This – is – really – IM-PORTANT!'

Always there's this London, which is presumably meant to be a stylised version of the London that actually exists. But it's really a stylised version of the London that exists in a book called *London for Deluded Shit-at-Writing Beardy Dickheads*. There's a spin-doctor moneyman property developer who lives in a castle made of steel and glass: he eats canapés, swaps bons mots with an American capitalist and secretly plans to turn a cherished playground into a nuclear dumping ground (or it might have just been toxic waste – can't remember). These portrayals are so cack-handed that even people who despise yuppies and all their works will start to rethink their position: hey, if this utter numpty hates yuppies, maybe they're not so bad . . .

It's forever an 80s where super-yuppie parties in large English gardens are invaded by cartoon lefties who grab the mike and yell: 'Four million unemployed! Four million unemployed!' The better to convey the fact that, while super-yuppies were having parties, four million people were, in fact, unemployed. *Never* forget that.

Then come the kooks. Oh God, the kooks . . . in particular, the kooky ladies. With some grindingly awful outsider figures – like a cult which lives in a big house surrounded by the feral children of south London. Or the brother and sister who shag each other because they hate Thatcher.

In *Gideon's Daughter*, kooky Miranda Richardson – her son had died (can't remember how, but it was probably thanks to a decision by the moneymen) – showed spin-doctor-in-chief Bill Nighy another side to London: the subterranean pleasures far away from the canapés and poncey dinners. It was a secret place. Somewhere only she knew. It opened his eyes to another sort of life. He had not known that down-to-earth, albeit kooky, people could find such pleasure in their simple lives. Perhaps, after all, the future lies with the proles and not with the assorted celebs, spinners, spoiled brats and media barons with whom he thought rested the complete world. That's right: she took him to a curry house.

Yes! Curry! It can taste amazing, apparently. It can even make canapés seem unappealing. I know! Who'd have

thought it? And can he go back to his old life after this discovery? He cannot. Eat canapés, like some sort of
spin-doctor-moneyman-twat? Now he's had pakora with
yogurty sauce? Of course not!

He even missed his important meeting with a Berlusconi-
like Italian bigwig. *But he didn't care*!

So he arranged for this beautiful curry house to host one of
his renowned bashes, to show the capital's assorted advertis-
ing-moneymen-spin-doctor-celebs how shallow their lives
were. He really stuck it to 'em.

Spread now among the moneymen and the usurers and the
warmongers the revelation that is cumin, turmeric, chilli and
oil. Let's show the fuckers what life is all about. Take them to
a curry house. Order some poppadoms. Maybe some prawn
puree. I like those.

Thus revealed Poliakoff. Curry: it's fucking real.

Policemen cutting up dead people on the telly
Incessant.

Politicians called David
David Blunkett, David Davis, David Lammy, David Cameron,
David Owen . . . Need I go on?

True, David out of David and Goliath was good – he helped
the Israelites, who had latterly been sore-oppressed, to defeat
the Philistines, who were ignorant. (Although he did later
commit adultery with Bathsheba, wife of Uriah the Hittite,
which would have given the tabloids a field day.)

Thirty-one sitting MPs are called David. Of these, only one refers to himself officially as 'Dave'. Dave Watts, Labour MP for St Helen's North, has presumably adopted the matey sobriquet to avoid people bellowing Kinks lyrics at him in the street: 'I wish I could be like Dave Watts/Lords Commissioner of the HM Treasury . . .'

While we're on the subject of politicians' names, and very much in the interests of holding our leaders to account, here are some non-David MPs with quite funny names: Mr Bob Blizzard, Mr Andy Love, Mr Peter Bone and Dr Howard Stoate.

Now *that's* satire.

Porn, misleading use of the word

Porn gets everywhere these days. Even where it patently is not.

We are now dangled 'gardening porn' (porn involving hostas), 'car porn' (porn involving Jeremy Clarkson), 'gadget porn' (porn with Inspector Gadget) and 'gastro porn' (belly porn).

One episode of celeb-foodie show *Eating with* . . . was trailed by announcers as featuring 'Nigel Slater, the king of gastro-porn'. They repeated this three times, presumably in the hope that on at least one occasion we might mishear and think, 'Wow, porn's coming up.' You half expected to see a big flashing sign saying: 'Something quite porny! This way comes! Oo-er! We said "comes"!'

Anyone thinking the next programme would feature something of a stimulating bent might have been disappointed to see a speccy man talking about his dark, painful childhood being brought up by a cold, distant father. That's not porn. Or, if it is, only a tiny minority will get their rocks off over it.

It's surprising they don't trail the news as 'topico-porn'.

And the weather could be called 'Hot 'n' Wet'.

Maybe it could be introduced: 'Now here's Peter with some hot fucking.'

Porsche SUVs

Want an SUV so you can loom over other road-users like the US Army? But also want something sporty to accelerate ludicrously away from the lights before suddenly braking at the next roundabout?

Then the Porsche Cayenne is the car for you: two utterly pointless vehicles in one. No one likes you.

Power lists

The 2006 *GQ* Power List no doubt took hours of debate, discussion and – who knows? – research to conclude that the two most powerful Britons were . . . Tony Blair and Gordon Brown. Yes, the Prime Minister and Chancellor of the Exchequer: both quite influential, apparently.

Lately, a key fixture in power lists (and not just media power lists) has been Ricky Gervais. Everyone likes *The Office*, but I'm not sure in what sense Ricky Gervais exerts 'power'. What does he do – give out Asbos?

Or is Gordon Brown just really desperate for a role in the next series of *Extras*?

Prawnies

Prawnies, available fresh-fried in big paella pans from stands at markets, events put on by councils, festivals – all that sort of behaviour – are reconstituted prawn and fish meat, coloured and flavoured to give the taste and impression of prawns, then moulded into the shape of large prawns. They are, according to the blurb, 'a revolutionary new product', related to seafood sticks (the rubbery things with the pink coating).

But if you want a foodstuff that looks and tastes like prawns, why not try prawns? It's almost as if they are designed to look and taste like prawns.

Presenters speaking to the camera while driving their cars

There are enough dangers in the world already, without current affairs presenters trying to present pieces to camera while negotiating heavy traffic.

Has no one learned from the tragic maiming of Fergal Keane: 'I'm driving down to Kinshasa now, to . . . *Cows!* Aaaaarrgggghhhhhh!'

Price promises

Now, surely, if I were going to hike around town/the net checking whether somewhere else sells this item cheaper, I'd do it BEFORE COMING IN HERE TO BUY IT AND NOT AFTERWARDS LIKE SOME SORT OF TWAT.

Private members' clubs

Private members' clubs are the places for 'like-minded' leaders of the 'urban-hip revolution' to 'mix business with pleasure in a relaxing environment'. These burgeoning boltholes are places where media-savvy movers display their 'cool, don't-mess-with-me, *GQ*-reading suavity' (the *Independent*). They are for the guys at 'the forefront of a lifestyle revolution that has since become established hip-urban style' (the *Sunday Times*). Essentially: to get into a private members' club, you need to be a member.

There is very little parallel with the posh gentlemen's clubs of yore. Yes, the new private members' clubs are expensive and exclusive; but they have much cheaper furniture. Basically, it's lots of chaps with Johnny Vaughan accents who relish 'stylish fun with a strong whiff of naughtiness'. People who know the best way to enjoy a drink is to look up every time someone walks in the room and then look down in disgust because it's not Sienna Miller or someone from Oasis. It's a bit like Bertie Wooster's Drones Club, but with more cocaine meltdowns: 'I say, will you take a look at that, Jeeves. Adrian from Web Your Own Hole's got his trousers round his ankles and is rubbing his old feller on all the leather sofas. What a rummy rotter!'

It's the new intermediary way of living: not stuck at home in private, but not having to mix with the general public either. Shed London has 'zzed sheds' – private spaces with leather adjustable day beds for members to crash – and guest speakers so members don't have to 'schlep across the city' to indulge their interest in the arts, sport or science. M1NT, whose inaugural chairman was Dragons' Den's Duncan Bannatyne, is 'not just a bar, but a forum bringing together individuals at the top of their respective profession'.

(Bannantyne resigned as M1NT chairman after an almighty bust-up with his fellow 'like-minded' movers and groovers. Apparently he left shouting: 'M1NT? It's not even spelt right, you big twat!' Alright, he didn't.)

Even the University of London Union, that is the Student Union in London, has a bookable VIP area. Students are people who haven't even got a profession to be top of, but here they are mixing business (which they don't really have) with pleasure in a relaxing environment.

The king of this private members club scene is Nick 'Mr Hospitality' Jones, who started Soho House in 1995. On its launch, explains Shane Watson in a hilariously positive *Sunday Times* profile, Soho House was perfect for 'a new generation of thirtysomething media types looking for places that defined their suit-but-no-ties lifestyle'. People were 'crying out to be a part of Jones's world. He has pulled off that trickiest of all tricks – comfortable cool . . .'

She continues: 'Everything he does is modern, but not too modern, warm but not too cosy, neutral, in that leather-and-polished-wood way, but not bland. The Soho House brand has become a byword for a style that everyone feels at ease with and subtly boosted by . . .' By which point, Watson is all but offering him her teeth on a plate for a piece of the action.

Interestingly, as his work is a private members' club, when Nick 'Mr Hospitality' Jones wants to relax, he goes to the Gala Bingo with his mum. Actually, no, now I think about it, he probably doesn't do that. 'Housey housey!' That's not his catchphrase. 'Dirty Gertie – Number 30'. Equally, he probably doesn't say that much either.

Prostitutes in the workplace

'Okay, so the last item on the agenda is . . . whoring! What, Liz? Yeah, banging with chicks for cash. Let's get through this one quickly because I'm seeing Elastic Tatania at two. Ah, she understands me so well . . .'

Many modern, forward-thinking companies find that nothing greases the wheels of industry like the sex industry – the greasiest industry of them all. These days, a business deal is often not fully sealed unless both parties have sat together staring at young ladies' thighs doing business with a pole; then you celebrate your acquisitions and mergers by temporarily acquiring a prostitute and merging with her.

Sometimes, though, this libidinal atmosphere doesn't make female employees feel overly comfortable. Judging by the raft of sex-discrimination cases brought against City and Wall Street firms recently, it appears that when you put a bunch of men into a macho bearpit their attitude towards women sometimes suffers. Which is a shock.

In 2005 six women sued the high-ranking investment bank Dresdner Kleinwort Wasserstein for a total of £800 million, claiming that male bankers entertained clients in strip clubs, boasted of their sex-industry roistering and compared their female colleagues to the likes of Pamela Anderson. According to the lawsuit, one director even routinely brought prostitutes back to the office. (Really hope it wasn't open plan.)

Even if we do appreciate the importance of a thrusting business environment, this is surely taking things too far.

Public phoneboxes, state of

Will no one think of the junkies?

Pub toilet adverts for pub toilet adverts

'Reach an audience of thousands EVERY DAY!' 'It's clear why 12,000 panels like this one can reach an audience of 15 million.'

It makes a nice change from 'birds, eh?' pleas to consume WKD, or exhortations to purchase satellite devices that detect speed cameras. But it's not a good advert for adverts, as they have no adverts, just adverts for adverts telling you how effective their adverts would be, if they had any. Which they don't. And that's not a good advert for their adverts . . . them not actually having any.

Pay-and-display tickets too: on the back of the sticker, always and for ever: 'YOUR ADVERT HERE!' No, no, no, it's *your* advert there. Ad man, you're a bad ad man, man.

Q

Questioning the whole basis of fashion

At the Autumn 2005 Paris Fashion Week, designer John Galliano claimed to be 'questioning the whole basis of fashion'. This meant having his collection modelled by giants, dwarves, identical twins, fat women and body-builders (but mostly dwarves).

This really socked it to the notion of the fashion industry serving only the rich and the beautiful. Either that or he'd just seen *Time Bandits* on DVD and thought it might be a laugh. Certainly, it questioned the whole basis of fashion, but possibly not in the way he had intended.

As a target for satire, the fashion industry is not a difficult one to hit – a little like hitting a very big barn door with a large herd of cows. Taking potshots at its money worship and body fascism (and borderline actual fascism) could not be simpler. (Cathy Horyn in the *New York Times* reported that someone came up to her after Galliano's dwarves show and asked, 'So what did you think of the monsters?') Except you cannot convincingly satirise things which you in fact are. You cannot credibly live for bon ton in the pay of one of the four global behemoths that own all the fashion houses and simultaneously say, 'It's all bollocks.' That's like pointing at yourself in a mirror and going: 'Look at that twat! Just *look* at him!'

One also has to doubt the artistic veracity of someone who

based a previous show on silly-arse dystopian sci-fi flick *The Matrix*. (Although this does at least lend weight to the *Time Bandits* theory.)

Avant-garde fashion seeks to transcend overtly commercial concerns. This is achieved by having jagged edges and extra zips and spraying models with paint; all heroic artistic endeavours. The sponsors of such avant-garde doings? American Express (benefactors of 'uncompromising, experimental' Boudicca) and Gucci (owner-patrons of Alexander McQueen). Truly, Baudelaire's got nothing on these guys.

The whole notion of the avant-garde has taken quite a battering in recent years. There's e-Brit avant-garde jewellery advertised in the foyers of five-star hotels (there's even a whole website devoted to selling avant-garde jewellery), plus the Mercedes CLK 430 Cabriolet Avant Garde. Presumably for all those people who like their luxury motor to fuck with their head a bit?

Even Siân Lloyd is avant-garde. Commenting on the fact that her partner, Liberal Democrat MP Lembit Öpik, is seven years her junior, she said: 'I lead a showbiz life that is slightly different to others – maybe it is more avant-garde – but I think the balance in society has changed.' (That's Siân Lloyd, the weather-person. Not another Siân Lloyd who was one of the Weathermen.)

By the way, interestingly – and not a lot of people know this – when Gucci bought out Alexander McQueen, they didn't just buy his company; they bought *him* – his actual self. Say they wanted him to run down to Gregg's for some pasties, or ring up Isabella Blow and call her a stupid tart, or just to give him a slap, they could, quite legally. Not a lot of people know this because it is not true. But still . . .

Questioning whether George Clooney is real

'He acts, he directs, he's gorgeous, he's intelligent, he's politically committed: can he be real?!'

It will no doubt relieve the redoubtable Mr Clooney that we have an answer to that question.

And the answer is 'Yes'. Isn't it obvious? Look at him!

Queues on Everest

Have you seen the queues? Bloody atrocious. Don't know why they don't put more staff on.

The fact that Mount Everest is 'really high' need no longer be a barrier to having a fun day out for all the family. Like Chessington World of Adventures, but with less oxygen.

Everyone's been up there, including the first double amputee and the first *Playboy* cover model. The ascent is now littered with abandoned oxygen bottles, soft-drink cans and shredded tents. There are piles of human excrement; loo paper is referred to locally as 'white man's prayer flags'.

Oh, and corpses. One in 20 people who go up don't come back. That's not because they like it so much that they decide to stay. At the time of writing, 203 people had been killed on Everest since records began in 1922 – 11 of them in April and May 2006 alone.

Strangely, the queues for Everest do not appear to make it completely safe. In fact, they might help foster the illusion that climbing the world's highest mountain is a breeze. One experienced mountaineer recently told Radio 4's *You and Yours*: 'I was on the North Camp with people who had not worn crampons before.' Some people thought Sherpas were a type of van.

Others might be deluded that someone will help them to safety if something goes wrong. This is not necessarily true. When David Sharp had to stop after he became ill on his way down from the summit in May 2006, it has been estimated that as many as 40 climbers passed by on their way up the mountain. A few gave Sharp oxygen or supplies, but none attempted to rescue him. He died.

In 1996, two Japanese climbers came upon a frostbitten but still conscious Indian climber slumped in the snow. Although the Japanese were carrying food and oxygen, they ignored him. Higher up, they passed two more stricken Indian climbers, one conscious and kneeling in the snow. Again, they passed by. One explained: 'Above 26,000 feet is not a place where people can afford morality.'

How's that, then? You're just on your holidays. You're not the first ones to do it. Although Edmund Hillary recently said: 'On my expedition, there was no way you'd have left a man under a rock to die.'

Putting the summit before human life might be called a hollow victory. Ah, the views. What a mountain. What an achievement. Okay, I have trouble sleeping with the knowledge that I stepped over a dying man, but what memories!

Quick recipes

By strange coincidence, the British craze for cooking fancy food has coincidentally coincided with the craze for working into the evening and then feeling the need to pass out from drink. This has led to a craze for quick recipes.

So all food magazines advertise the 'Quick and Easy' aspect of their 'Tried & Tested Recipes'. (What, you've actually tried out the recipes? With this trying and testing, you are really spoiling us.)

In his book *Jamie's Dinners*, Jamie Oliver claims that, in the past fifteen years, the average time spent making a meal for the family has slipped from an hour to thirteen minutes. He then describes some extremely quick 'Five Minute Wonders', a section which should more accurately be called: 'Five Minutes, My Giddy Sweet Back Bottom'. He even adds a challenge: 'Each recipe has the time it took for me to make it – you never know, you might be able to beat me on some of them!'

Well, you try making beef with pak choi, mushrooms and noodles, for instance – which can apparently be done and dusted with coriander in five minutes 12 seconds – including slicing the red onion, slicing the ginger, finely slicing the chilli and brushing and tearing up the mushrooms and quartering the pak choi – without slicing the tops of your fingers clean off and leaving the kitchen a blood-spurting mess. Particularly when you've been drinking.

Really, your partner might as well have the car running for that mercy-dash to Casualty. Is this what he wants? A&E wards full of wannabe quick chefs! Is this part of his bold vision for public sector renewal? And your partner's in no fit state to drive a car – they've been drinking. Look at the fucking state of them!

Honestly, he comes across as such a saint. But really he's still a bastard.

R

Radio stations helping listeners through the week

I was recently awoken at seven in the morning, unbidden, after a fairly late night, in a hotel room by the sound of Simon Bates saying: 'Let's be honest, it's been a fraught week.'

Well, it hadn't been a fraught week. But it became one after being woken up by Simon-fucking-Bates. I thought he was dead!

And, anyway, it was only Wednesday. How fraught can a week have been after the completion of two of the seven days? Bearing in mind I wasn't holed up in the Holiday Inn Fallujah, but the relative comfort of Manchester.

Radios coming on in the morning when you haven't asked them to, telling you that it's been a fraught week: it's very much the modern way. Some radio stations are so obsessed with cheering you up through the working week that it's a wonder they don't just call themselves Prozac FM.

They come to cure you. I once heard Steve Wright in the afternoon announcing at the end of Coldplay's 'Fix You' that we had just heard 'Coooold ... plaaaay, Fiiiiiix Yooooouuuu . . .'

His slow intonation was presumably meant to sound all healing and emotional but it was more like he was waiting in a traffic jam and trying out the feel of the words in his mouth.

Without these stations, by Wednesday afternoon we would be crying into our hot chocolate. Thursday would be an existential desert. And Friday? By then we would be clinically dead. To reinforce the relief that the end of the week brings, one local radio station even has Feelgood Friday.* So the DJ says things like: 'Okay, it's Feelgood Friday . . . the weekend's nearly here. Here's a classic from Mr Michael Stipe and the boys.'

Sorry, but how is hearing 'Losing My Religion' supposed to make anyone feel good? It's a song about losing your religion – isn't that obvious? How's that going to make me feel good? I *hate* losing my religion (and I hate 'Losing My Religion'). And I *really* hate Mr Michael Stipe and the boys. We've endured *decades* of that whining jangly pap.

'Don't give up, you're nearly there – here's Joy Division's feelgood 1980 hit "Atmosphere". Don't turn away, in silence – Your confusion, my illusion – Worn like a mask of self-hate. Then we'll have the competition . . .'

*We presume Feelgood Fridays are not connected to the Friday wind-down routine favoured by *Corrie* actor Craig Charles, the poet, which he christened Naughty Fridays. That is, knocking off work to enjoy 60 rocks of crack and a selection of porn in the backseat of a car being driven from London to Manchester. As a way of rewarding yourself for getting through another week, it's certainly a step up from treating yourself to a Crunchie. But watch out for Very Very Tense Saturday.

Razor blades that can shave even closer than the hitherto closest-shaving blade, which was already really quite close (also: washing powder)

Shaving has certainly come on in leaps and bounds since men dragged flinty bits of flint down their hirsute faces, pulling out clumps of hair matted with animal fat and their own fetid blood. 'Aaaarrrgggghhhhh!' they would say. 'For fucking fuck's sake. That really hurt and now it's all stingy and raw and throbbing and raw.'

Then there were the so-called 'cut-throat' razors, but these took a dive in popularity after barbers started cutting people up and putting them in pies. That's when the safety razor was invented by King Camp Gillette, in 1895. (Hur hur, King Camp. He's called King Camp.)

And bang! The race was on – to make the safety razor bigger, better, closer and, crucially, more expensive. Along came lubricant strips and 'spring loading', 'open cartridge architecture' and handles with 'knurled elastomeric crescents'. First there was one blade, then there were two. Then there were three, then – you can see where this is going. Now there are five – yes, five. Count 'em. And weep.

The new Gillette innovation has five razor blades in it. *Five*. Not four – like the Wilkinson Sword Quattro – but five. Five. Can't you count? I said five. It's very exciting.

Now, some people might suggest it's probably impossible to get closer than existing razors in a way perceptible to the naked eye. They might say it's a colossal waste of a billion dollars and the full-time efforts of a hundred people to go round developing new five-blade razors like the old ones were going out of fashion, which they are. Perhaps these people would agree with Roger Hamby, of the Cutlery Allied Trades Research Association, who said: 'The Holy Grail of closeness was reached 30 years ago with the first twin-blade razors.' But what do 'some people' know?

The names of these babies alone should be enough to reassure us of their scientific veracity and general goodness. Sensor – you know what it's all about. Mach 3 – the blade that is so manly it has a name vaguely reminiscent of strafing

Afghan villages. Mach 3 Turbo – it vibrates! Mach 3 Turbo G-force! (Don't know what that one does.) The five-blader, which has 75 patents on it and is made in a Class 5000 clean room in Berlin, an environment purer than an operating theatre, is called Fusion. Yes, it has capacities so mind-boggling it can only be described by conjuring up the spirit of jazz rock. Dark magus!

Also: washing powder.

Ready meals

Should you stray off the modern food-Nazi holy-eating track for a sneaky fix of bubbling additive-paste, you might need to develop the appetite of a particularly picky three-year-old. Because these things really ought to be called ready-for-another-meal-in-an-incredibly-short-space-of-time meals. Or 'snacks', as I believe such meagre portions were termed in the olden days.

For this reason, 'Where's the rest of my fucking ready meal, you chiselling shysters!?' is a phrase which should be heard shouted by disgruntled customers at supermarkets throughout the land as they stomp down the aisles, pushing over stacks of promotional Pringles and turning off the fridges.

'Serves 2'! Serves two *what*, exactly? Cockatiels?

I HAVE GIVEN YOU FOUR POUNDS AND FORTY-NINE PENCE – AND I *DEMAND* SUSTENANCE!!

Real Football Factories, The

In the feral, vicious world of cobbled-together 'Real' documentaries riding in the slipstream of anything remotely popular (*The Real Desperate Housewives/Footballers' Wives/Brokeback Mountain*), *The Real Football Factories* is The General – a fat-necked psycho going toe-to-toe with your telly who NEVER runs. You NEVER RUN. 'Ave it! Pie-eaters! Etc.

This clip show's claim to be a serious study of football hooliganism was undermined somewhat by its sole sociological analysis being a professor claiming: 'The Midlands is a strange area; it sort of falls between London and the North.'

Presenter Danny Dyer spends most of the 'ARD-'ITTIN' DOCUMENTARY ABAHT RIGHT NAUGHTY FIRMS 'AVIN' PROPAH FACKIN' TEAR-UPS dressed in a rudeboy trench-coat, 'snout' dangling from his yap, strutting through underpasses on council estates, randomly stringing together words like 'PROPAH', 'FIRMS', 'FACK' and 'ABAHT'.

'Dunno whevva you've seen a movie called *The Warriors*,' the Britpop actor gorblimeys while loitering outside Upton Park tube station in his trenchcoat looking TASTY, 'S'about a New York gang travelling through the city by subway, bumping into rival mobs along the way. PROPAH FILM! Now that's pretty much what it was like here in the 80s, as rival firms fought battles at train stations like King's Cross and Euston.'

Sat in a pub with some PROPAH hooligan nutcases, though, his mask slips. The studied sneer quivers, his top lip giving off micro-actions that silently scream: 'Don't cut me! Not the face! It's my livelihood! Not the face! Not the face!'

PROPAH DOCUMENTARY!

Dyer, of course, also starred in the real *The Football Factory* – the 2004 film of the book of the fight. It, too, is straightfor-wardly about fighting at or near football grounds. It opens with a fucking great big fight scene. It continues with some more fight scenes. It culminates in a big fight scene.

The film was advertised as being about fighting, with a

DVD extra called 'Fight Scene': arty stills of burly blokes knocking shit out of each other under a thumping soundtrack with snatches of dialogue from the film dotted through it like 'Don't fuck abaht – just ping 'im'. To sum up: *The Football Factory* is about fighting.

Except, according to director Nick Love, it's not: 'The thing I love, and will never get away from, is men bonding. They're not gay or anything. It's deep male friendship. I'm obsessed with male friendship. It doesn't mean it's a gay film. You just do it nice and gently and subtly and everything.'

The Football Factory's portrayal of male relationships is indeed subtle – the relationships being expressed wholly by them hitting each other.

Love's next film was *The Business* (also starring Dyer), a lads' own voyeurism flick about 80s villains living it up on the Costa del Geezah – the money, the drugs, the manly man-on-man fisticuffs, the clobber, the casual glassing of waiters, the improbable plot and terrible dialogue, the sub-Ritchie pop-video direction, the wooden performances, the male bonding with fists . . .

Forthcoming is *Outlaw*, due in 2007, about 'what happens when crime victims take the law into their own hands'. Its website describes it as a 'challenging and thought-provoking . . . exploration of social complexities in contemporary Britain'. But don't worry, it also pledges 'anarchy and off the wall naughtiness', which isn't nearly so complex.

But we probably shouldn't hold out much hope for a challenging take on Asbo Britain, given that the film's logo involves a hoodie-wearing youth hanging from a gibbet and balaclavas with blood dripping off them.

And the website features an online game called Nonce Hunter: 'Use your pistol, assault rifle and sniper rifle to kill those evil nonces and get to have a shot at Fred West and Ian Huntley.'

PROPAH FILM!

Recruitment videos

In the War on Terror, the recruitment videos of the opposition have the considerable advantage of a medieval fundamentalist ideology to fall back on. A tack which sadly isn't available to the British Army.

The recruiters' job has traditionally involved making joining up seem like a 'fun' and 'exciting' thing for go-getting youngsters to do. A fan club called My Camouflage aims to hook 13-to-17-year-olds into the camouflage-wearing habit. Admirably, its website doesn't attempt to hoodwink youngsters into thinking that war is just a large-scale computer game. Oh no, that's wrong: 'Play our new tank game. Command a tank and take on the enemy to battle for the highest score.'

Unfortunately for the recruiters, though, the 'fun' side of being a soldier is still difficult to convey. The new ads focus on the less warlike aspects of joining the army ('It's not all gun-related mayhem; sometimes it's preparing breakfast too'). But sadly, in times of war, one inescapable fact of army life is – yes, that's right – war. It just keeps cropping up.

But maybe these videos should be more honest and open about the true craziness of military life. Even without tackling the grotesqueries of the battlefield, there are excitements enough on the training ground. There's that footage of the 42 Commando Royal Marines filmed at their base at Bickleigh Barracks, near Plymouth, all naked – except for two men dressed as a schoolgirl and a surgeon – in their initiation ritual which involves fighting with rolls of matting tied to their arms and being kicked unconscious in the face.

According to the army establishment, this was 'fun' that got 'out of hand'. (And who among us hasn't seen a happy get-together descend into bare-knuckle fighting with mats taped over both arms?) A shocked Colonel Bob Stewart, who commanded the British forces in Bosnia, protested: 'This is nothing to do with training . . . Why are they naked, for goodness sake?' Well, to make it more 'fun', obviously.

Or there is the case of mixed-race 17-year-old recruit Americk Hayer, who claimed that on his final day of basic training up a mountain in Cumbria he was kicked in the head 'like a football', causing his gun magazine to pierce his tearduct and leave his eyeball hanging out. 'I was just screaming, "My eye, I'm blind!" He grabbed me by the scruff of my neck and kept on kicking me,' said Hayer.

Other rituals include 'babooning', in which the backsides of new soldiers are beaten until they are as red as baboons' bottoms. Meanwhile, recruits in a mounted regiment are stripped and covered with food which a horse eats off their bodies. Come on, what's not to like?

Knowing how much teens like their drugs, maybe a compilation of all these scenes – men dressed up as schoolgirls and surgeons, eyeballs hanging from gaping sockets, naked bodies with mats tied around their arms, red-raw monkey-man posteriors – might tempt in a few curious souls otherwise dissuaded by, you know, the war and that. Try telling them they'll get to drop some 'heavy shit'.

Restaurant service charges

Different from a tip in several key ways: it's not voluntary and it doesn't often get to the staff. Many establishments either split the service charge with the staff or just keep it all for themselves. So it's not even a 'service' charge, a charge in appreciation of the staff, who might reasonably expect to get paid properly anyway. It's just a charge: someone asking you for extra money for no reason whatsoever which they will then simply keep. You can see why they don't call it that on the menu.

Restaurant service charges that only apply to parties of more than 10 people

More service, certainly, but only because there is more stuff *being served*. You thieving shits.

Romantic comedies

'I really loved *Maid in Manhattan*' is a phrase one never hears. Or 'I really loved that film *Wimbledon*.' This is because romantic comedies are commissioned on the basis of a six- or eight-word premise, which then everyone who is involved neglects to expand into an actual script. Com does not ensue. Nor does rom.

The king of such films is Matthew McConaughey, a man who can smirk quizzically in posters next to Jennifer Lopez or smirk quizzically in posters next to Sandra Bullock. He was recently seen smirking quizzically in posters next to Sarah Jessica Parker for *Failure to Launch*: she's falling in love, but he still lives with his parents! Oh, and he's a boat broker, hence the title – it's applicable both to his familial situation and to the boats that, as a boat broker, he brokes. It's almost like literature.

Here's Matthew McConaughey on the difficulty of finding the right motivation for his romcom characters: 'Sometimes, in a romantic comedy, the male is sometimes the foil – meaning do I pull to the left? Do I pull to the right? Which way do I go? I don't know what to do!'

Coming soon: *Staying away from the Herd*. Wealthy socialite Sandra Bullock is smitten after meeting Matthew McConaughey at a high-class masquerade, but then she discovers he's not a Wall Street banker but herds cattle. Can this relationship ever be a dung deal? You'll be laughing till the . . . well, you know.

McConaughey on the chemistry between himself and leading ladies such as Kate Hudson, his co-star in *How to Lose a Guy in 10 Days*: 'If you've got chemistry, you kind of know what's going to happen, but you enjoy going along for the ride . . . We have similar senses of humour, man. Sometimes I do things that she doesn't think are funny, but she's laughing because I think they're funny while sometimes she'll do things that I don't think are funny, but I'm cracking up because she thinks it's funny.'

Coming soon: *She's So My Dad's Date*. Matthew McConaughey plays the son of ageing womaniser Sean Connery. There's trouble in the family when son falls for father's new girlfriend, played by Lindsay Lohan. Age-gap comedy extreme!

Here's Matthew McConaughey on finding the right tone as a romantic comedy actor: 'It's just standing up for your man, meaning the character. And that's my job as an actor, to look at my character, what does he do, and stand up for that. That's my job. Whatever my man does, it's to stand up for him . . .'

Coming soon: *That's No Lady*. Matthew McConaughey is smitten with new girlfriend Cameron Diaz . . . but is she really all she seems?

And Sarah Jessica Parker on what was surprising about working with Matthew McConaughey: 'You know what surprised me is he writes a lot. I didn't know he was a writer. He writes a lot. He really works on the script a lot. He really thinks about it. He breaks it down. I probably would have – if you'd given me truth serum before the rehearsal process – probably thought it comes pretty easy to him, which it does at the same time.'

Coming soon: *Secure Unit*. Starring Matthew McConaughey and Kirsten Dunst. He's a prison visitor – she's a real nut!

More McConaughey on getting the acting tone right good: '. . . and let him believe in what he's doing and let the comedy come from, for instance, in this movie, let him believe in what he's doing but let the rest of the world go, "No, no, no." And he's going, "Yeah, what's wrong with it?"'

Coming soon: *My Big Fat Racist Wedding*. Starring Matthew McConaughey as a black lawyer betrothed to white girl Mandy Moore. When is he gonna find out that daddy's in the Klan?

S

Salt lobbyists

The salt lobby is working tirelessly, heroically, day and night. On behalf of salt. The rights of salt. To be sprinkled on potatoes. To be utilised in the boiling of vegetables. Or used as a major ingredient in salty snacks.

'I'm lobbying – for salt!' This is what they say.

The Salt Manufacturers Association are keen to teach us Salt Sense. It's a beautiful thing, and sensible.

Cut salt at your peril: this is the salt lobby's prime message. Cut salt and you could be cutting your life – '37% increased risk of death from heart disease,' says new study.

Here's a picture of a running woman with the caption 'salt if you exercise'. She eats up her salt . . . and so should you.

Here's an elderly lady eating a salty meal with salt on, captioned 'salt and the elderly'. Don't take away her salt. It's all she's got.

And here's a salt gritter (caption: 'salt for gritting icy roads') which would, let's face it, be nothing without salt. Isn't it obvious? Stop using salt and icy, skiddy, mangled carnage will result. Do you see now?

Luckily, the salt lobby is now being recognised. The Food Standards Agency had wanted to cut the recommended daily salt intake from 10g to 6g per person within four years (their concerns: stroke, heart disease, blah blah blah). But the government, presumably not wishing to discriminate against salt, watered down the targets to 8g a day.

I call this a long-overdue victory for salt.

'Salt: nothing else is so dependably salty' is one slogan the salt lobby might consider adopting.

Or: 'Salt: suck it and see!'

'Sassy' songs about body parts

You're playing with your bits,
I'm playing with my bits,
Ooh baby, I betcha wish you were playing with my bits,
Instead of your bits . . .
My bits, my bits, my bits, my bits, my bits, my bits.

That sort of thing.

Ralf Schumacher

Poor Ralf. Everyone's just interested in his freaky big brother – the robotic winning-machine who has been known to deliberately drive into opponents (Jacques Villeneuve), or, at the Monaco 2006 Grand Prix, made his car stall on the final qualifying lap so that his competitors would be forced to slow down and thus stand no chance of beating his fastest time. Then had a huffy about being called a cheat.

But spare a thought for Ralf, living in nutty Michael's shadow. Because he's a freaky robotic winning-machine, too. And he wouldn't like us to forget that.

Shopped-up service stations

It's like pulling off the motorway for a wee-wee and ending up in one of those airport departure lounges that are one huge duty-free shop so you are fine if your needs are served by perfume, Scotch and chocolate truffles. But if you are after a bread-based snack, you've got to join a queue for the next hour or so to be awarded a stale croissant.

Okay, at Roadchef you can buy a bread-based snack at a shop, the entrance of which is just about distinguishable because of the word 'SHOP' emblazoned above it. But the shop doesn't stop in the SHOP. Outside the shop, it's also a shop! There's 'SHOPS' within 'SHOPS'! Shop shit all over the place. The whole central aisle is taken up with shop shit. You can't actually move, let alone relax.

People actually have to squeeze around each other to avoid the massive piles of water guns, Daleks, remote-control cars, travel mugs, monster trucks, Swingball kits, watch stands, remote-control dinosaurs, vast vats of candy floss and popcorn (to keep things calm and puke-free on the backseat). It's like a shop-shit warehouse sale. With the added bonus of a slightly psychotic guy from the AA blocking your entry to the toilet until you pretend you're already a member. (He knows you're lying, but short of hurting you – which, believe me, he has considered – there's not much he can do about it. His life is a long series of disappointments, adrift in a sea of shop shit.)

I'm knackered already – that's why I pulled up in the first place – so I'm not really going to feel utterly refreshed by a veritable shitstorm of shop shit. Honestly, these shitty shopped-up shitholes full of shit shop shit really should just shut up shop and shit off.

Sixpack secrets

Sixpacks sex you up. That's a fact. According to *Men's Fitness*, the 'abdominals are the Top Trump trophy muscles and the ones that drive women wild ... the abs may have come to symbolise masculinity'. Having phenomenal abdominals will 'improve your sex appeal and help you achieve your goals' (although the 'other goals' men might have besides having sex remain undisclosed). This is why, at some point or other, all men must uncover the secret of the sixpack.

So how does one go about acquiring these bristling sex muscles of sex? As previously explained, it's a secret. You can 'crunch' until you're blue in the face, but if you skip the secret stuff, the stuff known only to the chosen few, you are but a modern-day Sisyphus, forever pushing that boulder towards the unattainable peak.

Luckily, some secrets are too much to bear alone, so certain masters of the field have elected to pass on their sixpack lore to the chosen few. There are books with titles like *The Abs Diet: The 6-Week Plan to Flatten Your Stomach and Keep You Lean for Life* by David Zinczenko and Ted Spiker.* And fitness magazines offering 'From Fat to Flat – In Six Weeks!', 'Get Hard Abs' or 'Abs: Don't Think You Don't Want Them 'Cos You Do Really, Deep Down, Even if You Say You Don't, You Do Really . . .'

I feel almost guilty for going further here, such are the enormous implications, but I found my personal revelation came on reading the *Men's Health* issue offering: 'Rock Hard Abs: Jason Statham reveals his sixpack secrets'.

Inside, 'Hollywood hardman' Statham reveals: 'The key is explosive action: if I'm doing a press-up, I go down slow and bang, push up.'

After fully assimilating this news, one must then progress

on to the next piece of deep knowledge learned from his friend, martial arts expert Ras Butten: 'He uses punching combinations,' Statham says. 'He'll call out "one", a straight left. Then "one, two" – left, right – or "three" – left, right and a left hook. I can do that in a hotel room, anywhere.'

So that's it. The secret for achieving all your goals revolves around the fact that you can punch thin air in a hotel room.

*Other titles include *My Abs Are OK, Your Abs Are OK* by Vince Grundtzenecker. There's also *Make Every Day an Abs Day* by Bunt Masterson. Another alternative is *Abs: The Cosa Nostra Way* by Nico The Chip. Finally, there's *Neat Abs for Invading and Mating Good* by Clay Harbourmouth.

Sky Three
The channel for stuff that somehow isn't good enough to get on Sky Two (see **Sky Two**).

Sky Two
The channel for stuff that somehow isn't good enough to get on Sky One.

Smell of Subways, the
Not underpasses, the green-and-yellow, long sandwich shops. Many of their stores pump a 'bread-cooking smell' into the street. It is there to entice you in. Come in, Jason and weary sailors on your way home, it is meant to say, come in and enjoy our irresistible long sandwiches. You will not be dashed

on the rocks of fast-food oblivion; many of our subs have a very low fat content. You could also consider our meal deals, which represent considerable value. So, come in, come in. One of our lovely green-attired attendants will sprinkle sliced olives on your selection while wearing a plastic bag on their hands, if you like. It is the heavenly sphere of thin-hammed delights in here. Come, smell the cooking bread smell of our bread, cooking; you cannot resist . . .

But there is a problem. And that is that this phenomenally unpleasant, nauseating smell makes me want to vomit. It's the sort of bread-cooking smell you can imagine being created in a lab (I don't know how they actually create it), probably by the same guy who does the frozen French-bread pizza slices (this smell has got that bastard's sticky fingers all over it).

So, as an enticement to come and partake in some long sandwich goodness, it's clearly not aimed at me. Because, for me, the desire to consume a long sandwich with some thin-sliced smoked ham in it is always – always – going to be outweighed by the desire not to yak up all over my own shoes in the street. It's as if the sirens, instead of singing beautiful songs of an enchanting timbre, were barking the words to 'I Could Be So Good For You'.

Snack-a-Jacks, the name but not necessarily the product

The product I am not prepared to take a line on, for I am confused. My brain says it's wrong. Salt 'n' vinegar rice-cakes, it says. Screw that. Stupid idea. But my hands disagree with my brain and put them in my mouth, and I enjoy them. Is that good? I don't know.

The nutrition Nazis would crap on about salt and preservatives and what-not interfering with the basic rice and corn goodness – but who wants to eat plain rice cakes? Except babies, and they don't know anything about food. And, for me, it's nothing to do with health anyway: it's the taste and texture (I know!); I'm like a moth to cloth; I bakes for them rice cakes. You can see why this is an issue for me.

Anyway, they are not really helping me out with the name. To be purchasing something called Snack-a-Jacks feels somehow foolish and undignified. Snack-a-Jacks? It's a name, frankly, that only a prick could love. Luckily, Snack-a-Jacks are usually in boxes or on shelves and thus liable to self-service, and not, say, behind a counter, like Rennies and fags. If I had to ask for them, they certainly wouldn't be selling any Snack-a-Jacks to this snacker, Jack.

As for the new Snack-a-Jack chocolate orange flavour? *I'm trying to be on your side here, Quaker, but you just keep taking the piss out of me.*

Soap characters loosely based on Osama bin Laden

Nothing says daytime TV like a medievalist mass-murderer who wants to establish a worldwide Caliphate.

So full marks to long-running NBC soap opera *Days of Our Lives* (the one that supposedly starred Joey from *Friends*) for finally developing a character based on Osama bin Laden. Clearly, it would have been better if *EastEnders* had got there first, but you can't have everything. (Phil Daniels: 'I brought them kids up on me oah-n.' Osama: 'We love death. The US loves life. That is the difference between us.')

The character was created by Kola Boof, author of the forth-coming novel *The Sexy Part of the Bible* (please note: don't look for the sexy part of the Bible; you'll be sorely disappointed) and, she claims, a former mistress of bin Laden, having been held by the terror-lord against her will for four months in Morocco in 1996.

Really stripping away the layers and getting to the heart of her creation, the writer said: 'This character wants to take over the world.'

Clearly Boof has had some terrible experiences – having also been marked for death by the Sudanese-based National Islamic Front in response to writings critical of Islam. We can only thank God she has managed to work through it in the only way appropriate.

More fortunately, it appears she never personally met Osama's late bad lieutenant in Iraq, Abu Musab al-Zarqawi. But still, maybe she could be tempted to introduce a Zarqawi-esque character into *Days of Our Lives* too. Perhaps the skanky younger brother, like De Niro's Johnny Boy from *Mean Streets*, only always getting into beheading-related scrapes. She could sum up his motivation thus: 'This character wants to behead everybody.'

Incidentally, according to al-Qaeda expert Jason Burke, when bin Laden heard of his wildcard follower's death he might have felt 'sneaking relief'. How truly awful must some-one be for bin Laden to find them irresponsible? 'He was a bit of a handful, really,' says Osama. 'Just trouble from the word go. That kind of guy we just don't need . . .'

'Sold' signs

The property is no longer 'For Sale'. This is surely the point at which to take down all those big, fuck-off, multicoloured signs outside it. Not put up a new one.

Want to buy this house? Tough shit, you can't. It's not for sale. You should have been here last week. Go and buy another house. 'Cos you ain't buying this one. Want it? I bet you do. But you can't.

Soundtrack albums from shit films with shit soundtracks

Who – *who?* – emerges blinking into the foyer, dusting off a confetti of fumbled Revels and Butterkist, after sitting through, say, 'Can Pierce Brosnan's master thief resist one last big score with tough cop Woody Harrelson on his tail?' crappy adventure flick *After the Sunset* and thinks: 'Hey – great film, must get the soundtrack.'

'Music from and inspired by . . .' That's 'inspired' in the financial sense rather than in the actually-having-seen-the-film sense.

Toon-based, FIFA-sponsored footie-fest *Goal!* seems to have spent more time totting up potential soundtrack sales than writing the script. Mexican ball wizard Santiago Munez (he's poor, but he's moral) goes for a very, very, very, very long run along the Northumberland coastline, the waves crashing in and the music thumping away as he runs on and on and on and on and on. Plot-wise, a few seconds would have done – but how then could one crowbar in all of a pumped-up remix of Oasis's 'Cast No Shadow'? What's the Story? I can't remember – there's just this bloke running all the time.

Even good films generally have no necessity for a sound-track release. Who cheers themselves up by popping on the available-at-all-good-record-stores soundtrack to *The Elephant Man*?

Are there really flatmates and couples, staring down the end of another evening's TV braindeath, saying to each other: 'Let's make a night of it. I'll nip out and get a box of two-for-one Cava and some tabs – you slap on the soundtrack to *Jean de Florette*.'

Or: 'Which track from mentalist-insomniac-psycho-factory-worker thriller *The Machinist* do you like best? I really like "Miserable Life", but I *love* "Trevor in Jail".'

'They're both great, but on balance I definitely prefer "Where is My Waitress"?'

'Yes! The posing of the question, the lack of resolution – it's quite, quite beautiful. Do any of us know the whereabouts of our waitress, really? That's what he's saying. Where is *your* waitress? Where is *my* waitress?'

TV's at it too, with CD spin-offs from *Cold Feet*, *The Forsyte Saga*, *Ideal* and *The Virgin Queen*. 'That quite good drama of Elizabethan power-plays certainly enlivened our Sunday evening viewing – let's get the background music from the bits when they were walking down corridors.' 'Cool. We could walk down our hall.'

Even computer games have soundtrack albums now – the various volumes of *Grand Theft Auto* have their own section in music stores. 'Do you know, later, I think I might pimp some women for a bit and then crash my car.' 'Ace. You'll be wanting to put this on then.' 'Cheers. You motherfucker.'

As a general rule, if it's not a musical, it probably doesn't need a soundtrack album. Actually, that holds for most musicals, too. Particularly *Chicago*.

South Bank Show Little Britain Special, the

The crying shame of this programme is that many of the best bits couldn't be jimmied into a mere hour and were anyway either too interesting or too worthwhile to warrant inclusion. Until the suits at ITV get their blummen silly act together, here is a transcript of some of the prime offcuts:

EXT. LOCATION SET IN THE BACKGROUND. MATT AND DAVID IN LEOTARDS, SITTING ON PLASTIC CHAIRS. WALLIAMS IS WEARING BLACKFACE (NOT FOR THE SKETCH THEY'RE ABOUT TO SHOOT, HE JUST IS).

BRAGG: Tell me about the new characters you're working on.

WALLIAMS: Well, we're very excited about a West Indian character we've been developing.

LUCAS: Yes, she's a fat black witch who lives on an estate – she's called Mama Shakalakaboo.

WALLIAMS: (*loudly*) Aaaahm gon' put a spell on you!

LUCAS: Ha! She's always putting spells on people.

WALLIAMS: And chanting. Mama Shakalakaboo! Mama Shakalakaboo!

BOTH: Mama Shakalakaboo! Mama Shakalakaboo!

LUCAS: Then there's Ray. He's got a club foot.

Fade.

INT. KITCHEN AREA OF WRITING OFFICE. MATT AND DAVID SIT AT A TABLE ON WHICH ARE VARIOUS POTS OF YOGURT.

LUCAS: Strawberry yogurt.

WALLIAMS: (*smiling affirmatively at Lucas and nodding his head*) Yes, we've certainly had one of those.

LUCAS: Or raspberry?

WALLIAMS: Hmm.

LUCAS: Fudge even? (*Pause. Glances at Walliams.*) Or sometimes we don't even have yogurt. (*Both shake their heads.*)

Long pause. Lucas and Walliams smile awkwardly at the camera.

BRAGG: Do that anecdote you always do about how you met at the National Youth Theatre.

WALLIAMS: What? Christ, even I'm sick to death of that one. (*Long pause*) Do you want to see my cock?

BRAGG: What?

WALLIAMS: Do you want to see my cock? I'll show it to you.

BRAGG: What, no, I really don't think that's –

WALLIAMS: Go on, I'll just pop it out.

BRAGG: No, really, definitely –

WALLIAMS: I'll just get it out *a bit*. (*Fumbles with himself.*) There he is!

BRAGG: What? Jesus!

Cut.

INT. DRESSING ROOM OF LITTLE BRITAIN THEATRE TOUR. LUCAS'S DRESSING ROOM. HE IS HOLDING A CARD THAT SAYS 'GOOD LUCK' ON IT. WE FAINTLY HEAR PRE-SHOW SHOWBIZ HUBBUB FROM THE COR-RIDOR.

BRAGG: So here you are, playing to packed houses of schoolchildren right across the nation. How does it feel?

LUCAS: It's very interesting and pertinent you should ask that, as we're actually doing a book about precisely that.

WALLIAMS: Yes, I just think everyone out there just really wants to know how we're feeling right now, doing a tour, being on the telly, being in the papers, being so very, very popular. Matt and David. What are they feeling? What are they thinking?

BRAGG: Well, not to try to scoop your book too much, but what *are* you thinking?

WALLIAMS: Eh?

BRAGG: This thinking. What is it you think about?

Long pause.

WALLIAMS: There's, ah . . .

Long pause. Walliams and Lucas exchange looks.

LUCAS: Well, you spend quite a lot of time thinking about pretty ladies, don't you?

WALLIAMS: Not 'arf! (*mugging*).

Long pause.

LUCAS: The model for the book is *Feel* – by Robert Williams. Are you familiar with it?

BRAGG: No.

LUCAS: It's a chance to answer our critics. The ones who say we're just socialites doing jazz hands.

WALLIAMS: We don't do that. Not even a bit.

LUCAS: And anyway, where are the so-called victims? We haven't had a single letter of complaint from an incontinent old woman. I'm sure they're quite capable, if they're offended, of saying: 'Come on now, I'm an incontinent old woman, and I say no, that is wrong.' But they don't.

WALLIAMS: Exactly. Or take fat black women – please do! Eh? Not 'arf! (*Pause*) But, anyway, they're quite capable of speaking up for themselves. All the fat black women I've met – well, seen, I've seen some on the telly – they've all been pretty feisty. (*Pause*) Rusty Lee.

LUCAS: Rusty Lee. She had a right gob on her.

WALLIAMS: Ooh, Rusty Lee. Do you remember Rusty Lee?

LUCAS: We love Rusty Lee.

Pause.

LUCAS: A million plastic-figurine-buying children can't be wrong. So nay to the nay-sayers, that's what I say.

WALLIAMS: And if not, well . . . aaaahm gon' put a spell on you! (*Widens his eyes and glares at the camera in triumph.*)

LUCAS: (*chanting*) Mama Shakalakaboo! Mama Shakalakaboo!

BOTH: (*chanting*) Mama Shakalakaboo! Mama Shakalakaboo! MAMA SHAKALAKABOO! MAMA SHAKALAKABOO! MAMA SHAKALAKABOO!

Fade.

Stag weeks

Not just stuck with people from the office. But stuck with people from someone else's office. For a week. And they're off the leash and up for Fun with a capital 'Fun'.

Mere stag 'nights' now have the same quaint associations as powdered egg. 'I'm getting married in the morning . . .'? Not when you can sing: 'I'm getting married in about six months – just after I've shagged my way round half of the New Europe.' Let's face it, there's no more fitting way to see off your single status than by furthering a Baltic state's slide towards sex industry gangsterism.

Companies like Prague Piss-Up are finding much of Eastern Europe now ripe for exploitation. They've just launched the offshoot Tallinn Piss-Up – combining the two is a 'double-header'. In Tallinn now, any non-sex-related businesses are losing trade and being eaten up by criminal enterprises; to meet the demand, women are shipped in from Estonia's poor, depressed north-east to service Marcus from the office who is up for trying out some stuff he's seen on the internet.

This, increasingly, is the New European way: hordes of Elvises, hunting alcopops in packs, all hoping to service their Little Elvises. Love me tender? Thanks to the fantastic exchange rate, love me for not much tender at all. But what the staggie boys should bear in mind is that unbridled sensual delight does not necessarily lead to a life of total fulfilment. If it did, John Leslie would be king of the world. (And he's not.)

Nevertheless, it would still be much easier if they could compact the week's worth of stag activity back into one evening: a couple of hours of racing go-karts against strippers in Budapest casinos; then going for a curry with whores; that kind of thing.

At the start of the evening you could draw straws to see whose turn it is to come out as gay or be kidnapped.

Steak Bakes

Present a dilemma. I don't want to cast aspersions – but if you've got some top-quality steak, you're not going to go round putting it into what is essentially a flat pasty. That would be a waste. So I remain dubious.

Similarly, you're unlikely, generally, to bake steak. Who gets a nice piece of prime beefsteak and then pops it in the oven? It's not the done thing. Gregg's bake all their stuff – it's there in the name; Gregg's the Bakers. But is this just baking being taken too far? Baking taking an obsessive, some might say irrational, hold on Gregg? Like he's only one step away from baking soup or something?

I would firmly maintain that this product has been created purely because it rhymes: steak bake. (Gregg like rhymes: 'It's the way we bakes it that makes it.') Except – and, as you can see, I've given this some thought – for the existence of Pepper Steak Slices, Ginster's righteous take on the steak bake.

But I'm not sure we can take Ginster's word for it. They'll stick anything in a slice. Spicy chicken, mushrooms – I'm sure I even saw some broccoli in one once. Some Travelodges have a whole raft of Ginster's products in a big fridge in the foyer, in lieu of actual catering. There's stuff in there you'd never dream of. Stuff related to Scotch eggs in a sort of product-of-kissing-cousins sort of a way. Real fucked-up shit. So I rule the Steak Slice inadmissible.

'Stress-busting', the phrase

It's interesting that, in this day and age, you are even obliged to try to reduce your stress in an aggressive way.

Bust that stress! Get it down on the floor and really stick one on it! Faster! Really fuck it over! You're not good enough! You're not good enough! There isn't time! There isn't time!

Summer bodies

'Beach panic! Beach panic! Beach panic!'

Summer used to be a time to relax. To feel mellow and laid back, even. Enjoy a bit of sunshine. Beaches were often seen as the ideal places on which to enact such soothing operations. 'Life's a beach,' as the saying used to go. But now beaches are places of ungovernable paranoia, as young women are commanded to have 'summer bodies for the beach'.

You've got to get your body ready for summer. Don't, for fuck's sake, leave it to its own devices. That way lies ruin and derision. Which means, according to the women's magazines, getting in training in the middle of winter. Of course, tans tend to be at their best in autumn, when people start covering up. It's a fundamental flaw in this whole 'seasons' thing which we are now thankfully doing our level best to eradicate. By introducing artificial tans that make people look like they have covered themselves in toffee.

And it's not just tans, but having a toned belly, non-manky toenails, exfoliation, etc. This whole getting ready for summer is a bloody nightmare. But it's all important if you are not going to end the summer sad and lonely, with nothing to look forward to but winter and maybe autumn.

Superloos on trains

Don't work/not super.

Supermarket flowers

It's a hopeless and forlorn sort of concept, even before you consider their pre-supermarket life cycle: farmed in Colombia by sweated labour, backs to the sun and faces to the earth, wages – topped up with all the free toxic chemicals you can inhale – as pitiful as the blooms; all those wasted, wasted air miles to get them here. That's an oppressive enough litany for coal or iron ore, but for a flower?

Simply of itself, it's quite melancholic: supermarket flowers. In fact, I'm surprised somebody hasn't written a sad song incorporating the gift of supermarket flowers as the potent signifier of an empty, artificial relationship. It could be called 'Supermarket Flowers'.

If anyone now writes one, there'll be no legal comeback from me. It's the sadness I can't bear. That's all.

Surprise visits to Iraq

You would think Prime Minister Nouri al-Maliki might not be in need of any more surprises, what with trying to govern Iraq and all. But in June 2006, George Bush met al-Maliki during a trip to Baghdad that had been kept secret from everyone, including al-Maliki. Visiting the US Embassy for a video teleconference with Bush, he instead found himself being greeted by the leader of the free world in person. Surprise!

In photographs, al-Maliki was squirming like someone forced to shake hands with the man now sleeping with his wife. This ambush, after all, proved that Bush needed no permission to enter his country – why, it's practically America! A thought bubble above al-Maliki's head might have said: 'I wonder how you would take it if I entered your country unannounced. Would you freak? Oh, I rather think you would. I've got popularity issues enough here, without this doofus turning up.'

The Iraqis have probably learned by now to keep the biscuit cupboard well stocked, given the regularity of surprise visits from Western politicians. If it's not Bush, it's Condoleezza Rice or Donald Rumsfeld or Tony Blair or Dick Cheney or some other representative of the forces that aren't trying all that hard not to look like an occupation. Maybe after one too many of these visits, they will blow a fuse and burst: 'Look, why don't you just do it? If you like it here so much. You try running it. No? Really? Why not? You want to go home? Oh, really . . .'

Following the Bush visit, the Americans would soon surprise al-Maliki again. After the massacre at Haditha, which allegedly saw Marines responding to a casualty by killing 24 innocent civilians in cold blood, al-Maliki called the incident a 'horrible crime', adding that the occupying forces often showed 'no respect for citizens, smashing civilian cars and killing on a suspicion or a hunch'. The US response? White House press secretary Tony Snow said al-Maliki had been 'misquoted'. The hapless PM must have been awestruck. He thought he had said something, but he hadn't! Those crazy guys . . .

But his own government also has a couple of surprises in its arsenal: tens of thousands arrested with only 1.5% convicted of any crime; Finance Minister Bayan Jabr's alleged links to Shia death squads (taking the whole Iron Chancellor thing a shade too far). Other occupation shockers: rising deaths from malnutrition and preventable diseases. Electricity and water supplies worse than before the invasion. Half the workforce unemployed with many gaining their sole source of income from selling US Army-base junk on the streets (which is a metaphor but also real – inspired!) . . . All things considered, the last thing on the average Iraqi's shopping list is 'more surprises'.

Perhaps the ultimate punchline to all this: amid the notable non-rebuilding of the vast majority of Iraq, work on the new US Embassy is go, go, go! Building at the 104-acre complex on the banks of the Tigris (prime real estate many believe the US never paid for), known locally as 'George W's palace' (features: the biggest swimming pool in Iraq, a state-of-the-art gym, cinema, numerous US food-chain outlets), is officially a secret, but cranes filling the skyline give the game away. It's like, you know, the Iraq War was this massive folly, and here's an actual massive folly! (It's a metaphor but it's also real – again.)

Or maybe it will be put to good use, as George W's palace! Seriously, maybe as a last surprise for the Iraqi populace, on his retirement from the presidency, he will go and live among the people he has liberated from tyranny. Maybe between eating at the massive Pizza Hut and swimming in the biggest swimming pool in Iraq, he could go and stand next to the struggling Iraqi government as they try to quell the civil war, winking at them.

T

Tables which are in fact adverts

This amazing innovation from Coffee Republic sees, say, a large ad for the DVD of *Capote* encased in the tabletop – a circular ad covering all but a small border round the edge, laminated so as to repel spillage and righteous defacement.

Well, that's a relaxing pit stop, then. I had been hoping to slip an Americano and a brownie down my neck, rather than have an advertisement rammed down it with all the charm of a pissed wrestler.

This surely points the way to a bold new future. Have you considered putting adverts on the inside of the mugs? Tattooing the insides of patrons' eyelids? Threats of violence?

Talking, Big Conversations, 'open and honest debates', 'grown-up discussions', etc

Really, is it any wonder no eligible young people ever vote ever any more ever at all, not even some of them? Have you seen politics lately? Since 1997, those in charge have quite diligently sent out the message: 'Okay, we're taking the politics away now ... any thoughts, just pop them on the Big Conversation web-forum. Do we still have that? Oh no, that's right – these days it's "Let's Talk". As in "Let's Talk About

Sex Baby", the early 90s hit by Salt-N-Pepa . . . except that Let's Talk is no place for sex talk. Got that, kids?'

You can see where the alienation starts creeping in – it's when they open their mouths. Certainly, whenever I hear Patricia Hewitt talking, I do not hear someone remotely like anyone else I have ever met. I hear a countess made of metal. Which is a turn-off. It's a simple lesson that probably should be on the national curriculum: politics is now only open to those who have already achieved great things. Great things like working for an MP or a lobbyist. Or a think-tank. As for the electorate, just imagine a smiley giant in a yellow waterproof (a bit like a lollipop man) standing outside Parliament with his palm raised towards you, repeating: 'Nothing to see here . . . Move along . . . Nothing to see here . . .'

Luckily, some of the great and good (Brown, Cameron) are concerned about why young people hate their leaders (Brown, Cameron). The Power Commission, fronted by Helena Kennedy and Emma B off Radio 1, even had a Power Inquiry into why young people feel so powerless. Among the recommendations to solve the problem of young people not voting: lowering voting age to 16. To make, er, loads *more* young people not vote! And they did slightly miss the opportunity, I feel, to name their report: 'Why Do Young People Feel Powerless? I'll Tell You Why Young People Feel Fucking Powerless – It's Because They Are Powerless! Christ On A Bike . . .' That was just the draft title. (Other rejected titles included 'Jesus Wept' and 'NO–ONE–FUCKING–CARES'.)

It's true, though: the politics has been taken away from the populace – when many, many, many young people protest because they suspect that invading Iraq might not be the best idea ever, they are patted on the head and told to go home because they don't understand the reality of the situation.

And it's not just the electorate. The politics has been taken away from the party members, and the politics has even been taken away from the members of parliament: when 100 MPs wanted to recall parliament over Blair's refusal to call for a ceasefire in the Lebanon, they were ignored. If you're a member of parliament, in Parliament, the mother of all parliaments, and you're having the politics taken away from you, that's got to hurt.

And what of parliament? It's a mother. Of all parliaments. But is there such an amazing 'democratic tradition' to water down as we're led to believe? All adults, regardless of property or gender, have only had the right to vote for less than a hundred years. Last time I looked, the House of Lords was still there, and the civil service and the police were not democratically accountable to the people – but in fact to the very self-serving elite at the top of politics who are frantically trying to make themselves as unaccountable to the people as they can manage. So making democracy *less* democratic doesn't seem the way to go here.

Nevertheless, despite these reservations, in the spirit of participation, we some have further recommendations to get the young ones energised by the expected next general election contest between Cameron and Brown:

- having manifestos available on podcast read out by the Two Pints gang
- putting voting booths inside tanning salons
- replace party politicals with booty-bumping R&B videos to play on channels like Booty Bump Toons 4U

- have the leaders do a swear-off: Cameron says: 'Cock and balls!' Brown responds: 'Piss that shit up.'
- have a Faceparty (look up what that means)
- have a PCP orgy

Anyone who doesn't agree with these findings can feel free to write down their thoughts on a piece of paper and then burn that piece of paper.

Television on mobile phones
Far too small.

Testing children to make them clever
Tests used to be a way of seeing whether children were learning stuff rather than, say, just picking their noses and flicking it. Nowadays, children learn stuff so they can pass tests, so everyone can see that they are good at passing tests. If the first is the horse pulling the cart, the second is more like the cart pulling the horse and then making it sit a test.

Children are now made to sit tests on the morning they enter school. Then, in the afternoon, they are made to sit a test on what they have learned from that morning's test. Get that sandpit out of here! What do you think this is: fun? Or maybe we could test them on their sandpit abilities . . .

It's a testing situation. One which has intriguing ramifications for the nation's psyche. According to a 2004 report from the Qualifications and Curriculum Authority, Britain's education system is now so geared to cram-based learning that children have little 'reading stamina' for whole books. Reading a book from cover to cover? No chance. Not even a short one. (They were fine with turning over the paper, but . . .)

Thai-infused crisps

Now we know what those Thai families who live above pubs serving delicious meals through the evening get up to during the daytime. They tirelessly infuse crisps with their special 'fresh Thai spices'.

Brits have always loved crisps. And they increasingly love Thai food. So what's not to like about Thai food-flavoured crisps? This was presumably Walkers' thinking when it dipped into the market with their Sweet Thai Chilli Sensations. When this was matched by McCoys Specials' Thai Sweet Chicken, Walkers hit back with its most ambitious flavour yet: Gently Infused Lime and Thai Spices. (I'm not totally sure of the chronology, to be honest – I've been paying attention, but not that much.)

This flavour made plain that, when you infuse crisps with fragrant essence of Thai, roughness and hastiness will not do. Gentleness is the key. And, of course, 'freshness'. Those Charlotte Church Walkers ads make a big play of the 'fresh-ness' of the Thai spices that go into Walkers' Thai-infused crisps. Although I can't really see what's so great about fresh spices if you are then going to crush them up with salt and MSG before sprinkling them on crisps and vacuum-packing those crisps in foil packets. Crisp packets, in fact.

Chips in curry sauce? Now that works. Sort of.

Noodles in bags? Could work.

Sandi Thom

Yes, her internet-grassroots-word-of-mouth success was partly helped by words from the mouths of her PR company. Yes, she wishes she was a punk-rocker – but she hasn't got around to buying any of the right gear, so you do have to question her commitment on that score. Yes, the post-MySpace success of 'I Wish I Was A Punk Rocker (With Flowers In My Hair)' does make you question whether the whole kids-taking-over-the-music-industry revolution has altered things one iota.

But the truly fucked-up thing about Sandi Thom is her grasp on history. She studied at Liverpool's Institute of Performing Arts, but I'm saying those teachers filled her head with lies. Her hit's title expressed her urgent desire for a new youthquake to combine the punk and hippy movement legacies. But punks and hippies hated each other. You can't have punks with flowers in their hair. They wouldn't be punks. Flowers in the dustbin, that was more their thing. And not just when they were 'a bit over', either. And what are these new self-hating punk-hippies going to do? Gob on themselves?

Sandi Thom did her thesis on the history of popular music but her recall of dates is all over the shop. After all, wasn't revolution more strictly in the air in '68 rather than '69? Or maybe she is referring to the 1969 Green Revolution that brought Colonel Gadaffi to power in Libya.

Who knows?

Toy cars

Are aspirational these days. They're all big Mercs and Audi TTs. Visit any toy shop looking to gift-up a little person, and you'll find all the household names in the die-cast mini-motor universe – Matchbox, Siku, Hot Wheels – wholly obsessed with premium motors.

There's seemingly a ban on ordinary cars – the sort most people drive, the sort most children might ever see. No Mondeos or Yarises or Focuses or Kias – or even any Golfses or Lexi (that's the plural of Lexus, by the way). Xsara Picasso? Not on your giddy arse. The message: 'Hey, I know you think he's good, but sorry, kid, your dad's a loser.'

You'll be falling over huge delivery lorries branded with DHL or UPS logos, but searching high and low for an ambulance. You can still get fire engines – except they have to be either 40-foot long with 18 retractable ladders and called Flame Tamer, or have 'TURBO' written down the side.

What next? Conservatories for dolls' houses? Marbles made out of actual marble? My Little Gated Community? Doctors and Nurses could become Senior NHS Management Consultant and Drug Company Rep. Simon Says: 'Swarofski Rocks!'

Matchbox? You might as well call yourselves Hegemonising The Kids.

Trailers for programmes that are on the telly now

A blipvert trailer of a programme advertising the fact that said programme is on 'Next' or even 'Now' – that is, as soon as this trailer and the announcer announcing that the programme is starting get out of the way, the programme will start.

Surely trailers should trail programmes that will be on in the future, rather than those which are on in the present. I don't think of that as a complicated point.

Donald Trump

US *Apprentice* supremo Donald Trump – and this is true – claims he grows those amazing trademark eyebrows *on purpose*. They are alpha-male stag antlers designed to intimidate opponents in negotiations. Okay, but what about the stupid hair?

Big Don has a holiday website called – and this is equally true – www.gotrump.com.

He also has a property website called www.parp.org. Okay, he hasn't. But gotrump is real. In fact, I'd highly recommend listening to Trump's welcome speech on the homepage, where he shouts at you like an evangelical car salesman pumped up on sales after a sales seminar at a power-selling away-day: 'There's nobody better – there's nobody even close.'

Advanced megalomania – that definitely puts me in the holiday mood. Although I would be even more enthusiastic if they had animated the eyebrows.

TV sponsorship slots

Once upon a time, there was a clear delineation between the television and the adverts. The television programmes would stop and then Nanette Newman would try to sell you dish-washing stuff. Then *Shine on Harvey Moon* would come back on. But now there's television sponsorship slots: the bits in between the shows and the ads which are actually more ads, but somehow more parasitic and insinuating.

These ads are virtually eating their way into the pro-grammes, which can make the relationship between the two feel quite disorientating. There's *Mums on Strike* (the reality show where mum fucks off to a spa, leaving dad in charge – with often HILARIOUS results) being sponsored by Bernard

Matthews Turkey Ham Slices, like that's the stuff to really help teary mums through the day. Processed turkey cut into very, very thin slices. Or the weather coming to you from Powergen – neatly pointing up the link between energy usage and the climate doing a breakdance.

Weirder still, *The Simpsons* on Sky is sponsored by Domino Pizza and on Channel 4 was until recently sponsored by Pizza Hut. You thought *The Simpsons* quite explicitly satirised the brain-dead excesses of American junky food – as represented by such outlets like, well, Pizza Hut. But no, apparently Homer is a role model who should inspire us to declare: 'Hmm, I'll have some of what he's having . . . Hello, yes. Pizza Hut? I get *how many* items with the Coronary Fuck-Bucket? I'm in! D'oh!'

The 118–118 twins are of course much-loved comic characters – in their own diseased minds. There you are, watching *ER*: it's quite emotional; a man has of course died; nothing is going well for anyone. Then a kiddie gets shot. Oh, and now here are two freaky cackchops scraping chairs along the floor saying, 'Noi, noi, noi!' If that doesn't inspire you to ring directory enquiries, I don't know what will. ('Yeah, I'd like the number for the 118 guys. Oh, this is the number, is it? They're out running? Could you just tell them that the avenger is coming for them. That's right. I'm going to fuck them up. Thanks . . .')

Is there any way the mutton-chopped athleticists could be any more annoying? Maybe if they broke into your house and shouted, '118—118!' at you while you were having sex. That might do it.

What next? Product placement *within* the actual programmes?! I ask you!

Two Pints ... out-takes shows

Lazy telly. Even by the standards of telly.

And how do they decide which takes to use for the real show? Do they just keep going for take after take until they get one that is resolutely unfunny? 'Mark it! That's the one!'

U

'Über', the prefix

As in 'über-trendy', 'über-cool', 'über-stylish' and, of course, 'übergruppenführer'.

The question we must always ask ourselves before embarking on any leisure activity is: will this put me in a higher social position than my contemporaries? Otherwise, what's the point? After all, it's not a game.

These days, you can read an 'über-hip novel' surrounded by 'über-cool kids' in an 'über-flash drinking environment'. You can mix it on the high-end ski slopes with the 'über-stylish powder hounds'. Or dine at Mayfair's 'über-trendy' Umu restaurant, spending a hundred quid a head (which is in no way 'über-priced'). Or you can leave 'cattle class' and use private hospitals to become (according to *Times* writer Janice Turner) an 'über-consumer'.

Surprisingly often, cutting an 'über-dash' means flashing some 'über-cash'. And, logically, if one is not an 'über' then one is, dismally, an 'unter'. You never pay a hundred quid a head for your dinner? That's sad. It's probably not your fault, but you really do deserve to be enslaved. Are there any railways that still need building?

Stratifying humans into 'unders' and 'overs' seems a satisfyingly simple way of dividing society. And don't we all like simple ideas? But sometimes it gets tricky. One recent *Sunday*

Times news analysis piece referred to Neets (people not in education, employment or training) as 'a class of über-chavs'.

But surely that's weird. Shouldn't people who are more chavvy than your average chav be lower down the pecking order and so, logically, 'unter-chavs'?

Or maybe Britain's poorest and least educated are so grimly barbarous that they attain a new power. Yes, that's it. I see now. Neets are a super-strength mutation – like the Uruk-hai to the Orcs!

Is this how elements of the British mediocracy really think? Of course not!

As a necessary interlude in proceedings, here are some Christmas-cracker jokes:

Q: Where can one go to buy racially pure vegetables?
A: From the über-market!

Q: What was the racially superior Swedish pop sensation called?
A: Über!

Q: What is the racially pure Welsh market town situated near the English border?
A: Übergavenny!

I could go on.

'Übersexual', the phrase
Sadly, not all 'über' talk refers to innate superiority deriving from income banding. It's sometimes more fatuous than that.

In late 2005, advertising company JWT decided there was a new, higher form of man: the 'übersexual'. New York 'trendspotter' Marian Salzman (the company's executive vice-president and director of strategic content) even wrote a book about it (yes, you can write books about anything these days).

In *The Future of Men* she killed off 'metrosexuals', the poofy, preening straight men who were once hailed as the future of men (Salzman invented them, too). Their replacements – the 'übermen' – are very much the best men. 'The descriptor "über" was chosen because it means the best, the greatest,' says Salzman. 'Übersexuals are the most attractive (not just physically), most dynamic, and most compelling men of their generations.' Verily, these people shit confidence.

'Übersexuals' look after themselves, but not obsessively so. They care, but they have muscles and sometimes whiff of things that aren't grooming products. In case you are wondering, she doesn't mention the size of their willies – that poignant issue is left hanging, as it were.

Clearly, she needed other examples apart from George Clooney. Here are some of them:

Er . . . there's Donald Trump ('a man who is certain about what he wants and sets out to get it, no holds barred'), Bill Clinton ('a supremely confident, decisive leader. And he has supremely sexy hands'), Arnold Schwarzenegger ('He has succeeded in every challenge he's faced'*), and – we promise you this not made up, not even a bit – Guy Ritchie!

So let's just clarify: Guy Ritchie is allegedly one of the 'most attractive (not just physically), most dynamic, and most compelling men' of his generation. Okay, he was only at number nine in Salzman's top 10, but still . . . If you are lauding a near-perfect new breed of man and Guy Ritchie is one of your prime examples, you might be well advised to throw your own head off at the hopelessness of it all. But no. Apparently, 'gravitating toward strong women tends to be an über trait'. As is, presumably, being able to put up with abject ridicule from the moment you wake until the moment you fall asleep.

Of course, Arnie had 'sexy hands' too. That's 'sexy' as in hands that – according to numerous allegations – could not be in the vicinity of women's breasts without 'decisively', 'dynamically' and 'compellingly' grabbing hold of them.

Superman returns!

UK Music Hall of Fame, the

The UK Music Hall of Fame is a bloody liar. Inducting the Eurythmics in 2005, Bob Geldof bigged up Annie Lennox's voice before adding that it was 'redundant to point out Dave Stewart's virtuosity as a musician of a higher order, one that immediately makes him one of our greatest guitar players'.

There are hoary blues guitarists touring the pubs of West Yorkshire who are greater guitarists and generally musicians of a 'higher order' than Dave Stewart.

The UK Music Hall of Fame is also a bloody fraud. Because it is just *based* in the UK. It's not about UK music. I'm not saying there needs to be one for UK music – because there doesn't; we're busy. I'm just wondering what the fucking difference is to the Rock and Roll Hall of Fame, from which the concept is borrowed. How many halls of fame do Bob Marley and Elvis need to be inducted into exactly?

Or is it all just an excuse to remind people of the existence of Dave 'higher order' Stewart?

What is this? The UK Music Hall of Titty Beards?

Understanding business

Everyone thinks we should 'understand business'. We have no business not understanding business. We should very much make it our business. To understand business. Personally, I make it my business scrupulously to avoid business. But that's my business.

Gordon Brown wants 14-to-16-year-olds to understand business by attending Enterprise Summer Schools, where they forgo any summer-job cash opportunities to attend a kind of business boot camp. (Gordon Brown has never met any 14-to-16-year-olds. Not even when he was fourteen to sixteen.) Here, they will look at pie charts. All summer.

Sir Alan 'Sir Alan' Sugar wants business to be taught in schools from an early age. Talking to one interviewer, he read from an imaginary Janet-and-John-style book that he keeps in his head: 'Mummy gets £100 a week from Daddy because Daddy goes to work.' (Mummy eventually ends up bashing Daddy about the head because he's 'never there'. Daddy, it transpires, has been spending those evenings when he claimed he was Auditing entertaining Clients at Strip Clubs. Then Daddy robs the Pension Fund. Actually, now I think of it, I don't think Sir Alan 'Sir Alan' Sugar's story continued quite like that.)

It seems that nobody these days considers business to be a very boring thing that other people do. In olden days, at least business types marketed themselves as dull but necessary. Now they have to be fun and sexy, too. All those boardroom pay rises must be going to their heads. If the opening credits of *Dragons' Den* are to be believed, it's got quite a lot to do with waterskiing.

In *The Apprentice*, according to the *Sunday Times*, Sir Alan 'Sir Alan' Sugar 'made business look sexy' (I'm having difficulty again!). Certainly, *The Apprentice* contestants appear to think Sugar is not a prat but some kind of elemental warlord – like the hero in a Kurosawa epic.

But other businesspeople say this is wrong, that Sugar is a prat after all and that he might lead people to misunderstand business. 'Young people will be turned off because they think they will be shouted at by a horrible, fat, old, rich bloke,' said former CBI overlord Digby Jones (a fat, horrible, old, (quite) rich bloke).

One thing I have learned from *The Apprentice* is that even people who are really into business don't understand it. Most of the contestants haven't got a fucking clue. About anything. Set them a simple task like 'go and buy these items in London for the cheapest price' and they will flap around like an elderly person suddenly commanded to drive Formula One. Unless I'm missing something and one key business skill involves being fairly average but shouting loudly that you are, in fact, not average. 'Average? Me?! Get out of here! I'm the best. I know I'm fucking everything up and no one likes me, but I'm the kind of guy who gets things done and can get on with anybody. Buy stuff, people! Buy stuff!'

Aspiring businesspeople being numpties brings us neatly to *Dragons' Den*. Or, as we like to call it in our house, 'Please God no, please don't tell me she's mortgaged her house and ploughed it all into the Solar Travel Juicer. She's got kids.'

Dragons' Den unintentionally completely destroys the Thatcherite dream. On the one hand, we have the poor, deluded hopefuls who really believe that by giving it a go, they will enter the bright, goodies-strewn world of entrepreneurialism, rather than just get eaten alive. And then we have the Dragons – and a more charmless bunch of bastards you'd struggle to assemble.

Ah, but no. They are heroes. A bit like, er, rock stars. Duncan Bannatyne is so keen to propagate business, he has founded a magazine, *The Sharp Edge*. One editorial summed up the key things to remember about being in business. There were only three points. And two of them were 'remember to have fun'. That would be where the waterskiing comes in, then.

Bannatyne says business involves 'tough challenges (as tough as the notorious ridge in the Lake District which shares my magazine's name). And to cut it on your own takes a sharp edge too: quick thinking needs hard decisions.' In a few lines, he drops four heroic adjectives – 'tough', 'sharp', 'quick' and 'hard' – which rather suggests sex as imagined by a 13-year-old boy who still plays war.

The Sharp Edge magazine also featured a glossy spread on the potential rewards of flogging your guts out for years at a stretch (bigger watches, basically).

Peter Jones, meanwhile, refers to himself as an 'ultra-preneur'. The hideous yellow mansion featured in the credits with the stone lions on the gates? That's his ultrahouse. Architecture and social critic Jonathan Glancey called it 'Kentucky fried Georgian'.

So let's get all the young people down to Uncle Gordon's boot camp. They can practise foreclosing and workplace bul-lying for a bit, then Duncan Bannatyne can come and give a lecture. He would glare at them with those big eyes of his, before declaring: 'I bet you want a watch as big as mine. Oh look, time for waterskiing.'

Unnecessary digitisation

Virgin's new Pendolino trains have special tiny screens set

into the carriage walls just above the windows, telling you whether seats 045 and 046, say, are AVAILABLE or, conversely, NOT AVAILABLE.

The screens are tiny. The carriage lights are set into the wall just above them – and thus shine directly over the faint LED lettering, which sits on/merges into a light grey-green background. Even with 20/20 vision, you have to squint to read them, leaning in right over the top of the double-seat.

So maybe a more efficient, faster, easier method of discerning whether a seat is AVAILABLE or NOT AVAILABLE would be to look at the seat and decide whether there is someone sitting in it. (Or, conversely, NOT SITTING IN IT.) Old-fashioned, perhaps, but less likely to require the utilisation of binoculars.

Digital scales, meanwhile: the only people who need those are Heston Blumenthal and drug dealers. By which, we don't mean to imply that Heston Blumenthal has anything to do with drugs. It's just his food that's on drugs.

He pricks each chip individually to let the steam out. But he's not on drugs.

Unnecessary greetings cards

'For my wife . . . On Mother's Day'. Such messages are presumably intended to carry the subtext: 'For my wife – on Mother's Day, because, as you know, I tend to think of you as my mother'. Or maybe: 'Because I love you in much the same way as I love my mother'. In either case, don't expect a nice cup of tea.

I didn't realise Mother's Day meant giving cards to every woman in my acquaintance. How about: 'For my childless female friend, the one without kids, on Mother's Day, because you have the potential to be a mother – which is a great and beautiful thing. (Even though you do, as I think we have discussed before, get a bit irritating when you've had too much to drink.)'

'Congratulations on your divorce'. Presumably comes with the message: 'Roses are red/Violets are blue/You didn't get the house/But you did get the canoe . . .'

'Here's wishing you a happy St George's Day'. Great. A card which more or less suggests that I am a fascist.

Not forgetting:

'Congratulations on your teeth-whitening.'

'Happy Prom, princess.'

And, of course: 'Commiserations on the death of the life-partner you stole from me. Rot in hell, you fuck.'

Unofficial 'sponsors' of sporting events

It is one of the finest memories of 2006: settling down to watch a World Cup match with a newly opened tin of World Cup SPAM. What do you mean you didn't eat World Cup SPAM? It was the World Cup, for Christ's sake – when else are you going to eat World Cup SPAM? Wimbledon? During the Open? That's golf!

World Cup SPAM was, of course, just regular SPAM with the words 'World Cup' added to the label. It wasn't individually tailored for different countries: no 'Come on England/Croatia/Ghana/Deutschland über Alles' SPAM; just generic, all-inclusive World Cup SPAM. 'Now you can enjoy SPAM® in match-time sandwiches, on pizzas and in salads or straight from the barbecue as a SPAMBURGER® Hamburger!'

If you didn't wish to spend your half-time devouring

SPAM salad, there were many other unofficial 'sponsors' of the event, alongside the official FIFA-endorsed tat-hawking industry which raked in over a billion dollars.

Then there was 'in-urinal entertainment', as the promotional material for Wee Goals had it – Wee Goals being small plastic goalmouths with a ball dangling off them that sit in pub urinals so men can wee on them.

'The ball dangles tantalisingly from the crossbar of the Wee Goal. This is irresistible to the male of the species.'

It's 'your own wee beautiful game'. But there's a serious side, too: 'The good news being that the newfound focus on aiming reduces spillage, making the job of cleaning a lot less challenging . . . Obviously the urinal mat prevents foreign objects, such as cigarette butts and chewing gum, from clogging up the urinal – another urinal goal shared by many in the hospitality industry.'

It was an international festival of cashing-in in slightly odd ways. Manchester's Piccadilly Station boasted of being a venue in which to watch the match. It is certainly easy to get to – by train.

One Japanese restaurant in Camden, London, filled its window with a sign exhorting us to: 'CELEBRATE THE WORLD CUP WITH A TAKEAWAY!' This was audacious: beyond simply pointing out that, if you are watching the football, you will be less inclined to cook, so why not enjoy some of their prawn tempura. It was more than that: it was positing a direct causal connection between buying a takeaway and vicariously participating in a sporting event that was taking place hundreds of miles away. As John Motson put it during his commentary on the Germany–Argentina game: 'What a festival of sport. I expect they'll all be eating udon soup noodles in north London tonight, Mark . . .'

On the same busy road as the Japanese restaurant was a sauna/massage parlour displaying the handwritten sign: 'Come and watch the World Cup in our climate-controlled premises.' Don't know if they offered 'extras'. Maybe when it went to extra time? Or, as Motson put it: '. . . and then I expect they'll continue the celebrations by being wanked off by a stranger for money, Mark.'

But the best, and also the darkest, unofficial tie-in was the German undertaker who offered a discount for the duration of the tournament. Which full-blooded Englishman facing bereavement wouldn't want to capitalise on that? 'All I'm saying is – and I know everyone's upset and all that, but if you look at it rationally, if you just look at the facts for a minute, what I'm saying is – if we took Grandad out there to be buried, we could spend the considerable saving on, you know, tickets for a game.'

'Hello? How much? Is that all? Great. Of course, he was almost buried out there before, during the, erm . . . See you on Thursday. Come on England!'

The Times said the World Cup is not even about football but about 'the expression of a wondrous web of personal, national and geo-political plotlines that weave into an intoxicating drama'. How true, and nothing evokes this heady global spirit like processed meat, piss and death.

US versions of UK reality shows

Dancing on Ice becomes *Skating with Celebrities*, what with the original being too hard to understand.

V

'Various Things To Do Before You Die' lists

Whole series of listy travel books convey the message: 'Don't die before seeing Borneo. For then, you will not have lived.'

Or even The Menai Straits. The Menai Straits! Look, I've seen the Menai Straits, and I can honestly say I could have easily lived without seeing them. They were okay but, well, I haven't been back – which kind of says it all. I could see Anglesey on the other side. It was okay.

'Unforgettable Things To Do Before You Die'? Although there is not much point doing something 'unforgettable' just 'before you die' because you won't actually have too much opportunity to forget it. Maybe a subtitle should point out that: 'You might want to do them a while before you die, otherwise their unforgettable nature might be somewhat wasted on you.'

Of course, another way of saying 'Things To Do Before You Die' is 'Things To Do While You're Still Alive', which rather goes without saying, unless we are to assume that there are loads more boxes to tick off of 'Things To Do After We Have Stopped Living'.

The primary thing about these kinds of lists is . . . look, it's not going to happen. And if it did happen, you would quite clearly, and quite tragically, have set about methodically experiencing life with the spontaneous zeal of a solicitor's desk clerk catching up on invoices, which rather defeats the life-seizing object you are seeking to convey.

I don't want to die.

Village People, the, not being gay

In 2005 the Village People's lawyer protested that the whole gay thing surrounding the group was a travesty of the truth. The lawyer has decided the members need a more 'mainstream' image and barred inclusion of their songs in an upcoming gay rights documentary.

This is a bit rich, seeing as their hits included 'YMCA', which said: 'Get some bumming at the YMCA.' And 'In the Navy', which exhorted listeners to: 'Get some bumming in the navy.'

A little known fact is that, after their first flush of success, the boyz tried to update their sound. The 1981 album *Renaissance* (and this is 100% true) saw them morph into a hideous electro-pop outfit, styled as New Romantics. I hesitate to suggest you look up the pictures on the internet, so just try to imagine, instead of the Cop, the Indian or the Construction Worker, a black Steve Strange with a moustache/goatee combo standing with his legs apart, crotch thrust forward, like . . . well, like a member of the Village People.

And is this lawyer also maintaining that the New Romantic Village People weren't gay?

Jeremy Vine

In recent years, Jeremy Vine has evolved from the post-punk Paxo into 'The Man Who Lets Middle England Have Its Say'.

A media agency poll recently put him alongside David Cameron and Carol Thatcher as being 'Widely regarded as having a thoroughly modern middle-class touch.' This could be interpreted as: 'He seems pleasant enough, but is quite happy to host phone-ins about yobs not being hanged enough'.

Anyone still harbouring fears that the BBC has a left-wing bias should be directed towards Vine's show on Radio 2. It certainly sounds like left-wing, or even vaguely liberal, views are vetted with a precision that would make Joe McCarthy proud. If Vine had any scruples, he would shout at the callers: 'What do you think this is? Fuckwit FM?'

But the parading of tedious Middle England bigotry isn't the worst thing about *The Jeremy Vine Show*. A recent poll hoped to find the song with the most power to change people's lives. Listeners voted online for their ultimate life-changing track from a list of nominations that included: 'God Only Knows' by the Beach Boys, 'Chorus of the Hebrew Slaves' by Verdi, Jeff Buckley's 'Hallelujah', Aretha Franklin's 'Say a Little Prayer' and 'Imagine' by John Lennon. The winner, though, was Pink Floyd's *Dark Side of the Moon*. The album.

Vine said: '*Dark Side of the Moon* won hands down. People just love it. For its mammoth sense of scale and all the invention, it's still wonderful.'

Its mammoth sense of scale? Certainly, next to the other contenders it is likely to appear mammoth. That's because it's an album. With something like twelve songs on it.

Pink Floyd vocalist and guitarist David Gilmour was thrilled: 'It's fantastic. What can I say except be thrilled?'

Well, how about: 'Look, this is all dreadfully embarrassing – not as embarrassing as my solo albums, but really bloody well quite embarrassing. You see, *Dark Side of the Moon* is not a song, it's an album. Why don't you give the award for the song that has the power to change people's lives to, well, a song? One of mine off *The Wall*, say. Or 'No More Lonely Nights' by Paul McCartney. I played the guitar solo, you know. Toodles!'

Vittel Bottle Archery

Vittel Bottle Archery billboards ('ReVittelising the city') appeared like a creeping stain in summer 2006, encouraging fractious commuters to have cooling fun by taking premium water – which been pumped out of the French earth, bussed to Blighty, kept cold at all times and served in fancy plastic bottles that can't practically be reused – and spraying it at each other.

Of course, Vittel Bottle Archery can be played 'ONLY with the new Vittel bottle . . . Players MUST use the 750ml quick-release cap for speed, and special squeezy grips to increase shooting distance.'

With one point for a hit, it's fun for all the family. If all the family happen to be preposterous, trivial wankers.

Water is an increasingly charged issue: with the Chinese frantically re-rerouting rivers from the south to the north in a gigantic engineering project to boost declining supplies; Bolivian social movements fighting pitched battles in the streets to stop Surrey-based water companies (backed by Labour) tripling prices; real droughts and British pretend droughts caused by water leaking from pipes that simply can't be fixed because, well, there's a pricey fat-cat lunch to pay for. So . . . using energy to extract, bottle and transport water, and then squirting it away for fatuous fun is a symbol. For something or other.

One particularly vigorous proponent of archery was, of course, Henry VIII. During his reign, he made practising it mandatory for all men of fighting age and banned all other sports on Sundays. He also liked big lunches (his waistline was 56 inches) and thoroughly enjoyed wasting stuff: like wives.

W

Web 2.0

Haven't finished reading the first one yet.

Wembley

Far be it from me to have concerns about national pride, but when Jon Bon Jovi is righteously laying into the competence of our construction projects, lo, we may have pause for shamed thought. If the permed warbler, a cowboy, on a steel horse he rides, denounces the failure to complete the new Wembley Stadium on time as 'a shambles', surely even the most liberal and internationalist among us must momentarily reflect upon Stephenson's *Rocket* and Monty?

The Jovi, having played the last gig at the old Wembley, were due to open the new one in high style – that is, by playing 'Bad Medicine'. But the gig had to be cancelled as the almost a billion-pounds stadium languished unfinished. Blaze of Glory it was not.

Jon Bon Jovi lamented: 'I'm broken-hearted – it's a shambles.'

Not to take his pain in vain, one amusing side-effect of the Wembley farrago was that the bookies managed to mug themselves completely over the issue.

When Multiplex announced there was only a 70% chance of the stadium hosting the 2006 FA Cup final on 13 May, Irish firm Paddy Power opened a book on whether the new stadium would be ready in time. More than 60 workers from the Wembley site placed bets that it wouldn't – with nearby Paddy Power branches taking wagers totalling around £10,000 in just two days before betting was suspended.

A Paddy Power spokesperson said: 'I suppose we should have reacted quicker when we saw men in hard hats placing big bets in the Wembley area.'

Bon Jovi, who were not implicated in the betting scandal, played in Milton Keynes instead.

Here's that FA mismanagement timeline in full:

1994: FA bigwigs convene to discuss crumbling national stadium. Should they rebuild Wembley, which nobody can get to, not even if they live in Kilburn? Or should they whack up a new stadium near Birmingham that everyone in the country could reach quickly? After two and a half hours of heated debate, talks stall. It's time for lunch.

1995: Lunch.

1996: Lunch.

1997: Action! Ah, no, lunch.

1998: Coffee, petits fours.

1999: FA bigwigs finally announce decision. Wembley will be demolished, then rebuilt at a cost of £475 million. Internationally renowned architect Sir Norman Foster is asked to knock up one of his fancy building doodles. He's told the plans should also feature an athletics track, accommodation just like Chelsea FC's successful hotel venture Vacancies, and a fountain spouting free beer.

2000: An independent assessor has a quick look at internationally renowned architect Sir Norman Foster's plans. He spots that many of the 90,000 seats would have restricted views, while the roof would cover only three of the proposed athletic track's eight lanes, rendering any race ever run in the rain a total farce. Foster is told to bugger off and come back with a better plan, one which doesn't bother with the hotel or the running track, and includes seats that face the pitch.

2001: Plans in. They'll do. Multiplex contracted to do the job on the basis of a two-page letter which reads, 'We will build big building.' Demolishing work begins. Building work signally does not. Cost of project now £660 million.

2002: Builders begin construction . . . of nine-skin spliffs as they sit around doing sod all. Well, the ones who aren't queuing up outside the bookies to take the 9/1 on Wembley not being completed by 2005 are, anyway. Cost of project now £900 million.

2003: Builders decide to 'make good' by putting down some hard hats for goal posts and making 'stands' out of three old sofas and an armchair that they found in a nearby skip. 'Will this do?' they ask.

2004: FA bigwigs discuss whether it will do.

2005: Lunch.

2006: Germans host World Cup, utilising five brand-new stadiums, including the tastefully refurbished Olympiastadion in Berlin and Munich's showpiece Allianz Arena, which cost £190 million, is made from 2,874 hi-tech panels which change colour to reflect who is playing at the time, and took about a fortnight to construct. Meanwhile, at Wembley, some bricks have been placed on top of one another, making quite a high pile of bricks, actually.

Football Association? You Give Great British Construction Projects a Bad Name.

William, King, Court of

What do we really know about our future king? Well, we know that, as the eldest son of the eldest son of the sovereign, his arms are differenced by a label of three points unlike the arms of other grandchildren of the sovereign (if granted) which are differenced by a label of five points. That much is certain. But what do we know of William, the man. Is he a prince among men? Well, yes, he's a prince. But what else?

We know he's in the army, but isn't mad keen on the colour scheme: 'Everything is khaki this and khaki that,' he told a pal, who then told a newspaper. 'It's all completely army.'*

We know that when things get a bit army in the army, he passes the time by dressing up as a 'chav', tipping up to a Sandhurst party wearing a tracksuit and hilarious 'bling jewellery', which is popular among his less wealthy future subjects. As a 'source' told the *Sun*: 'It's not often you see the heir to the British throne trying to put on a silly accent while dressed as a chav.'

We know – because he told Ant and Dec, which is the closest thing we have to a constitution – that the geography graduate (no sniggering) likes *The X-Factor*, *I'm a Celebrity . . .*, *Pop Idol* and, particularly, *American Pop Idol*. Well, to be fair, it's the only way he'll ever get to vote for anyone.

We know that the future King Bill is a 'die-hard traditionalist' (royal biographer Brian Hoey) in thrall to his grandmother ('what the Queen says, William does'). So the prospects of any self-imposed scaling down into a European-style bicycling monarchy looks thin – unless you mean accidentally on purpose cycling over some foxes.

But what of William's future court? Through the ages, princes have used their boundless power and riches to suck the greatest talents of their generation, the science-and-arts movers and shakers, into their orbit. William hasn't done that.

One of his best mates, Guy Pelly, eschews all arts, with the exception of the art of getting his bits out. This serial exposer (hobbies: 'impersonating the Queen and mooning') has the nickname 'The Naughty Waiter'. This is not much to do with waiting – although he did work as one in Acton for a bit. No, it's more about being 'naughty'. Yes, It's a Right Royal Cockout whenever Guy's about. The twat.

Another close mate is James Murray Wells. He's 'thrusting' (*ES* magazine), having made a fortune in online spectacles. Which doesn't mean spectacles in the Guy Debord/ Situationist sense. He's not following the 60s French thinker's example and seeking to strip away the illusions of heartless modernity to bring bourgeois society crashing to its knees. No, he just sells glasses.

Murray Wells, 'a joker' often found 'frolicking' with The Naughty Waiter, broke his leg on Christmas Eve 2005 when trying to climb into a girls' boarding school in Westonbirt with Pelly – 'on the hunt for skirt'. There wasn't any skirt, though, with it being the school holidays. The twat. And, if there had been any skirt, it would have been the skirt of a schoolgirl, presumably fairly perturbed at being woken by a couple of pissed assholes, one of whom was probably naked. The twats.

You will be pleased to hear that William's 'good Christian' mucker Natasha Rufus Isaacs – when not 'working at Sotheby's and nipping around town in her Audi' – 'brings some much-needed Bible-study to the Court'. Does she bring up the bit about everyone having to give up their riches to enter the Kingdom of Heaven? Not sure that she does.

Other great mates include polo-playing, 'chiselled' Luke Tomlinson, one of Otis Ferry's comrades in storming Parliament to defend fox hunting. Undermining democracy in the name of bloodlust? It's what the great British monarchy is all about!

William's girlfriend Kate Middleton – 'a "boys" girl' – is apparently 'one of the few women who find William's boorish sense of humour amusing'. This raises the slightly terrifying possibility that, of the brothers, Harry is not the boorish one. And what's with all these women not finding the future king's shit jokes funny? Are they stuck up or what?

And there we have it, the Court of William: a load of hoorays sitting around bullying women, occasionally reading the Bible but mostly just watching *The X-Factor*. Casting thousands of votes with *our money* while one of them keeps getting his cock out 'for a laugh'.

God Save the King!

*The British monarchy has a long and noble tradition of going all 'army'. Henry V, obviously, and Richard the Lionheart, who was so 'army' that he kept going to war against his father in league with his brothers, then going to war against his brothers with his father. If things ever looked like going a bit 'not army', he'd fuck off to the Middle East to slaughter Muslims. He was a bit like Wayne Rooney in the World Cup: if you didn't let him have a war, he would only start injuring himself in training. Sometimes, the monarchy goes a bit 'navy'. George V went so 'navy' that he got loads of tattoos and a parrot. In more recent times, Prince Philip served on battleships in the Second World War, and was present at the Japanese surrender in 1945. 'Come on, you slitty-eyed nippos, sign!' is *not* what he found himself shouting uncontrollably at the ceremony.

Willyoujoinus.com

Willyoujoinus.com wants to get everyone together under one umbrella, in a friendly environment inside the same environmentally friendly tent – academics, eco-warriors, Lenny Henry. A counter on the home page shows the number of barrels of oil and gas consumed globally during your visit. And let me tell you, it's loads. That counter's whizzing away. There are loads of scary stats on there, and a moderated discussion board on which you can get really quite worried. Oh, and it's been put up by Chevron. The oil company. The one that sells oil.

At first, I wasn't sure whether they wanted us to join them in donating hundreds of thousands of dollars to Arnold Schwarzenegger and the California Republicans who in turn coincidentally forgot their promises to regulate the oil company's activities more tightly. Or whether they needed help, after buying Texaco, in maintaining their massive legal/PR offensive against a class action from the people of the Ecuadorian Amazon, where, after destroying vast areas of pristine rainforest, Texaco left behind 600 open toxic-waste pits that continue to leak into the watertable, producing what Amazon Watch has christened the 'Rainforest Chernobyl'. Or even whether they wanted us to join them in being implicated in the murder of protesters in Nigeria. But no, apparently they've got all that covered.

It really is all about joining them to save the planet. And who could do more in the global struggle against rapacious cash-hungry behemoths plundering the Earth than the very rapacious cash-hungry behemoths that are doing all the plundering? They're ideally placed. All they need to do is have a quiet word with themselves and bish, bash, bosh – teepees!

We're all pushing in the same direction here, and that can only be a good thing. The coming century is undoubtedly going to be a stretch – in terms of energy, water, etc; there's a lot of shit to sort out here. Who can we rely on to sort things out equitably and without major bloodshed? Well, how about the oil industry? When have they let us down before?

These people have money to burn, too – always a boon in times of need. Shell and BP both recently notched up £10-

billion-plus profits (all of which would be wiped out if the social and environmental costs of their emissions were taken into account). And BP cares so much it has even changed its name – from British Petroleum to Beyond Petroleum – to highlight its commitment to clean energy. Okay, the company is currently under investigation by a grand jury over the spillage of 1.2 million litres of crude at the Prudhoe Bay field, the largest ever in Alaska's North Slope region – which doesn't exactly scream cleanliness. But don't worry, because 'recently appointed head of BP's US operations, Robert Malone, has made cleaning up the firm's public image a top priority' . . . Er, surely cleaning up the oil should be the top priority?

BP has also recently explored buying large chunks of the controversial, some believe semi-criminal, Russian oil group Rosneft, whose flotation would – according to lawyers representing the Yukos oil group – turn the London Stock Exchange into a 'thieves' bazaar'. If they are right, this would potentially see BP embracing the brave new world of money-laundering and gangsterism. Money-laundering? That's definitely moving beyond petroleum.

So what of that carefully sculpted ethical petrochemical image? A company source explained: 'If you took all your decisions on the basis of reputational risk, you would never do anything.'

Sometimes never doing anything might be preferable. Like all of us, the oil giants' minds are heavily concentrated on the melting polar ice-caps, the crumbling ecosystems, the livelihoods destroyed. Unlike the rest of us, though, their response has involved making immediate plans to start drilling for newly accessible oil under the North Pole: 'Come on guys, let's get Klondyke! Let's pump all the oil out . . . and burn it!'

And no one in the boardroom lets out a sustained yell of

primal pain then throws themself out of the window, leaving tufts of bloodied charcoal wool suit on the shattered glass as they fall 40 storeys to the pavement below.

All told, asking that lot to save the environment would be like getting Dastardly and Mutley to join your campaign to save pigeons: you could never be sure their hearts were really in it.

Other corporate websites you might enjoy include: justmakethechequeouttolarry.com and fuckinghellthechinesearecoming.org

Work experience
Employment arrangement that enables companies to shift their training costs on to middle-class parents.

Working Lunch
They should make the people behind business magazine pro-gramme *Working Lunch* go on *Dragons' Den*: 'It's a business programme that goes out when all the business people are either at lunch or working. Hence the name; it's ironic. Either that or it's a reference to the fact that the presenters are work-ing through lunch. Don't know.'

'You know what? I'll pass.' ('Me too. I think it's mental.' 'I'm in!' 'What!?' 'Only joking. Anyway, what's that freaky make-up Evan Davies is wearing? He's weird.' 'You can talk, Theo, you put the shits up kids.' 'I don't.' 'You bloody do.')

To be fair, the BBC does seem to realise the futility of the enterprise by not making very much effort with *Working*

Lunch. There's a rotating staff of presenters comprising jack-of-all-trades types and people they probably found lying around in cupboards. The title sequence and set – all blue and floaty and full of fish – make totally no sense. It is plausibly a left-over from a fish-related panel game which never saw the light of day. (It could have been called *A Question of Fish*.)

They sometimes draft in presenter Paddy O'Connell from infantile celeb-worship show *Liquid News*. To draw a line between that programme's camp frippery and the high-minded seriousness of *Working Lunch*, O'Connell . . . puts on a pair of glasses. Maybe this wafer-thin divide should just go altogether: 'Uh oh, looks like Jen's down in the dumps again – and look, so's the yen!'

A *Working Lunch* stalwart is BBC everyman Adrian Chiles. He performs a sweeper/holding midfielder role at the Beeb – bridging the gaps, filling the holes, presenting pretty much every type of second-tier show going. One minute he's on a *Match of the Day 2* sofa looking bored – quite rightly – as Graeme Le Saux does some slow, careful talking; next he's on *Working Lunch* looking incredibly bored – quite rightly – as someone from PriceWaterhouseCoopers talks about VAT allowances. Then he's on *The Apprentice: You're Fired* trying to interpret those strange barking noises made by Sir Alan 'Sir Alan' Sugar. Then he's doing footie phone-ins on Five Live. Then he's doing *The One Show*. Then he's at the World Cup interviewing ex-players in dark corners underneath stadia.

There's nothing Adrian Chiles can't do – I firmly believe that. And there is no situation into which he is unable to work in a reference to his beloved West Bromwich Albion. The weather? Easy. And all those dancing programmes. I expect if the Beeb do another *Good Sex Guide*-type thing, Chiles will be in there, banging away, working in a reference to his 'Baggies'.

I personally hope to see him on the next series of *Celebrity Fame Academy*. I want him to have hair braids and a neckerchief on his head, do a strange shuffling dance backed by a guitarist with a KFC bucket worn as a mask and call himself Sweet Chiles O'Mine. It's just a dream I have.

World according to Clarkson, the (not the book)

Here be the manifesto of I, Jeremy Charles Robert Isambard Denim Clarkson (hon. Ph.D./pie):

I have no clean pants. I cannot work the washing machine.

No to pesto! Say no. To pesto.

Over a lifetime the average man wastes 394 days sitting on the lavatory. That's 56 weeks. They are the happiest and most peaceful 56 weeks of a chap's life. I love being on the lavatory more than I love being on holiday.

Hold on a minute.

One of my special stares.

I'm actively encouraging you to call me a bad-tempered, fat, balding slob with a gay car and a fondness for vulgar home appliances.

Hold on a minute.

That tall bloke with the long hair whose name nobody knows. Not even me. James, maybe? Anyway, I control him. He keeps a tiny little paint-brush in his car to wipe dust off the switches, and on one occasion he dried his underpants in a mate's microwave. (He had a spare pair; he wasn't naked.)

A man who looked like Robert Plant once gave me a lift to the local pub in what was undoubtedly a Renault Scénic.

I asked a squaddie in Basra why he had joined up. 'Because

I wanted to kill people.' Now he isn't even allowed to hit anyone with a stick.

Being Surrey, of course, the pub had been bistrofied. It was also spinning round quite a lot. And then the next thing I knew I was in a bed.

World leaders, messianic

You might have thought that, given the choice between a messianic leader and a non-messianic leader, most people would realise that the latter was safer by far. Sadly, though, some populations can't resist the lure of leaders with delusionally apocalyptic ideas of saving the world by getting their God on, who think there is a big man up there telling him to bring about a clash of civilisations. Which is a shame.

The build-up of tension between America and Iran has been particularly intriguing in this regard, being a clear stand-off between one person who believes in the coming messiah and another who believes in the coming messiah – albeit, problematically, a different messiah.

The Iranian uranium enrichment programme has focused attention like little else on the messianic thoughts of elected president, and world-renowned Holocaust denier, Mahmoud Ahmadinejad.

Just before announcing that Iran had gatecrashed 'the nuclear club', he disappeared for several hours to hold a mystic meeting with the Hidden Imam, an arcane figure who has apparently been hiding in 'grand occultation' since the 10th century and who Ahmadinejad believes will soon return to earth, and embark upon a climactic face-off with all enemies. The subsequent all-singing, all-dancing show put on by way of celebration was great, a bit like a *Eurovision* interval show, but with added uranium.

Luckily for everyone, nobody in the 'infidel' West would ever dream of getting caught up in anything so dangerous and irrational as a clash of civilisations. Excepting, perhaps, the current administration ruling the United States. The born-again President George W. Bush has, after all, said that he invaded Muslim countries because his Christian God told him to. How do we know this? Because he carefully explained this to a gathering of Muslim leaders. According to Nabil Shaath, Palestinian foreign minister at the time, at a meeting in 2005: 'President Bush said to all of us: "I am driven with a mission from God. God would tell me, 'George go and fight these ter-rorists in Afghanistan.' And I did. And then God would tell me, 'George, go and end the tyranny in Iraq.' And I did."' I would like to have seen their faces after that.

Bush actively considered destroying Iran's capabilities with a nuclear bomb – the first used in anger since 1945. According to *New York Times* reporter Seymour Hersh, senior military officials tried to remove the nuclear option, as such an insanely inflammatory act might not play well with the world's 1.2 bil-lion Muslims. The White House insisted the option must be retained. Using information from his Pentagon sources, Hersh said of Bush: 'It is his mission, his messianic mission if you will, to rid the world of this menace . . . He thinks he's the only one now who will have the courage to do it.'

'Courage': yes, that's definitely what he's got. Responding on Radio 4's *Today* programme, BBC Middle East corres-pondent Jeremy Bowen pondered that maybe the situation was not totally as dire as it seemed to be: 'Are they telling [Hersh] the truth or is this some kind of disinformation oper-ation?' he wondered. 'It could suit the Bush administration for people to believe they are not rational when in fact they are.'

It's sort of comforting to know that actions which appear irrational could, in fact, actually hide a deeper rationality. That's much better. And, certainly, these guys are not usually in the habit of taking fairly hairy risks about that kind of thing. Except, perhaps, for the time when the CIA handed instructions to the Iranians about how to build an atomic bomb.

According to *New York Times* reporter James Risen's book *State of War*, in 2000 the CIA began the really quite flaky Operation Merlin, an intriguing experiment aimed at throwing Iran off the scent that involved passing on nuclear secrets – Russian blueprints for a crucial component known as the TBA-480 high-voltage block – but first making them slightly wrong. It had worked with other weapons designs and, so, the thinking went, it could also work for nuclear bombs – sending Iranian scientists down a dead-end for years. It's like a fun trick, but a fun trick that sort of passes nuclear secrets to Iran.

What could possibly go wrong? Well, what reportedly went wrong was that the CIA's Russian scientist, a defector who lived in the United States, spotted the CIA's intentional flaw and, rather misunderstanding the nature of his mission, added a helpful note tipping the Iranians off to the problem. It was, one could definitely assert, a mistake. But an honest mistake. We've all made them. Although ours don't usually involve passing nuclear secrets to Iran.

In this intriguing mêlée, Seymour Hersh identified 'a wild card' – 'and that is: Tony Blair.' You might have thought there were enough wild cards here already, but no.

Hersh identifies the British PM as the great imponderable who could turn the situation one way or another. Luckily, Blair – perhaps realising his status as leader of the most secular nation on earth – has always successfully tempered Bush's excesses in the past and never himself engaged in missionary rhetoric. Except, perhaps, for calling the Iraq War 'a turning point for the world' and in lumping together all varieties of troublesome Arabs in one 'arc of extremism'.

During the run-up to that war, Blair studied St Thomas Aquinas and adopted an I-have-seen-things tone that led many to believe he had, in fact, seen things – as in, documents revealing imminent danger to the West posed by Saddam Hussein's regime. But it later transpired that he didn't see those things. Maybe he saw other things. Things that weren't actually there.

'People have just got to make up their minds whether they believe me or not, I'm afraid,' he said. He didn't say 'whether they believe *in* me or not'. He didn't say that. Recalling this tense period afterwards, one Downing Street official said: 'He did not think he could walk on water.' So, you know, it's all good.

At their meeting in June 2006, Pope Benedict urged Tony Blair to try to cool things down and fight for a diplomatic settlement in the Iran crisis. He apparently said: 'It's all getting a bit too messianic now, even for me. And I'm the Vicar of Christ. I believe in transubstantiation and think I'm infallible. Which should give us some sense of the scale of the problems we're now facing.'

As a gift, Tony Blair handed the Pope two Mozart CDs (which he presumably picked up at the garage when he was filling up with petrol). Maybe he should have thrown in a copy of his favourite album: Free's *Fire and Water*.

X

Xanax addicts

What's wrong with Hollywood people these days? Getting addicted to Xanax, Vicodin, Ambien or other assorted mother's little helps: it's not very James Caan, is it? Oxycontin sounds like a zit cream.

Certainly, on one level, an addiction to prescription painkillers does have logic on its side. If taking drugs is a way of killing the pain, then clearly the ultimate painkilling drug would be the painkiller. It's kind of the motherlode. But the outlaw chic that drug use supposedly confers on the user is somewhat diluted by the 'prescription' element.

Did Francis Ford Coppola and crew film *Apocalypse Now!* on drugs that made your legs wobbly and your speech slow and slurred? They did not. They used high-octane cocaine. These were very much the go-getters of the age. Would they ever have made it up the river pumped up on Xanax? No, they would just have wobbled about in the hotel room for a while. Then they'd have had a kip.

Xenu

The Church of Scientology's theory of Xenu, its highest level of wisdom, must be imparted only to those who have ascended to the zenith of human development (that is, people like Tom Cruise). This is because lesser people trying to process the revelations may die; that is actually the stated reason. But we will now reveal to you what OT (Operating Thetan) level Scientologists pay probably hundreds of thousands of pounds and devote many years of effort to learn. Be brave. Gird thyself, or turn away, damn you . . .

Basically, humans are made of clusters of spirits (or 'thetans') who were banished to Earth some 75 million years ago by an evil galactic warlord named Xenu. Suspecting rebellion due to overpopulation, Xenu – ruler of a galactic confederacy which consisted of 26 stars and 76 planets (including the Earth, which was then known as Teegeeack) – duped citizens into attending 'income tax inspections', where he drugged them and shipped them off to Teegeeack. They wore clothes 'which looked very remarkably like the clothes they wear this very minute' (wrote L. Ron Hubbard), and were shipped in planes which were exact copies of Douglas DC-8s, 'except the DC-8 had fans, propellers on it and the space plane didn't'.

Through the Scientology process of 'auditing', the thetan – who has lived through many past lives and will continue to live beyond the death of the body – can free itself of 'engrams' and 'implants' (the accumulated crud of ages) and thus recover its native spiritual abilities – thus gaining control over matter, energy, space, time, thoughts, form and life. This freed state is called Operating Thetan.

How are you feeling? Dead yet? Do you still want a free stress test?

Scientology claims to be the 'study of truth'. Which is almost amusing. The Church was founded in 1954 by L. Ron Hubbard. Tired of his unsuccessful attempts to be a pulp writer (he had also previously flunked college and was discharged from the US Navy), he told acquaintances: 'I'd like to start a religion. That's where the money is'; and 'If a man really wants to make a million dollars, he should start a religion.' So he started a religion and got rich. The richer the Church got, the more Hubbard could deal with his own stress – ultimately de-stressing by cruising around the Med in his own liner with lots of foxy women in uniforms attending on him. (Since Hubbard's death in 1986, the Church has been run by David Miscavige.)

How did Hubbard discover the 'Space Opera' that is the Xenu revelation? The revelation came to him in 1966/7, when he conducted a series of 'audits' on himself to unearth what he believed to be his hidden or suppressed memories, using an E-Meter (the primitive lie detector used by Scientology in its stress tests/'intensives'). In a letter of the time to his wife Mary Sue, Hubbard said that, to assist his research, he was drinking a great deal of rum and taking a cocktail of stimulants and depressants ('I'm drinking lots of rum and popping pinks and greys'). His assistant, Virginia Downsborough, revealed that he 'was existing almost totally on a diet of drugs'. Well, it was the mid-60s: everyone was at it. But you wouldn't let 'I Had too Much to Dream (Last Night)' by the Electric Prunes become the basis for a religion, would you?

The Church now claims 10 million members in 159 countries and more than 6,000 churches, missions and outreach groups. Volunteers sign contracts donating a 'billion years' of labour. Scientology charges for virtually all its services: intensives, the little chats about your engrams, can, according to Janet Reitman in *Rolling Stone*, 'cost anywhere from $750 for introductory sessions to between $8,000 and $9,000 for advanced sessions'. Being registered as a religion, of course, means the Church is tax exempt.

Anyone thinking critically within the Church is marked down as a Potential Trouble Source. Anyone trying to leave has to go through a year-long 'route out' process, during which they are put under immense pressure to stay. Critics outside the Church have been intimidated with litigation, and also by more direct, old-fashioned methods.

Katie Holmes was, of course, famously told by the Church to remain silent while giving birth to Tom Cruise's child (lest the trauma induce engrams in the baby). A spokesperson for the Church claimed they actually meant the delivery staff, and Katie could make the occasional noise if she absolutely needed to. Oh, that's okay then. Except that the average woman would probably appreciate a few words of encouragement from delivery staff during labour. It really hurts.

But what do we non-Scientologists – or 'common, ordinary, run of the mill, garden-variety humanoid[s]' (Hubbard) – know? Who are we to question the right of people to be black-mailed, brainwashed, separated from their families while having their heads filled with horseshit about aliens? Each to their own. Or, as Kabbalah-worshipping freak Madonna put it: 'If it makes Tom Cruise happy, I don't care if he prays to turtles.'

Thus speaks the voice of reason.

X-Factor winners who don't stand in line

After becoming the first *X-Factor* champion in 2004, Steve Brookstein was saddened to realise that winning the ITV talent show was not a fast track to a credible, independent career in music. Instead, it would mean demeaning himself as Simon Cowell's plaything, producing cruiseship covers of slushy standards. But . . . he had his own songs! He wasn't just a puppet! Didn't they understand? He was Steve Brookstein, not A.N. Other.

This is a common mistake of songwriting contestants in *X-Factor*, *Pop Idol* and *Fame Academy*. They write their own songs and sometimes want to sing those songs. They don't want to play by Simon's rules. And Simon doesn't like people who don't play by his rules.

The viewers who engage in this process are after, without sounding too derogatory, light entertainment. Quite reasonably, Thom Yorke solo albums are not their bag. So, sorry, but once Kate Thornton has put her arm around you in front of an audience of millions, it's probably a bit late to be asserting your artistic credibility. Imagine it instead as a bird flying away over the horizon, heading for some wetlands in Eastern Europe. Never to return.

Brookstein's rebel status saw him swiftly plummeting down the rubbish chute, eventually to land on top of fellow 'credible' talent-show winners like David Sneddon and Alex Parks.

A kindly message to any future winners: do *exactly* what they say. Or they *will* make you burn. They'll fry you like an egg.

Y

Youth Alpha

Youth Alpha is essentially the Alpha Course – that is, learning all about Jesus in a subtle, touchy-feely, Shloer and cheese sort of a way – only for much younger, much more impressionable people. If the Alpha Course gets God into adults who, for whatever reason, find themselves feeling coldly adrift in a world that doesn't care, then aiming it at teenagers, all of whom, virtually without exception, feel coldly adrift in a world that doesn't care, is the getting-God equivalent of shooting fish in a barrel. Or even loaves in a barrel.

Young people are attracted to Youth Alpha by youth-centred methods such as cinema ads, text messages and people talking to them about Jesus. Once enrolled, they first participate in discussions based on the Alpha book *Questions of Life*, which mostly features questions about the Lord Jesus. Then, on a weekend away, they are shown a video about the Holy Spirit, and are invited to receive the Holy Spirit.

Not having seen the video, I can't help wondering how they depict the Holy Spirit. I hope they have used some serious CGI effects and it's not just shiny-eyed Alpha leader Nicky Gumbel with a sheet over his head going: 'Woo-oooh!'

Who is Youth Alpha aimed at? 'The main deal is that if you are interested in getting some of life's big questions sorted, and want to work out what you believe, then come along.'

It helps if your 'main deal' involves listening to people talking about Jesus. The 'big questions' will definitely veer quite markedly in that direction. You won't be doing a compare and contrast on, say, Rousseau and Lenin. It will be mostly Jesus under consideration. Primarily, if not exclusively, this will be a Jesus situation centring heavily on the teachings of Jesus (that is, the mythical Christian Jesus who ascends to heaven and all of that; not the historical Jesus, the Jewish anti-Roman revolutionary millenarian – just so that's clear).

Some Christians, though, believe that the Alpha Course, while incorporating a lot of Jesus (as I think we were discussing previously), doesn't focus nearly *enough* on Jesus. The website for Ian Paisley's European Institute of Protestant Studies features a discussion piece by the Rev. Paul Fitton, asking: 'The Alpha Course: Is It Bible-Based or Hell-Inspired? Does its teaching rest solidly and squarely upon the authoritative rock of Holy Scripture or does it teach error in the name of Jesus?'

Now this might be disappointing news for young people attending Youth Alpha courses and labouring under the misapprehension that they are learning all about Jesus, but, sadly, it turns out that the course is more Hell-Inspired than Bible-Based. That's got to hurt. Like hell.

On the plus side, they do provide snacks, although the Rev. Fitton doesn't go into that side of things much.

Youth news

Part of the government's remit to BBC 3 was that it should provide, among other things, a 'commitment to news and current affairs'. Ideally, the document continued, it should 'condense the news into 60 seconds – otherwise it just gets boring'.

And so was born *60 Second News*, which arrives, as they explain every hour, 'on the hour, every hour'. At the end, though, they waste some of their valuable seconds saying, 'We'll be back in an hour.' The news they pack into that minute relates, surprisingly often, to Tom Cruise.

Meanwhile, the news on London alternative radio station XFM is accompanied by an ambient techno whirr which renders what is being said impossible to hear.

Maybe, in the future, we could have the headlines whispered by a small boy under the new single by whoever the contemporary equivalent of the Kooks is.

'Shhh, there's a war on,' he mutters. 'Shhh.'

Z

Zane, presenters whose names contain the word

Zane Lowe. Alex Zane. Those two, mainly. It's weird, how many people do you know with the word 'Zane' in their names? And then these two ball-aches come along at almost the same time. Billy Zane's okay, he's keeping Kelly Brook out of the country. But those other two . . .

New Zealand indie-rock dude Zane Lowe refers to himself, live on Radio One, as 'The Zipper'. What kind of tosser gives himself a nickname? Well, Sting is one tosser who gave himself a nickname. Then there's The Zipper. Sadly, when he calls himself The Zipper, I start to wonder whether I will become The Gipper. What kind of tosser calls himself The Zipper? The Zipper? The Twat, more like. Captain Twat, even. You could get a suit made up.

For all these and many other reasons (his band Breaks Co-Op, his voice, everything else), he deserves to be banished to a small, rocky island for all eternity to ponder long and hard about what he has done. Let's say Rockall – the most finely named of all the small rock islands.

And as I say, Alex Zane too.

Z-list celebrities saving the planet

Saving the planet is one of the major challenges facing the planet. Luckily, the celebrities know the score and are fighting – literally fighting – to do their bit. It's almost – *almost* – enough to make you think.

Here's Gaynor Faye, in a short newspaper Q&A, asked what she wishes people would take more notice of. 'The environment,' she answers, no doubt quick as a flash. 'I do as much as I can, but there are so many things we're doing that are destroying the world.' Answering a question about what she does in moments of weakness, she reveals, 'Go shopping and buy too many things which sit in the wardrobe.' In a nutshell, her philosophy is this: 'Live for today and have no regrets.' Live for today, don't care about tomorrow. While doing as much as you can for, er, tomorrow.

Eco-tourism is a big deal: we can see the world without ruining the world. Asked about it by *The Times*, writer and philosopher Alain de Botton contributed a small essay about . . . himself. 'I am drawn to large empty spaces, particularly deserts,' he began, before going on to explain absolutely nothing about eco-tourism. 'Travel offers a constant lesson in humility,' he concluded.

Following Al Gore's rousing example, Leonardo DiCaprio's environment film reveals an interest that dates back to the filming of *The Beach* – yes, the Danny Boyle film that was marred by protests from environmentalists after the production team uprooted indigenous plants to widen the beach. The beach wasn't wide enough for *The Beach*, you see.

Then came the news that *Dirty Dancing* star Patrick Swayze was so devastated by people destroying the planet that he cries about it all the time: 'I cry frequently at the way we're destroying the planet. We are heading for disaster until and unless we do something about it.'

Guess what he's planning to do about it. That's right: make a documentary. Don't laugh. A man is dying here.

There could be hope. If only governments would stop ignoring the advice of Tracey Emin. In March 2006 the *Independent* asked a series of minor celebrities/public figures if there was hope for the planet. Emin said: 'We need more research and development in the things like electronic cars. Research is desperately needed in so many areas in this country but is ignored by the Government.'

Yeah, that's really sticking it to them. Sadly, Emin continued: 'It is not just governments who have responsibility – it is people like myself, who are aware of what they are doing wrong, yet still do it. Much more needs to be done to let people know what they are doing.'

So, unless I am mistaken, when asked for your opinion on how we can avoid Armageddon – as well as calling for research into 'electronic cars'; which would be hard because there's NO SUCH THING – you are forthrightly demanding that more needs to be done to tell people like you what is going on. If only people like you could be forced to listen to what is going on, then – and only then – will you properly be made aware of the problem. Essentially, your opinion is that you – at some point soon – must be made to have an opinion.

But if you are a Z-list celebrity and you find yourself being asked your opinion on global change, and your opinion is that you must be forced to have an opinion, because people, like you, don't do anything, you might actually first consider getting an opinion. Otherwise, what you are doing is WASTING EVERYONE'S FUCKING TIME.

Acknowledgements

Many thanks, of course, to Scott Murray and Dorian Lynskey for their contributions. To everyone at Little, Brown/Sphere: our valiant editor Antonia Hodgson, Sean Garrehy, Jenny Fry, Tamsyn Berryman, Daisy Malaktos, Andy Edwards, Andy Hine, Sarah Shrubb. To our agents Kate Jones and Karolina Sutton at ICM. To telly types Stuart Prebble, Pip Banyard, Joel Wilson, Stephen Mangan. Thanks for various suggestions/pointers to Karl, Rick, Ian and Alexis. Most of all, eternal gratitude to our immediate families, for their understanding and support.